IMAGISM
& THE IMAGISTS

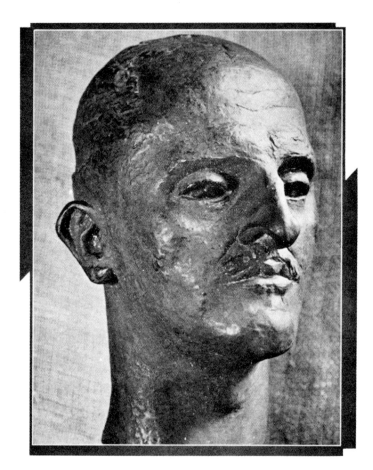

T. E. HULME
FROM A BRONZE
BY JACOB EPSTEIN

IMAGISM & THE IMAGISTS

A Study in Modern Poetry

By
GLENN HUGHES
Professor of English
University of Washington

BIBLO and TANNEN
NEW YORK
1972

Originally published by STANFORD UNIVERSITY PRESS, 1931

Reprinted by Arrangement by

BIBLO & TANNEN BOOKSELLERS & PUBLISHERS, INC.

63 Fourth Avenue / New York, N.Y. 10003

Library of Congress Cataloging in Publication Data

Hughes, Glenn, 1894-1964.
    Imagism & the imagists.

    Bibliography: p.
    1. English poetry--20th century--History and
criticism. 2. American poetry--20th century--History
and criticism. 3. Imagist poetry--History and
criticism. I. Title.
PR605.I6H8 1972   821'.9'1209   72-7421
ISBN 0-8196-0282-5

For
KARL GREEN
wherever he may be

PREFACE

IT MAY be, as W. B. Yeats once said in my hearing, that, "The only real Imagist was the Creator of the Garden of Eden." This book, however, is about a group of modern poets who have called themselves imagists, and who, by means of their poetry and propaganda, have created a considerable impression on the reading public and on many other writers. Imagism, I think, may be characterized as the best-organized and most influential "movement" in English poetry since the activity of the pre-Raphaelites; and although it is still operating dynamically, its propaganda is completed, its illustrative poems have been officially admitted to standard anthologies, and the storm of criticism which it aroused has subsided.

It seemed to me, when I undertook this study, that a certain advantage can be obtained by chronicling a literary movement soon after its climax, before the principal participants forget the motives and the events essential to it. I still believe, having completed my work, that there is much to be said in favor of this idea. I am greatly impressed, however, with the fact that, whereas one acquires by this method of approach unusual insight into motives, as well as much valuable data which might later prove unavailable, one is sorely hampered by convention and a sense of personal decency which do not permit the setting down of a large number of facts (chiefly biographical) necessary to a complete understanding of the poets involved. It seems inevitable, therefore, that no literary history can be perfect, for the contemporary historian withholds facts and the later one cannot discover them!

The present work is necessarily a combination of history and criticism, but it is intended to be chiefly the former. As far as possible I have maintained an impartial attitude toward the work of the imagists, and have given the reader both sides of controversies. In fact I have, in my quoted criticisms, leaned rather to the adverse than to the favorable, in order to illustrate the full force of the opposition which imagism met and overcame. I have of course expressed my personal opinion of certain poems, but such evaluation must be considered incidental rather than fundamental to the study as a whole.

The first problem confronting me was one of limitation. The group of poets whom Ezra Pound invited to contribute to *Des Imagistes,* the earliest imagist anthology, included several who had no particular interest in imagism as a movement, or even as a poetic point of view. It seemed advisable, therefore, to accept the personnel of the later group organized by Amy Lowell and represented by three anthologies published in three successive years. I have not concerned myself with poets who merely happen to write imagistically—to do so would be to open up a limitless field. And besides, there is no absolute standard by which one may determine whether or not a poet is an imagist. All such classifications are arbitrary. The imagists I am writing about are the six who adopted the name and stuck to it until their common aims were realized, and a seventh, Ezra Pound, whom I have included because of his importance to the movement as organizer, propagandist, and aesthetic philosopher. It may be urged that

William Carlos Williams is more of an imagist than D. H. Lawrence, and that James Joyce and Ford Madox Hueffer (Ford), besides having contributed to *Des Imagistes*, are as much worth writing about as some of the seven who appear in my study. These statements I cannot deny. I merely reiterate that my limitation is an arbitrary one, and is historical rather than aesthetic. And then, as F. S. Flint once said in another connection, "Seven is in many ways an appropriate number where poets are concerned."

For the opportunity to execute this study, which I believe will prove useful to students of modern poetry, I am indebted in the first place to the John Simon Guggenheim Memorial Foundation, for it was as a Fellow of that Foundation that I carried on the necessary research in Europe during the winter of 1928–29. Next, I am deeply indebted to imagist poets themselves, Richard Aldington, H. D., John Gould Fletcher, F. S. Flint, D. H. Lawrence, and Ezra Pound, all of whom were extraordinarily kind in discussing with me the subject in hand and in placing at my disposal a large number of books, periodicals, and private documents. For various favors, which I greatly appreciate, I wish also to thank Herbert Read, T. S. Eliot, Harold Monro, Miss Sylvia Beach, Yvor Winters, Professor William Leonard Schwartz, Carey McWilliams, and Baron Paul d'Estournelles de Constant.

G. H.

SEATTLE, WASHINGTON
July 1, 1930

ACKNOWLEDGMENTS

For permission to reproduce certain material, I wish to acknowledge gratefully my indebtedness to the following holders of copyright: Covici, Friede, for poems by Richard Aldington; Houghton Mifflin Company, for poems by Amy Lowell; Alfred A. Knopf, for poems by D. H. Lawrence; Horace Liveright, for poems by H. D. and Ezra Pound; The Macmillan Company, for poems by John Gould Fletcher; Man Ray, for photographs of H. D. and Richard Aldington.

G. H.

CONTENTS

ILLUSTRATIONS

PART I
IMAGISM

I ≈ THE ORIGINS
OF IMAGISM

A SEARCH for the origins of those poetic ideals which culminated a few years ago in an Anglo-American movement known as imagism leads us very far back into literature, as far back, indeed, as the beginnings of poetry. In this study, as in most others, we are faced with the trite but startling fact that nothing is as new as it appears at first to be. Everything has a string of precedents. Imagism, like nearly all movements in literature, was a reaction against the poetry of the immediate past, at least of the immediate past in England and America. Its sources of inspiration were, chronologically, of two sorts: ancient and modern. The ancient literatures contributing to its ideals were: Greek, Latin, Hebrew, Chinese, and Japanese. The modern influence was French.

Not that all the poets who participated in the movement were affected by the same literatures; each poet was the product of a particular combination of sources, and the chief source varied with the individual. Yet the platform on which the imagists eventually took their stand was not such a jumble as might be supposed from the diverse origins of its

[3]

elements. It was a harmonious structure, for the simple reason that its elements were not superficial but basic, not regional but universal. Hardness of outline, clarity of image, brevity, suggestiveness, freedom from metrical laws—these and other imagist ideals could be drawn from Greek as well as from Hebrew or Chinese.

The modern influence, that of the French, was of special importance, for besides reinforcing the imagists' belief in their neo-classicism, it offered them examples of organized poetry movements. It not only clarified their ideals but also gave them a method of propaganda.

The principal forerunner of imagism was "symbolism." To account for "symbolism" we must go back to the 1860's, when a group of French poets declared war on romanticism. French poets are always forming groups and declaring war. They love principles, and above all they love fighting for them. The poets who took arms against the romantics called themselves Parnassians, and during the decade 1866–1876 they published three anthologies of poetry under the general title of *Le Parnasse Contemporain*. Among the contributors were José-Maria de Hérédia, Stéphane Mallarmé, Villiers de l'Isle Adam, Leconte de Lisle, Sully Prudhomme, Paul Verlaine, François Coppée, and Catulle Mendès. Their ideals were orderliness (that is, exactness of form) and objectivity. Guided by a materialistic philosophy, they tended to present descriptively the phenomena of the external world and to suppress undue personal emotion.

But there were those among the Parnassians who could not content themselves with objective realism, and who, in their development along more spiritual lines, became the inspiration of a new school, the "symbolists." The two Parnassians mainly responsible for the symbolist trend were

Verlaine and Mallarmé, both of them disciples of an earlier Parnassian, Charles Baudelaire, who is therefore considered the actual "father of symbolism." As early as the middle of the century (*Les Fleurs du Mal* appeared in 1857) Baudelaire had struck the note which was to echo through "symbolism" and imagism, a note of modernism well illustrated in his poem, "Correspondances," by the lines:

> Il est des parfums frais comme des chairs d'enfants,
> Doux comme les hautbois, verts comme les prairies,
> — Et d'autres, corrompus, riches et triomphants. ...

But although these Parnassians were direct and powerful precursors of "symbolism," their influence was equaled by that of the individualist, Arthur Rimbaud, who in the early 'seventies conceived a poetry destined to serve as an inspiration to many of the most characteristic symbolists. It was Rimbaud who wrote:

> Mais fondre où fond ce nuage sans guide,
> — Oh! favorisé de ce qui est frais!
> Expirer en ces violettes humides
> Dont les aurores chargent ces forêts?[1]

It remained, however, for other poets to crystallize the ideals of these pioneers into a doctrine, and to give the doctrine a name. In 1885 the word symbolism was first used as a rallying point for poets of the new order, and the leader of the organization, as well as the inventor of the name, was Jean Moréas. In close association with him were Paul Adam and Gustave Kahn, the latter a pioneer in the domain of vers libre.

---

[1] From the poem, "Comédie de la Soif," by Rimbaud, in *Les Illuminations*, 1872–73.

6

The avowed purpose of the symbolists was to combat the realistic materialism of the typical Parnassians, and to free French poetry from the tyranny of conventional form. They did not repudiate the objective method of presentation, but they endeavored to give their images of externality a spiritual, a symbolic value. Description for its own sake they opposed; literal directness they replaced with suggestive indirectness. They favored individuality, but not the romantic sort, with its emphasis upon egoistic emotions.

From 1885 until 1900 "symbolism" was the dominant force in French poetry, and practically every poet of ability who wrote during those years came under the influence of its ideals. There were parallel movements, that of the so-called decadents being one, but all these overlapped with and were submerged by "symbolism." So general was the symbolist doctrine and so varied were the characteristics of its adherents that eventually the significance of the term became extremely vague, and a restatement of principles was inevitable. It was impossible to unite all the symbolists under one banner; they had drifted too far apart. And particularly wide was the gulf between the exotic experimentalists (disciples of Tristan Corbière, Jules Laforgue and Arthur Rimbaud) and the classicists, who favored a return to ancient law and order.

The first official announcement of a regrouping came in 1891, when the classicists issued a manifesto. Their spokesman was Jean Moréas, and those who seconded him were Raymond de la Tailhède, Charles Maurras, Maurice du Plessys, and Ernest Raynaud. They called themselves the "École Romane," and dedicated their efforts to the recovery of the formality and restraint of Greek and Roman masters as exhibited in the work of sixteenth- and seventeenth-century French poets. So effective was their propaganda that many other symbolists reacted to it and modified their style. Henri de Régnier, Laurent Tailhade, and Paul Claudel are three important poets who have shown themselves susceptible to the neo-classical idea.

The radicals went their own way, evolving one "ism" after another, but tending always toward greater freedom of form and novelty of content. There have been the "cubists" (Guillaume Apollinaire, Max Jacob, and André Salmon), the "fantasists" (Tristan Derème, Franc Nohain, Vincent Muselli, Paul-Jean Toulet, Georges Fourest, and Francis Carco), the "unanimists" (Jules Romains, Georges Duhamel, and Charles Vildrac), the "dadaists" (Tristan Tzara, Francis Picabia, Jean Cocteau, Paul Dermée, Nicolas Beauduin, André Breton, Louis Aragon, and Philippe Soupault), and, most recently, the "sur-realists," who are only dadaists with a difference. MM. Breton, Aragon, and Soupault form the link between dadaism and sur-realism.

With the exception of the last two, which appeared after the War, all these groups may be considered forerunners of the imagists. Between them they offered to alert English and American writers every conceivable poetic ideal, old and new, and the imagists were the first to take advantage of the offer, the first to base their own work on the successes of modern French experiment and to interpret for English and American readers the spirit as well as the technique underlying those successes.

That a majority of the imagists drew direct inspiration from the symbolists is indisputable, and recently an attempt has been made by a French critic to determine in detail the connection between the two schools. M. René Taupin, in an accurate and exhaustive study entitled *L'Influence du*

*symbolism français sur la poésie américaine (de 1910 à
1920)*,[2] spends considerable time tracing the rise of imagism,
giving proper credit to Hulme and Pound, then indicates the
importance of Remy de Gourmont and the lesser importance
of Jules de Gaultier in furnishing the English with an
aesthetic, and, finally, traces the influence of specific symbolists on specific imagists. His judgments in this matter are
based upon admissions made by the imagists themselves as
well as upon evidence found in their poems. Without pre-
senting the evidence, so carefully prepared by M. Taupin,
we may summarize his findings as follows:

Ezra Pound, though familiar with many modern French
poets, owes most to Gautier, Rimbaud, Corbière, and Laforgue; secondary influences in his case are Tailhade and
Jammes. F. S. Flint, like Pound, was, in the early days of
imagism, an omnivorous reader of French poetry, but the
poets who influenced him most strongly were Émile Verhaeren and Jean de Bosschère. The fact that he made a
number of translations from both these writers lends support
to such an opinion. Although Amy Lowell made critical
studies of several of the symbolists and read widely among
the others, M. Taupin considers that the vital French influence on her work came from Henri de Régnier and Paul
Fort. John Gould Fletcher ran the gamut of "symbolism,"
reflecting at one time an imitative admiration of Rimbaud,
at another time of Corbière and Laforgue, again, and, most
consistently, of Verhaeren. Naturally enough, M. Taupin
finds it difficult to specify the French influences in the work
of H. D. and Richard Aldington. These two imagists, as
we shall emphasize later, were dominated by ancient classical

[2] Paris: Champion. 1929.

poets, and were therefore not so susceptible to modern Continental style. H. D., however, is compared with Henri de Régnier and Mallarmé (the comparison not implying necessarily an influence), and Aldington is credited with having absorbed the French spirit as a whole rather than with having taken lessons from particular poets. Remy de Gourmont is mentioned, rightly, as having contributed largely to Aldington's general conception of the French point of view.

Having indicated thus briefly the foreign sources of imagism, we may now turn our attention to its native origins. At the outset we find ourselves concerned with the activities of a comparatively unknown man, T. E. Hulme, an aesthetic philosopher who quite reasonably may be called the "father of imagism."

Hulme was an Englishman, born in North Staffordshire in 1883. After a high-school education he entered Cambridge University, but soon afterward, in 1904, he was "sent down" from that institution because of some escapade. The next two years he spent in London, studying independently. In 1906 he went out to Canada, worked for three months on a ranch, and then returned to England. He next went to Brussels, where he remained seven months, teaching English and studying French and German. From Brussels he returned to London, where he devoted himself to an intensive study of philosophy, a subject in which he had long been interested, and in 1912 he was readmitted to Cambridge University, partly through the efforts of the eminent French philosopher, Bergson, who expressed great admiration for Hulme's intellect and a firm confidence in his future.

Dominated by restless independence, however, Hulme left the University soon after his readmission, and went to Berlin, where for nine months he devoted himself to

German philosophy and psychology. Again he returned to London, and in 1913 he published his translation of Bergson's *Introduction to Metaphysics*.[3] Three years later appeared his translation, with a critical introduction, of Sorel's *Reflections on Violence*.[4]

The only other work of Hulme's published during his lifetime consisted of articles contributed to periodicals, and a group of five poems which were printed under the exact if somewhat amusing title, "Complete Poetical Works of T. E. Hulme," as a supplement to Ezra Pound's *Ripostes*.[5] Concerning these poems we shall have more to say later.

Hulme went to the War in 1914, was invalided home in the spring of 1915, returned to the front late in the same year, and was killed in September 1917. It may be mentioned that he was not averse to war; he was enthusiastic about it. He even wrote articles designed to form an intellectual defense of militarism.

Our chief interest in Hulme, however, lies in the fact that during the years 1908–1912 he was the center of a shifting group of writers, painters, sculptors, architects, and philosophers over whom he exercised a considerable influence. Hulme had the qualities of leadership. He was vigorous, aggressive, and original.[6] He was also blessed with a sufficient income to allow him to devote all his time to study and controversy.

It was in 1908 that Hulme founded the Poets' Club, and

[3] London: Macmillan.

[4] London: Allen & Unwin. 1916.

[5] London: Elkin Mathews. 1912.

[6] Hulme's great friend, Jacob Epstein, the sculptor, said of him, "He was capable of kicking a theory as well as a man downstairs when the occasion demanded." See the foreword to *Speculations*.

although none of the poets who became officially the imagists were members of this early group, it was at its meetings that the first experimental imagist poems were read and discussed, among these being Hulme's own poems.

Early in 1909 Hulme made the acquaintance of F. S. Flint, who had been writing a series of articles in advocacy of vers libre, and out of this acquaintance developed a new dining-and-talking society (unnamed), which thereafter held regular meetings on Thursday evenings at a restaurant in Soho, the Latin Quarter of London. The first meeting took place on March 25, 1909, and according to Mr. Flint those present were T. E. Hulme, F. S. Flint, Edward Storer, F. W. Tancred, Joseph Campbell, Miss Florence Farr, and two or three others whose names no one recalls.

In a brief article entitled "The History of Imagism," which appeared in the *Egoist* (London) for May 1, 1915, Mr. Flint tells of the activities of the group, and throws some light on the origins of the Imagist ideals:

> I think that what brought the real nucleus of this group together was a dissatisfaction with English poetry as it was then (and is still, alas!) being written. We proposed at various times to replace it by pure *vers libre*; by the Japanese *tanka* and *haikai*; we all wrote dozens of the latter as an amusement; by poems in a sacred Hebrew form; .... by rimeless poems like Hulme's "Autumn," and so on. In all this Hulme was ringleader. He insisted too on absolutely accurate presentation and no verbiage .... There was also a lot of talk and practice among us, Storer leading it chiefly, of what we called the Image. We were very much influenced by modern French Symbolist poetry.

He goes on, then, to recall that on April 22, 1909, Ezra Pound, whose *Personae* had been published on the previous Friday, joined the group. "He was very full of his troubadours." Mr. Pound's initiatory gesture was to read in clarion tones his stirring "Sestina: Altaforte," whereupon the entire café trembled.

The group died a lingering death at the end of its second winter. But its discussions had a sequel. In 1912 Mr. Pound published at the end of his book, *Ripostes*, the complete poetical works of T. E. Hulme, five poems, thirty-three lines, with a preface in which these words occur: "As for the future, *Les Imagistes*, the descendants of the forgotten school of 1909 (previously referred to as the School of Images) have that in their keeping." In that year Pound had become interested in modern French poetry; he had broken away from his old manner; and he invented the term *Imagisme* to designate the aesthetic of *Les Imagistes*.

We may note, therefore, that although Mr. Pound did not start the discussion of "the image," he was the first to employ the derivatives of this term in print. He introduced them to England in the preface to Hulme's poems; to America in the November 1912 issue of *Poetry* (Chicago), wherein appeared three poems by Richard Aldington, with a biographical note classifying him as an "imagiste." To the January 1913 issue of *Poetry*, Pound contributed some literary notes from London, and one of these was to the effect that "The youngest school here that has the nerve to call itself a school is that of the Imagistes." In the same issue appeared three poems signed "H. D., Imagiste." It was Pound who, acting as *Poetry*'s London representative, obtained the poems from Aldington and H. D. and sent them to Chicago. Thus much for the origin of the name, the French form of which was soon Anglicized—though not until Pound had deserted the group for another "ism."

The development of imagism as a movement will be followed in another chapter. Meanwhile let us return to

Hulme and his ideas, which are fundamental to our study. During the years immediately preceding the War, Hulme wrote a great deal, but most of his writing was in the form of brief notes, intended solely for his own reference. In only a few instances were the notes expanded into fairly complete essays. After his death this mass of material was turned over to Herbert Read, now recognized as one of the best minds of his generation in England, and after the most arduous labor, Mr. Read succeeded in editing for publication the bulk of these notes. They appeared in a single volume in 1924, with the title, *Speculations*.[7]

Later, after a final sifting, another collection of brief but illuminating and intensely suggestive fragments was arranged by the same editor, and was published under the title "Notes on Language and Style," first as an article in the *Criterion*, the quarterly review edited in London by T. S. Eliot,[8] and more recently as a chapbook in America.[9]

It is not only presumptuous but decidedly unjust to both Hulme and the reader to attempt to summarize the great store of ideas which are packed into these notes. They could inspire scores of books. As a matter of fact, had their author lived a few years longer, they would unquestionably have been expanded into at least half a dozen volumes of extraordinary interest. For the purposes of this essay, however, we must indicate merely the main tendencies of Hulme's thought and reproduce sufficient excerpts to illustrate the depth of that thought and the power of its expression.

[7] London: Kegan Paul; New York: Harcourt, Brace.

[8] Vol. III, No. XII, July 1925.

[9] Number twenty-five, University of Washington Chapbooks. Seattle: University of Washington Bookstore. 1929.

A considerable portion of *Speculations* is taken up with a discussion of humanism; in fact, the subtitle of the volume is "Essays on Humanism and the Philosophy of Art." The basic contention is that we have reached the end of a humanistic period (which began, of course, with the Renaissance). A good thing to have done with, too, is Hulme's attitude, for in his estimation humanism is a disease, a weakness which carries within itself the seed of its own destruction.

The inevitable result of humanism, he says, is romanticism, and the exaltation of the individual. "We introduce into human beings the *Perfection* that properly belongs only to the divine, and thus confuse both human and divine things by not clearly separating them." To the humanistic attitude he opposes, of course, the religious, and to romanticism, classicism. He is careful, however, to note that he uses the word religious in a special sense, as a "way of thinking," which may find expression in myth, but which at the same time is independent of myth. In other words he means an attitude based upon a belief in absolute values, in the light of which "man himself is judged to be essentially limited and imperfect." Following from this, "A man is essentially bad, he can only accomplish anything of value by discipline—ethical and political. Order is thus not merely negative, but creative and liberating." Hence classicism.

Hulme goes to some length in his contrast of these two general attitudes, and, in the course of his argument, gives an interesting exposition of Egyptian, Greek, and Byzantine art. He makes clear why Greek art and nineteenth-century art are enjoyed by the same persons—because they are natural, because "the lines are soft and vital"; he also makes clear why the hard, geometrical lines of Egyptian and Byzantine art are reappearing in twentieth-century art—because the age of humanism is over, and personality has again been subordinated to law.

On the other hand, he does not mean to imply that the new art will necessarily resemble closely the art of previous classical periods. Being the product of its own age, not an imitation, it probably "will culminate, not so much in the simple geometrical forms found in archaic art, but in the more complicated ones associated in our minds with the idea of machinery." The similarity between the new and the old will be in the common "tendency toward abstraction." Nor does he believe that the modern inclination to make use of mechanical forms is caused primarily by our mechanical environment. The fact that we live in an age of steel is of some artistic importance, but it is not the main reason for our increasing enjoyment of mechanical form; the main reason is an inner change, "a change of sensibility."

Coming to the subject of poetry, he makes some significant comments on its romantic and classic aspects. He says: "What I mean by classical in verse, then, is this. That even in the most imaginative flights there is always a holding back, a reservation. The classical poet never forgets this finiteness, this limit of man. He remembers always that he is mixed up with earth. He may jump, but he always returns back; he never flies away into the circumambient gas. You might say if you wished that the whole of the romantic attitude seems to crystallize in verse round metaphors of flight. Hugo is always flying, flying over abysses, flying up into the eternal gases. The word infinite is in every other line."

He feels certain that we are at the end of a period of romanticism. The nineteenth century saw its climax, and "We shall not get any new efflorescence of verse until we get a new technique, a new convention, to turn ourselves loose in." But of course he realizes that public taste for a tradition survives beyond the period of which the tradition was the natural expression. "For every kind of verse there is a corresponding receptive attitude . . . . while the romantic tradition has run dry, yet the critical attitude of mind, which demands romantic qualities from verse, still survives. So that if good classical verse were to be written tomorrow very few people would be able to stand it."

Continuing on the same theme, he makes a series of statements which have been proved remarkably true during the past two decades, and which have a definite bearing on the reception met by those imagist poems which correspond most nearly to Hulme's ideal of the new classicism:

The dry hardness which you get in the classics is absolutely repugnant to them [i.e., to most readers]. Poetry that isn't damp isn't poetry at all. They cannot see that accurate description is a legitimate object of verse. Verse to them always means a bringing in of some of the emotions that are grouped round the word infinite.

The essence of poetry to most people is that it must lead them to a beyond of some kind. Verse strictly confined to the earthly and the definite (Keats is full of it) might seem to them to be excellent writing, excellent craftsmanship, but not poetry. So much has romanticism debauched us, that, without some form of vagueness, we deny the highest.

In the classic it is always the light of ordinary day, never the light that never was on land or sea.

But the awful result of romanticism is that, accustomed to this strange light, you can never live without it. Its effect on you is that of a drug.

His plea for modern poetry is, therefore: first of all, abolish the conception of man as a god; next, eliminate vagueness and reliance on the "infinite." "The great aim is accurate, precise, and definite description." "It is essential to prove that beauty may be in small, dry things."

He is fully aware of the difficulties faced by the neo-classic poet: the difficulty of seeing accurately, and even more, the difficulty of recording accurately in words. His sense of the inadequacy of language is very strong. Over and over he emphasizes this point. "Language has its own special nature, its own conventions and communal ideas. It is only by a concentrated effort of the mind that you can hold it fixed to your own purpose."

It seems to him that one must distinguish between imagination and fancy, and for the purposes of his own discussion he limits imagination to the realm of the emotions, and fancy to the realm of finite things. And it is fancy, he thinks, which must be the "weapon" of the modern poet. By means of fancy one is enabled to create the physical image which is the very basis of poetic expression. "Visual meanings can only be transferred by the new bowl of metaphor; prose is an old pot that lets them leak out. . . . . Fancy is not mere decoration added on to plain speech. Plain speech is essentially inaccurate. It is only by new metaphors, that is, by fancy, that it can be made precise."

And he concludes this essay with a reiteration of his belief that "a period of dry, hard, classical verse is coming," and that "a literature of wonder must have an end as inevitably as a strange land loses its strangeness when one lives in it. . . . . Wonder can only be the attitude of a man passing from one stage to another, it can never be a permanently fixed thing."

Now even from this inadequate and rather ruthless condensation of the principal essays in *Speculations*, it is plain that Hulme was much more than a vigorous and serious philosopher. He was, in his own sense of the word, and likely in the truest sense, a poet. He may have written only five poems as such; that is, five compositions in the nature of lyrics; and these were done only as exercises, for purposes of illustration—but from the mass of his notes one may pick dozens of the most astonishing poetic statements, as concentrated as the finest *hokku* from Japan, as penetrating as the epigrams of Wilde, as fresh and startling in their imagery as the best efforts of his associates and followers, the professional imagists.

The five lyrics are unpretentious, and their manner has been made familiar by hundreds of writers since, but if we think of Hulme as a philosopher, with a critical interest in poetry, writing in the days before the War, when the new poetic styles were really new, we will be able to appreciate their merit. Take, for example, the following:

AUTUMN

A touch of cold in the Autumn night—
I walked abroad,
And saw the ruddy moon lean over a hedge
Like a red-faced farmer.
I did not stop to speak, but nodded,
And round about were the wistful stars
With white faces like town children.

It is appalling to think how many times this poem has been rewritten, usually by amateurs, in the past fifteen years. Hulme, however, was not rewriting; he created it. Its content is slight, but its method is compelling.

"Autumn" is the first of the five. The last is more subtle and imitating it requires professional talent:

CONVERSION

Light-hearted I walked into the valley wood
In the time of hyacinths,
Till beauty like a scented cloth
Cast over, stifled me. I was bound
Motionless and faint of breath
By loveliness that is her own eunuch.
Now pass I to the final river
Ignominiously, in a sack, without sound,
As any peeping Turk to the Bosphorus.

This is, I insist, extremely good, and it was composed as a blackboard exercise.

The remaining three poems, which space does not permit to be reprinted here, may be found, as has already been mentioned, at the end of Ezra Pound's *Ripostes*, and also as an appendix to *Speculations*.

But even more striking and more valuable than these lyrics are the random notes of which I have spoken, and so important are they to this study that I have selected a number of them for inclusion here. Inasmuch as they were set down by Hulme for his own reference, and frequently without careful construction or order, they must be read as so many independent comments, as suggestions and embryos, though it will be perceived that most of them relate to expression and style, to the philosophy of composition:

Philosophical syntheses and ethical systems are only possible in armchair moments. They are seen to be meaningless as soon as we get into a bus with a dirty baby and a crowd.

Animals are in the same state that men were before symbolic language was invented.

Philosophy is about people in clothes, not about the soul of man.

The world lives in order to develop the lines on its face.

I shall call my philosophy the "Valet to the Absolute." The Absolute not a hero to his own valet.

I look at the reality, at London stream, and dirt, mud, power, and then I think of the pale shadowy analogy that is used without thinking by the automatic philosophers, the "stream of time." The people who treat words without reference, who use analogies without thinking of them: let us always remember that solid real stream and the flat thin voice of the metaphysician, *the stream of time.*

We may say that the reader habitually takes words as *x, without* the meaning attached.

Aphra[10] sees each word with an image sticking on to it, never as a flat word passed over a board like a counter.

Perhaps the nearest analogy is the hairy caterpillar. Taking each segment of his body as a word, the hair on that segment is the vision the poet sees behind it.

It is difficult to do this, so that the poet is forced to use new analogies, and especially to construct a plaster model of a thing to express his emotion at the sight of the vision he sees, his wonder and ecstasy. If he employed the ordinary word, the reader would only see it as a segment, with no hair, used for getting along. And without this clay, spatial image, he does not feel that he has expressed at all what he sees.

The ordinary caterpillar for crawling along from one position to another.

The hairy one for beauty, to build up a solid vision of realities.

The prose writer drags meaning along with the rope. The poet makes it stand on end and hit you.

A sentence and a worm are the most stupid animals and the most difficult to teach tricks. They have a tendency to crawl along; it requires genius, music to make them stand up (snake charmers).

The uncomfortable vision of all prose as merely a line of string lying on a paper.

[10] A character invented by Hulme to be the hero of a proposed philosophical allegory.

Never, never, never a simple statement. It has no effect. One must always have analogies, which make another world. Through-the-glass effect, which is what I want.

The process of invention is that of gradually making solid the castles in the air.

With perfect style, the solid leather for reading, each sentence should be a lump, a piece of clay, a vision seen; or, rather, a wall touched with soft fingers. Never should one feel light, vaporous bridges between one solid sense and another. No bridges—all solid: then never exasperated.

All styles are only means of subduing the reader.

Prose is a museum where all the old weapons of poetry are kept.

Whitman had a theory that every object under the sun comes within the range of poetry. But he was too early in the day. It is no use having a theory that motor-cars are beautiful, and backing up this theory by working up an emotion not really felt. The object must cause the emotion before the poem can be written. Whitman's theory, that everything in America must be glorious, was his snare, because it was only a theory. Minor poets, with their romantic jewels, make the same mistake from the other side—a lost poetic content.

Literature, like memory, selects only the vivid patches of life. If literature (realistic) did really resemble life, it would be interminable, dreary, commonplace, eating and dressing, buttoning, with here and there a patch of vividness.

Life is composed of exquisite moments and the rest is shadows of them.

.   .   .   .

It is difficult to refrain from quoting further, but the above excerpts serve to illustrate Hulme's power of expression, and also to furnish the reader with the fundamental statements of the imagist point of view.

I wish it were possible, but it is not, to prove exactly to what extent the various poets whom we shall consider later were indebted to Hulme and his theories. I have discussed the point with several of them, and they agree that the influence was considerable; but it is too much to expect of a poet that he will recall or be able to determine specifically the extent of influences which he felt many years ago. A small hint taken from another mind will grow in the receiver until it seems his own. It is a fact, at any rate, that three or four of the original group of imagist poets were acquaintances of Hulme's, and that they regularly indulged in conversation with him on the subject of poetry. Without detracting from their individual abilities, we may at least look upon Hulme as their common stimulus and, in that sense, the starting-point of modern imagism.

Herbert Read, in his introduction to Hulme's "Notes on Language and Style," makes two very interesting statements, one regarding Hulme's own sources, the other regarding Hulme as a source. They are as follows:

It is not claimed that Hulme's theories are in any wonderful way original. They owe a good deal, I think, to Remy de Gourmont's *Problème du Style*, and perhaps a little to Jules de Gaultier, the author of *Le Bovarysme*. More exactly, perhaps, they reproduce the metaphysical conceptions of Telesio and Campanella. But Hulme cared intensely for his ideas, wherever he may have derived them, and he worked hard to give them a personal valuation.

. . . . though attempts have been made to create an "imagist" poetry directly under the influence of Hulme's theories, and though these attempts have been of great value in the introduction of a clearer tone into poetic expression, they have remained comparatively obscure because they have not been the vehicle of any momentous intelligence. That does not alter the validity of the ideas or the possibility of their general application.

Our friends the imagists may feel that the preceding

statement is a trifle harsh, but on the other hand it is true that in England these poets are "comparatively obscure"; in America I should say they are comparatively well known. And as for "momentous intelligence," well, it would require unusual conceit to lay claim to that. Let us assume merely that they are worth writing about.

II ≉ IMAGISM AS
A MOVEMENT

WE HAVE located the germ of imagism in the writings and conversation of T. E. Hulme and his friends. We have now to trace briefly the development of that germ. Hulme's interest was in philosophy, particularly aesthetic philosophy. When he had formulated a philosophy of poetry, he turned to the theory of sculpture.[1] To make of imagism anything more than a set of theories, supported by a few modest examples of application, a professional literary man was required.

Ezra Pound joined Hulme's group early in 1909, and immediately assumed the literary leadership not only of this particular group but of all the young poets in London who were interested in the creation of something new. He was a very magnetic young man, come flaming from the shores of America (via Italy), slender, with a mass of reddish hair, bright, indescribable eyes (green rather than any other color), a quick mind, a good basis of languages and classical literature, a passion for the troubadours, and the self-confidence of the Devil himself. His room in Church Walk,

[1] At the time of his death he was writing a book on the work of Gaudier-Brzeska. The manuscript was lost.

Kensington (at eight shillings a week) soon became the center of the new poetry.

In 1911 Hilda Doolittle, another young American poet, arrived in Europe, and eventually in London. She had known Ezra Pound in Pennsylvania. Soon she made the acquaintance of Richard Aldington, a gifted young Englishman who had been studying at the University of London. Mr. Aldington was fascinated by Greek poetry; so was Miss Doolittle. They read poetry together. They began writing poetry, chiefly on Greek themes, in vers libre. They brought to life rhythms and images which reflected the beauty of an older age but which also expressed something very modern. These poems were greatly admired by Pound. He wanted to do something with them. But there were at the time scarcely any periodicals liberal enough to publish this sort of poetry.

In this same year, 1911, Miss Harriet Monroe, an art critic on the Chicago *Tribune*, returned to America from a visit to China, where she had been much impressed by the recognition given to poetry. She was inspired to do something to help poetry in America. In her spare time she set about raising five thousand dollars to subsidize a magazine of which she was to be the editor. She asked subscriptions of fifty dollars each from a hundred people, mostly business men. In a few months she had raised her quota and a little bit more. She then secured Alice Corbin Henderson as associate editor, and in October 1912 appeared the first issue of *Poetry: A Magazine of Verse*. Ezra Pound was appointed foreign representative and correspondent, and in this capacity he sent over the first imagist poems to reach America —three by Richard Aldington and three by H. D. (Hilda Doolittle).

The history of Miss Monroe's enterprising and courageous magazine is a book in itself, and cannot be incorporated
here. But we may remark that since 1912 practically every
new poet of value in England and America has found the
magazine a channel for his expression and, in many cases, the
means of introducing his work to the public.[2] The remarkable thing is that the editors have been willing to publish almost any kind of poetry, and have demanded only that a
poem be good of its kind.

To the issue for January 1913 Pound contributed, in addition to H. D.'s three poems, some literary notes, in which
he mentioned the imagists as a group. In the March number he went further, and set down the principles of imagism.
These were printed over the signature of F. S. Flint in what
purported to be an interview with an imagist but which as a
matter of fact was merely a statement by Pound. And following this, in the same number, appeared "A Few Don'ts
by an Imagiste," signed by Pound himself.

In the "interview" the four cardinal principles of Imagism are set forth as:

1. "Direct treatment of the 'thing,' whether subjective
or objective.

2. "To use absolutely no word that does not contribute
to the presentation.

3. "As regards rhythm, to compose in sequence of the
musical phrase, not in sequence of a metronome."

4. To conform to the "doctrine of the image"—which
the author says has not been defined for publication, as it

[2] A similar service was performed for several years by the *Little
Review*, edited by Margaret Anderson. The imagists were among the poets
who found its pages hospitable.

does not concern the public and would provoke useless discussion.

By these first three propositions the imagists judged all poetry and found most of it wanting. The test "will throw out nine-tenths of all the bad poetry now accepted as standard and classic; and will prevent you from many a crime of production."

As for the list of "Don'ts," which Floyd Dell, writing in the Chicago *Tribune*, thought worthy of incorporation in a constitutional amendment, here are some of the most striking items:

Pay no attention to the criticism of men who have never themselves written a notable work. Consider the discrepancies between the actual writing of the Greek poets and dramatists and the theories of the Graeco-Roman grammarians, concocted to explain their meters.

Go in fear of abstractions. Don't retail in mediocre verse what has already been done in good prose. Don't think any intelligent person is going to be deceived when you try to shirk all the difficulties of the unspeakably difficult art of good prose by chopping your composition into line lengths.

Be influenced by as many great artists as you can, but have the decency either to acknowledge the debt outright, or to try to conceal it.

What the expert is tired of today the public will be tired of tomorrow.

Let the candidate fill his mind with the finest cadences he can discover, preferably in a foreign language, so that the meaning of the words may be less likely to divert his attention from the movement, e.g., Saxon charms, Hebridean Folk Songs, the verses of Dante, and the lyrics of Shakespeare—if he can dissociate the vocabulary from the cadence. Let him dissect the lyrics of Goethe coldly into their component sound values, syllables long and short, stressed and unstressed, into vowels and consonants.

It is not necessary that a poem should rely on its music, but if it does rely on its music that music must be such as will delight the expert.

Don't chop your stuff into separate *iambs*. Don't make each line stop dead at the end, and then begin every next line with a heave. Let the beginning of the next line catch the rise of the rhythm wave, unless you want a definite longish pause.

The musician can rely on pitch and the volume of the orchestra. You can not. The term harmony is misapplied to poetry; it refers to simultaneous sounds of different pitch. There is, however, in the best verse a sort of residue of sound which remains in the ear of the hearer and acts more or less as an organ-base. A rime must have in it some slight element of surprise if it is to give pleasure; it need not be bizarre or curious, but it must be well used if used at all.

Consider the definiteness of Dante's presentation, as compared with Milton's rhetoric. Read as much of Wordsworth as does not seem too unutterably dull.

If you want the gist of the matter go to Sappho, Catullus, Villon, Heine when he is in the vein, Gautier when he is not too frigid; or, if you have not the tongues, seek out the leisurely Chaucer. Good prose will do you no harm, and there is good discipline to be had by trying to write it.

These precepts illustrate very well the acute poetic intelligence of Ezra Pound—an intelligence which has been amply manifested in his own poetry and, it must always be remembered, in the work of a great many of the best writers of today who have studied with him and taken his advice.

In this same article Pound refers to the "Image," and defines it as "that which presents an intellectual and emotional complex in an instant of time." He continues: "It is the presentation of such a 'complex' instantaneously which gives that sense of sudden liberation; that sense of freedom from time limits and space limits; that sense of sudden growth, which we experience in the presence of the greatest works of art." And finally, there is his concentrated affirmation that: "It is better to present one Image in a lifetime than to produce voluminous works."

These documents are important, for they constitute the first publication of an imagist credo. As Mr. Pound has explained to me in conversation, he was guided by a desire to formulate the points of agreement between the various imagist poets. The manifesto was not, could not be, an expression of the individualities of the poets. Their dissimilarities had to be carefully excluded. Had Mr. Flint, for example, drawn up the credo, it would have been based on French impressionism, says Pound; whereas H. D. and Mr. Aldington would have drawn up a purely Hellenistic one. The official imagist credo, however, was not prepared until the publication of the 1915 anthology, when Pound was no longer a member of the group.

Meanwhile there was the problem of an organ of imagist expression in England. In 1909 Ford Madox Hueffer (now Ford Madox Ford) had founded the *English Review*, and one of his avowed purposes was to publish the work of interesting new writers (he did publish work by Ezra Pound, F. S. Flint, and D. H. Lawrence); but after a year and a half, the magazine changed hands, and a new editor was installed. This circumstance was, according to Pound and others, a very great blow to modern English poetry. Hueffer was sympathetic toward the new poetry and could have been of great service to the imagists. What actually happened was that the latter, blocked by the conservative periodicals, were forced to take control of a small paper and make it their own. But this they did not succeed in doing until January 1914. In the meantime they found an outlet for a certain amount of their work in the *Poetry Review,* a monthly magazine, and in its successor, *Poetry and Drama,* a quarterly, published by Harold Monro in connection with his Poetry Bookshop. Mr. Monro, although not entirely in sympathy with the imagist point of view (his own poetry would prove that) has in many instances served the imagist cause. His bookshop, opened in January 1912, created a center of poetic interest in London, and from this center have issued periodicals and volumes of poetry in which the imagists have had a considerable if not a major share. *Poetry and Drama* suspended publication at the end of 1914, but five years later, the War having been concluded, its place was taken by *The Chapbook: A Monthly Miscellany,* certainly one of the most attractive series of pamphlets ever printed. Unfortunately, it, too, was suspended after four years of publication.

It was something to be able to secure the publication of a certain number of poems and critical articles in such charming mediums as those sponsored by Mr. Monro, but from the point of view of the imagists this was not enough. The entire group was boiling over with ideas, chiefly propagandist ones, and the only solution was a magazine devoted to their interests.

It occurred that in June 1913 a fortnightly paper, *The New Freewoman: An Individualist Review,* began publication. Its founders were Miss Harriet Shaw Weaver and Miss Dora Marsden, two women imbued with the spirit of the then raging feminist movement. But unlike Mrs. Pankhurst, whose paper, *Votes for Women,* was very much in the public eye, these two suffragettes contented themselves with a philosophical rather than an active political campaign. Miss

Weaver was inclined toward philosophical anarchism, and Miss Marsden was under the spell of Berkeleyan metaphysics. Miss Weaver had some money, and Miss Marsden was itching to preach. *The New Freewoman* was the result.

The eye of the imagists fell upon this paper, and the shrewd Mr. Pound convinced the two philosophical feminists that what they needed for their publication was an up-to-date literary department. Forthwith an agreement was reached under the terms of which the literary group was to do as it liked with the whole paper, except for the leading article, which was always to be written by Miss Marsden. Richard Aldington was installed as assistant editor (Miss Marsden retained the title of editor, although it was purely nominal), and the name of the paper was changed to the *Egoist*. The subtitle, *An Individualist Review*, was retained.

The first number of the *Egoist* appeared on January 1, 1914. It continued as a semi-monthly publication throughout the year. In January 1915 it became a monthly, and remained such until December 1919, when it suspended publication. In the last year of its life, however, only five numbers were issued.

With the July 1, 1914, issue, Miss Weaver appears on the masthead as editor, and Miss Marsden becomes contributing editor. This form is maintained thereafter. Beginning in the summer of 1916, H. D. and Richard Aldington are both listed as assistant editors; but in June 1917 their names are dropped (Aldington having gone to the War) and their place is taken by T. S. Eliot, who continues in this capacity until publication ceases.

It was a very amusing, and in many ways a very good, paper. To anyone interested in the imagist group it is little short of fascinating. And not the least amusing thing to one who looks through the complete file of the *Egoist* is the never-ending stream of abstraction contributed by Miss Marsden. Except for one or two occasions when illness intervened, she never failed to exercise her privilege of occupying the first page (and usually several other pages into the bargain). What she wrote had not the slightest connection with the other contents of the paper, and was studiously overlooked by most readers. As for the bulk of the contents, it was written by a small group, not all imagists, but largely so. Among the principal contributors were: Richard Aldington, Ezra Pound, F. S. Flint, H. D., John Gould Fletcher, D. H. Lawrence, T. S. Eliot, Amy Lowell, James Joyce, Huntly Carter, John Cournos, Allen Upward, Storm Jameson, Edward Storer, A. W. G. Randall, Wyndham Lewis, May Sinclair, and William Carlos Williams.

One of the most important non-imagist contributors, of course, was James Joyce, whose novel, *A Portrait of the Artist as a Young Man,* was run as a serial, and whose *Ulysses* would have appeared similarly had the editors been able to find an English printing establishment willing to set it up in type. Wyndham Lewis' *Tarr* was also run as a serial.

For the most part the *Egoist* was composed of short articles on modern poetry, painting, sculpture, music, and so on; translations of Greek, Latin, and French poems, and of prose pieces by Remy de Gourmont and other important modern Frenchmen; original poems by the imagists and their contemporaries; woodcuts and line drawings in the modern manner; and a page of frequently diverting correspondence. Many of the critical articles were pure propaganda for imagism—or at least advertising for the imagists —but the literary editors were not averse to printing counterblasts and attacks on themselves, so a reasonable balance was maintained. The sad thing was, of course, that the paper had such a small circulation: almost none outside of England, and very little there. But if it did not gain a large audience for these poets, at least it provided them with a safety valve.

About the time the *Egoist* transaction was being effected, the restless Mr. Pound was working at another scheme, namely, the publication of a volume of the new poetry. What he really wished to do was to promote the poems of Aldington and H.D. But at that date the output of these two was decidedly small. They were working along distinctively qualitative, not quantitative, lines. Between them they could not muster enough poetry for even the proverbial "slim volume." But their *entrepreneur* was not to be thwarted by any such circumstance. Selecting ten poems by Aldington and seven by H. D., he used these as a nucleus, and invited a number of sympathetic contemporaries to contribute the rest of the book. He tossed in six of his own poems (those which he considered the most imagistic), took five from F. S. Flint, and one each from Skipwith Cannell, Amy Lowell, William Carlos Williams, James Joyce, Ford Madox Hueffer, Allen Upward, and John Cournos. For good measure he added some "documents," which consisted of three frivolous poetic travesties written (obviously) by himself, Aldington, and Hueffer.

It was a rather wild and not altogether homogeneous collection, but at least it was held together by a spirit of revolt. Completed late in 1913, it was published in March 1914 with the title, *Des Imagistes: An Anthology*.[3] Who edited the book was not indicated. In England it was generally scorned, though one favorable review appeared in a London

---

[3] New York: Albert and Charles Boni; London: Poetry Bookshop.

paper, the *Morning Post.* A few insulted readers returned their copies to the Poetry Bookshop and abused Mr. Monro for having sponsored such a volume. In America, as Amy Lowell said later, "It was much, but very ignorantly, reviewed." Yet not quite all the blame should be put on the public. The title was affected and cryptic; the poems were based on a new technique; and there was no preface to explain the technique or to indicate the ideals of the poets.

Having launched imagism, even if not altogether successfully, Ezra Pound's interest in the movement began to wane. He was then, and is still, intensely afraid of belonging to a dead movement (if this contradiction in terms is permissible). He will lead a charge, but he will not remain to hold the gained position. To do so would mean for him stagnation. The moment a thing is accepted or even tolerated, Pound drops it like a hot cake. He abhors respectability. Not that he stayed with the imagists long enough to see them fully accredited; he deserted before such a calamity could befall. His interest swung to Gaudier-Brzeska and Wyndham Lewis, the first a young French sculptor living in London, the second a brilliant English painter, novelist, and critic. In conjunction with these two, Pound evolved a new "ism" more startling than imagism. This was "vorticism." New manifestoes were prepared and included in a huge pamphlet called *Blast,*[4] which was published on June 20, 1914. *Blast,* it was announced, would appear regularly, as a quarterly magazine. Actually, however, only one other issue ever appeared, and that not until July 1915. Both numbers were edited by Wyndham Lewis, and contained a good many of his own drawings and prose articles. Other con-

---

[4] London and New York: John Lane.

tributors were: Ford Madox Hueffer, Rebecca West, Ezra Pound, Jacob Epstein, Gaudier-Brzeska, and T. S. Eliot. There is not space in this chapter to describe in detail these very interesting, if extremely blatant, publications, nor to summarize the vorticist credo. At the moment I wish merely to note Mr. Pound's defection from the imagist idea.

But that idea was not to be let die. The little orphan was presently to be picked up, have its face washed, be given a square meal and a new suit of clothes, and be presented to the world as the smartest child in seven counties.

The fairy godmother, and a very rich godmother she was, too, arrived in London (from Boston) early in the summer of 1914, with a grand motor car, a chauffeur, and a maid. She took a suite of rooms at the Berkeley Hotel, gathered about her all the aspiring young poets (especially the imagistic ones), questioned them at length about their work, discussed modern French poetry with them (a subject on which she was reasonably well informed), dined them and wined them, and altogether took charge of things. She was no other than Amy Lowell, the large, affluent, blue-blooded, energetic, well-educated spinster poet of New England, who smoked cigars and worshiped Keats.

Miss Lowell had met some of these poets before, on her previous visit to London in the summer of 1913, and she had contributed one poem to *Des Imagistes*. In other words, she knew what was going on, and what imagism was, although until her 1913 visit to London her own poetry had been entirely of the conventional rime-and-meter sort.[5] As far as can be ascertained, the poem, "In a Garden," which Pound used in *Des Imagistes,* was her first attempt at vers libre.

[5] See her first volume of poems, *A Dome of Many-Coloured Glass.* Boston: Houghton Mifflin. 1912.

But at the time of her 1914 visit, she was wholeheartedly
in favor of technical experimentation and innovation, and she
set herself the task of "selling" the new poetry to the world,
at least to the American world. It was an opportunity which
in her astuteness she could not overlook. She envisaged herself in a triple rôle: first, as one of the principal poets of the
group; second, as business agent for the others; third, as
critical interpreter of the new poetry in America. To say that
she filled all three rôles with reasonable success is to state an
absolute fact.

It was not difficult to enlist a following from among the
young poets then in London. None of them had tasted any
large success, artistic or financial. How could they, or why
should they, hesitate to follow a fairy godmother who prom-
ised to bring them fame and if not fortune at least a few
shiny dollars? What impoverished young poet of Kensington could resist the hospitality of the suite at the Berkeley,
or the glowing confidence of its opulent inhabitant? As a
document of intrinsic charm and some historical importance,
let me reproduce here the menu of the so-called "Imagist
Dinner," given by Amy Lowell at the Dieu Donnes Restaurant on the evening of Friday, July 17, 1914, those present,
apart from the hostess, being Richard Aldington, John
Cournos, H. D., John Gould Fletcher, F. S. Flint, F. M.
Hueffer, Ezra Pound, and Allen Upward:

MENU

Hors d'Oeuvres Norvégienne

Consommé Sarah Bernhardt

Bisque de Homards

Filets de sole Lucullus

Cailles en Gelée aux Muscats

Selle d'Agneau Richelieu

Canetons d'Aylesbury a l'Anglaise
Petits Pois aux Laitues
Jambon d'York au Champagne
Haricots Verts Maitre d'Hôtel
Bombe Moka   Friandises   Dessert
Café

Is it any wonder at all that when Miss Lowell returned to America in September (the War hurried her departure from England) she carried with her the manuscript of *Some Imagist Poets?* The wonder is that she didn't carry off the poets as well.

Meanwhile, however, she had been compelled to choose carefully from among the poets. Some she could not get on with (in spite of the dinners); others were unwilling to subscribe to a fixed program, the imagist program, and one of Miss Lowell's contentions was that the group must stick together for a period of at least three years—must not desert the camp until the battle had been won. At any rate, the personnel eventually was determined, and the six poets who became the official imagists were: Richard Aldington, H. D., John Gould Fletcher, F. S. Flint, D. H. Lawrence, and Amy Lowell. In the name of the group, Miss Lowell signed a contract with Messrs. Houghton, Mifflin and Company for the publication of three anthologies of imagist poetry, to be issued separately at yearly intervals. This contract was fulfilled, and the anthologies appeared in 1915, 1916, 1917.

Another word regarding the personnel of the group: Richard Aldington and H. D. were indispensable to any group marching under the banner of imagism, for their work was the purest expression of that movement. Something similar might be said of Mr. Flint, for he was one of the earliest and most consistent professors of imagist principles.

That Amy Lowell should have included herself among the six needs no explanation. Why D. H. Lawrence "made one" has never been adequately explained. He had had nothing to do with the movement in its early days; he had not even written poetry which could be classified as imagistic. But Miss Lowell admired his work, and invited him to join her party. Lawrence thereupon developed a practical interest in imagism and contributed a number of poems which were at least admissible to the imagist anthologies. John Gould Fletcher enlisted chiefly because of Miss Lowell's persuasiveness. By nature he was strongly averse to identifying himself with any "school," and for several years he had pursued his solitary course, developing his poetry in his own way. He had refused an invitation from Pound to contribute to *Des Imagistes*. Before that, even, he had been invited to join Hulme's poetry-philosophy discussion club, but had declined, through shyness and an exaggerated individualism. But having resisted imagism, he could not resist "Amygism," as Pound labeled the movement when Miss Lowell became its leader. Why Pound himself was not of the "six," or why he did not make it seven, must be fairly obvious. He had already acquired new, and to him more vital, interests. As he said to me recently in conversation, "Imagism was a point on the curve of my development. Some people remained at that point. I moved on." Besides, it is patently impossible for him to play second fiddle to anyone, and Amy Lowell had planted herself firmly in the first fiddler's chair. By accident or design, the six imagists struck a national balance: three (H. D., Fletcher, and Miss Lowell) were Americans; three (Aldington, Flint, and Lawrence) were Englishmen. That is why the movement is, with peculiar justice, referred to as Anglo-American.

Miss Lowell did not insist upon editing the three anthologies for which she had contracted. Indeed, she preferred that the contents be selected by all the poets represented, acting as a committee and passing on each other's work. This plan was adopted, in most cases the poet's own selection from his work being accepted. The authors were arranged alphabetically.

To the 1915 anthology was attached a preface, unsigned, and purporting to express the principles of the group. This preface was written by Mr. Aldington, and was slightly revised by Miss Lowell. It explains that the six poets do not "represent a clique," but that they "are united by certain common principles, arrived at independently. These principles are not new; they have fallen into desuetude. They are the essentials of all great poetry, indeed of all great literature."

Then follows the famous credo, which has been reproduced so many times, but which nevertheless must be stated again to illustrate the final crystallized form of the ideas whose development we have been at such pains to trace. There are six points:

1. To use the language of common speech, but to employ always the *exact* word, not the nearly-exact, nor the merely decorative word.

2. To create new rhythms—as the expression of new moods— and not to copy old rhythms, which merely echo old moods. We do not insist upon "free verse" as the only method of writing poetry. We fight for it as for a principle of liberty. We believe that the individuality of a poet may often be better expressed in free verse than in conventional forms. In poetry, a new cadence means a new idea.

3. To allow absolute freedom in the choice of subject. It is not good art to write badly about aeroplanes and automobiles; nor is it necessarily bad art to write well about the past. We believe pas-

sionately in the artistic value of modern life, but we wish to point out that there is nothing so uninspiring nor so old-fashioned as an aeroplane of the year 1911.

4. To present an image (hence the name, imagist). We are not a school of painters, but we believe that poetry should render particulars exactly and not deal in vague generalities, however magnificent and sonorous. It is for this reason that we oppose the cosmic poet, who seems to us to shirk the real difficulties of his art.

5. To produce poetry that is hard and clear, never blurred nor indefinite.

6. Finally, most of us believe that concentration is of the very essence of poetry.

It will be clear at once to the reader that this credo is a summary of the fundamental propositions of Hulme and Pound, and is not in any respect an innovation. It did, however, serve this purpose: it furnished the sympathetic reader with a clue to the poetry which followed and set up a visible target for the reactionary critics to fire at.

The enormous amount of discussion which followed the publication of the 1915 anthology led to the inclusion of another preface in the volume for 1916. In this preface, unsigned, but written almost entirely by Miss Lowell, an attempt is made to clear up the misunderstandings which had arisen, and to explain in detail the principles of vers libre, of poetry based on cadence. But as this subject is to be dealt with later in a chapter devoted to the prose-poetry controversy, I shall not allow it space here.

The battle was fought out on every ground during 1915 and 1916. By the spring of 1917, when the last anthology appeared, it was deemed unnecessary to say anything more in extenuation of the imagist principles. The poetry was left to stand alone. In her *Tendencies in Modern American Poetry,* a book written shortly after the publication of the last imagist anthology, Miss Lowell gave a short account of the movement, and concluded it with this statement:

> There will be no more volumes of *Some Imagist Poets*. The collection has done its work. These three little books are the germ, the nucleus, of the school; its spreading out, its amplification, must be sought in the published work of the individual members of the group.[6]

We may say, then, that although imagism as an idea, or as a point of view, or even as a conscious method in poetry, goes back to 1908 in England (let us not here consider its foreign origins),[7] as an organized movement designed to affect the public taste, it dates from the publication of Pound's article in *Poetry* for March 1913. We may say also that although certain of the imagist poets have continued to write in the imagist manner, and a great many of their contemporaries and successors have done so too, imagism as a movement ended with the publication of the fourth anthology in April 1917.

The appearance of a recent volume entitled *Imagist Anthology, 1930*,[8] has helped to revive interest in imagism as a movement, though the intention of the volume is not in the least propagandist. Its purpose is merely to present in friendly juxtaposition specimens of recent work by various poets who have at one time or another marched under the imagist banner. Those who were found willing to attend

[6] Lowell: *Tendencies in Modern American Poetry*. New York: Macmillan. 1917. Page 255.

[7] Light is thrown upon the antiquity of free verse in Henry Lanz: *The Physical Basis of Rime* and B. R. Lewis: *Creative Poetry*, both published (1931) by the Stanford University Press.

[8] New York: Covici, Friede; London: Chatto & Windus. 1930.

this reunion in print are: Richard Aldington (the actual instigator of the volume), John Cournos, H. D., John Gould Fletcher, F. S. Flint, Ford Madox Ford, James Joyce, D. H. Lawrence, and William Carlos Williams. Forewords are contributed by Ford Madox Ford and the present writer.

In his foreword, entitled "Those Were the Days," Mr. Ford discourses whimsically on various literary movements in which he has participated, and takes pleasure in posing as a benevolent and witty patriarch. He is particularly happy in teasing "the late Ezra Pound." The serious theme beneath his persiflage is that militant movements are wholesome and necessary to the vitality of literature.

My own point, expressed in the other foreword, is that the imagist banner is here flaunted not as a challenge but as a symbol, and that the imagists are here mustered not for a charge but for parade. Even if two or three of the marchers seem to limp slightly, the parade is nevertheless a success, for there is sufficient fame attached to the names of these veterans to lend the occasion an air of triumph.

III ≋ THE CRITICAL REACTION

IT IS ALWAYS amazing to perceive what a furore a new, or revived, artistic credo can create, not only among the French, who, we know, draw swords and let fly fists over technical points of versification, but even among Anglo-Saxons and others of notably cold blood. The generous interpretation is, of course, that a great many people are really fond of art in some form, and therefore resent any attempt to modify the principles on which their pleasure is founded. Most English-speaking people into whose consciousness broke the first imagist anthologies had been nourished on romantic, rimed and metered verse. Their experience of poetry from Mother Goose to Keats and Tennyson had been unjarred by either looseness of form or hardness of content. A few had read Whitman, but not with affection, and certainly with many reservations as to the authenticity of most of his "poetry." More had read or heard poetic passages from the Bible but not with literary appreciation.

One might have expected a reasonable number of professional critics, as distinct from average readers, to perceive the essential merits (as well as the faults) of the new poetry.

But the records show that very few indeed, either in England or America, were sufficiently catholic in taste or acute in perception to evaluate intelligently what has since come to be recognized as good and relatively important work. Instinctive prejudice was in most cases the controlling factor. It is probably fair to say, however, that every incentive for a violent reaction was given by the imagists and their revolutionary contemporaries. Being young, they were consciously provocative and irreverent; being wise in the ways of literary revolts, they attacked with sensational boldness. It is obvious that they carried the fortress of America and are now safely encamped within the citadel. England they never carried. Five years at the most were sufficient to win places for their work in the best American anthologies and in college curricula. But after fifteen years imagist poetry goes begging in London. The romantic tradition is too strong.

It is very likely typical of the two countries that the one which protested most violently, yielded, whereas the one which merely ignored, still ignores. In spite of the publication of the imagist anthologies and the propagandist enthusiasm of the *Egoist*, not to speak of the publication of many volumes of verse by the several imagist poets, remarkably few comments on the movement have appeared in English periodicals. The effect is that of a conspiracy of silent scorn. Provincial papers have occasionally waxed sarcastic, but briefly. The friendly notices appearing from time to time have been contributed for the most part by eulogistic friends or by the imagist poets themselves. It has been either mutual back-scratching or oblivion.

The first serious and extended view of the movement was given by Harold Monro, and, although his article appeared in the *Egoist*, it was not by any means a eulogy. In fact its tone was rather severe.[1] Mr. Monro, unlike the majority of English critics, had been in close touch with imagism from its inception, and was therefore in a position to quarrel with it intelligently. At the beginning of his essay he recounts briefly the origins of the movement, and then proceeds to evaluate its results. He says:

> The English movement was from the first not broad enough. Several of the Imagists seem to have been struck partially blind at the first sight of their new world; and they are still blinking. Some simply made the discovery, and then started preparing their public before they had written their poetry. Others were so terrified at Cosmicism that they ran away into a kind of Microcosmicism, and found their greatest emotional excitement in everything that seemed intensely small. But, above all, Skepticism, having once attacked them, played havoc in their ranks. They found themselves obliged to reduce their production by 90 per cent, and they recommended everyone else to do the same. The forms they still felt they might use, the vocabulary that remained at their disposal, were so extremely limited; so much good material had to be thrown into the large wastepaper basket of *Cliché*, that they remained now almost unprovided with a language or a style.

Mr. Monro then proceeds to enumerate the other obvious difficulties faced by the imagists, and to record the losses which are inevitable in the case of a poetry based upon a theory of limitation. He is particularly annoyed by the statement in the credo that "In poetry a new cadence means a new idea." He asks, "Is one to believe that if one first design a poem, then the idea will be present by reason of the design? In their correct order these words should read: 'In

---

[1] "The Imagists Discussed," *Egoist*, May 1, 1915.

poetry, a new idea means (better *makes*) a new cadence.' "
Later he contends that imagism "is on the point of deciding
whether it intends to be taken seriously," and if it is to be
so taken, its poets must "reconcile themselves to bringing
imagination to the support of intellect." He concludes with a
series of critical comments on the various imagists, and on the
poems of the 1915 anthology, finding some cause for praise,
but more for censure.

Another, and perhaps more interesting because more
personal, article on the subject appeared soon after Mr.
Monro's. This was contributed by F. M. Hueffer to the *Outlook* (London) for July 10, 1915, under the title, "A Jubilee." What this title means is that in 1890 Mr. Hueffer
wrote his first book review and that in the present review of
the imagist anthology, *Some Imagist Poets* (1915), he is
celebrating the twenty-fifth anniversary of his initiation into
literary criticism. He takes the opportunity to sketch his relation to this movement and others. The article is worth
quoting from at length:

> I do not suppose that I have led a movement, though I dare say
> I have. There isn't, you know, any knowing in these matters. Sup-
> posing that I should say that my young friends the Imagists were
> children of my teaching. I expect that, with one accord, they would
> get up and say that they had never heard of me. The world is like
> that. But still, unceasingly, in season and out, for a quarter of a
> century I have preached the doctrine that my young friends now
> inscribe on the banner of their movement. So I may have led their
> movement—blowing, as it were, into a discordant gourd, in the dust
> of the wilderness, miles ahead, and no doubt unworthy to unloosen
> the shoe-latchets now that I am overtaken.

> What, then, is this doctrine? Simply that the rendering of the
> material facts of life, without comment and in exact language, is
> poetry, and that poetry is the only important thing in life.

He then goes on to say that he differs in some ways from the imagists—especially in their "sniffing attitude toward prose," and he quotes from the preface to *Some Imagist Poets* as follows: "We attach the term ['free verse'] to all that increasing amount of writing whose cadence is more marked, more definite, and closer knit than prose, but which is not so violently nor so obviously accented as the so-called 'regular verse.'"

Mr. Hueffer's comment on this statement is:

This is a survival of an ancient superstition descending from barbarous days when primeval savages first found that rhythmical grunts could be used for the accentuating of group emotions. I express this fact as incisively as I can because this pronouncement of the preface writer is a perpetuation of the greatest nuisance in the world. The fact is that cadenced prose is poetry, and there is no other poetry. Rhythmic prose, regular verse forms, and "free verse" itself as soon as its cadence is "more marked, more definite, and closer knit" than that of properly constructed prose—all these things are departments of rhetoric, which is a device for stirring group passion.

At this point the writer interpolates specimens of "rhetoric" and specimens of "poetry." He then continues:

Of the six poets printed in this anthology, only two—H. D. and Mr. F. S. Flint—have the really exquisite sense of words, the really exquisite tranquillity, beauty of diction, and insight that justify a writer in assuming the rather proud title of Imagist—of issuing, that is to say, that challenge, that they will rouse emotions solely by rendering concrete objects, sounds, and aspects. Mr. D. H. Lawrence is a fine poet, but he employs similes—or rather the employment of similes is too essential a part of his methods to let his work, for the time being, have much claim to the epithets "restrained" or "exact." (What I mean is that although it may be ingenious writing to say that a wave looks like green jade, Stephen Crane's statement as to waves seen from a small boat, "the waves were barbarous and abrupt," is the real right thing.) Mr. John Gould Fletcher, Mr. Aldington, and Miss Lowell are all too preoccupied with themselves and their emotions to be really called Imagists. It is no doubt right to be dissatisfied with the world, or with the circumstances of your life in childhood, or to make your mark in the world by writing as if you were Paganini or Tartini of the "Trillo." But that is really not business—though of course it is business as usual.

After some further remarks concerning Miss Lowell's cleverness, and Mr. Lawrence's "touch of greatness," he pays extraordinary tribute to Mr. Flint, "one of the greatest men and one of the most beautiful spirits of the country," and to H. D. ("We may put it to the credit of this out-of-joint world that it has produced H. D."), and concludes that "English letters may take heart while such poets are writing," and that "Their movement is about the only literary thing that much matters today."

This is biased criticism, no doubt, but it is intelligent, and it is significant as being one of the few sympathetic responses to the appearance of imagism in England. And it is undeniably true that Hueffer had a share in determining the course of imagism. His statement that his point of view differs somewhat from that of the imagists is corroborated by his own poetic credo, which appears in the preface to his *Collected Poems*,[2] and which was also published under the title, "Impressionism: Some Speculations," in *Poetry* (Chicago), in the issues of August and September, 1913, as a counterblast to the imagist credo.

The chief result of the imagist movement in England appears to have been the resurrection of the vexatious question, "What is the difference between poetry and prose?"

[2] London: Secker. 1916.

This is a ghost that will not be laid, for it is still comparatively easy to find learned discussions of the subject in London literary reviews. And the fact that imagism has been so largely responsible for this continuing argument leads me to introduce in another chapter (chapter iv) representative statements from the principal controversialists.

Meanwhile, however, let us study the critical reaction to imagism in America.

One of the first, and certainly one of the few, sympathetic echoes came from the Chicago *Tribune*, in the spring of 1913, shortly after the appearance of the imagist credo in *Poetry*. The notice is credited to Floyd Dell, then a little-known reviewer, and it read in part as follows:

> If this is Imagism . . . . we are for establishing Imagism by constitutional amendment and imprisoning without recourse to ink or paper all "literary" ladies or gents who break any of these canons.

There were others besides Mr. Dell who realized the essential value of the credo, but few of them expressed themselves publicly or so early in the game. As a matter of fact, the controversy did not start in earnest until the summer of 1915, following the appearance of *Some Imagist Poets*, for only then, under the auspices of a large publisher and with the energy of Miss Amy Lowell behind it, did imagism force itself on the attention of a great number of American critics and readers. The early propaganda in *Poetry* had reached a limited circle, and the first anthology, *Des Imagistes* (1914), besides having a small sale, contained no credo—supplied no platform, and therefore failed as a challenge. *Some Imagist Poets* flaunted its banners, and the enemy charged.

One of the most impetuous assailants was Conrad Aiken, who led off with a poetic diatribe, contributed originally to

the Boston *Transcript,* and reprinted on May 9, 1915, in the
New York *Sun:*

BALLADE OF WORSHIPPERS OF THE IMAGE

Ezra Pound, Dick Aldington,
 Fletcher and Flint and sweet H. D.,
Whether you chirp in Kensington
 Or Hampstead Heath, or Bloomsbury;
Birds of protean pedigree,
 Vorticist, Cubist, or Imagist,
Where in a score years will you be,
 And the delicate succubae you kissed?

You, of the trivial straining fun,
 Who ape your betters in mirthless glee;
You, whose meticulous clear lines run
 In hideous insipidity;
And you, forsooth, who shinned a tree
 To keep with the gaping moon your tryst,
Where in a score years will you be,
 And the delicate succubae you kissed?

Idols and images, every one,
 Crash down like ancient theory;
Where is the Vortex under the sun
 That spins not always emptily?
Cease these jeers at minstrelsy,
 You, who perish and are not missed,
For where in a score years will you be,
 And the delicate succubae you kissed?

L'Envoi

Pound, though your henchmen now agree
 To hail the Prince in the Anarchist,

> Where in a score years will you be,
>   And the pale pink dream blown mouths you kissed?

The refrain still lacks a reply, though the "score years" is three-quarters gone, and complete oblivion has not descended upon any of the imagists. The most that could be said in support of Mr. Aiken's implication is that most of the imagists have ceased to write imagistically.

About the same time, however, Mr. Aiken composed a prosaic and less impassioned critique of the same poets, and this was published under the title, "The Place of Imagism," in the *New Republic* of May 22, 1915. Here he accuses the imagists of being a mutual admiration society (a charge somewhat justified, it must be admitted), and insists that imagist verse at its best is charming, interesting, or delightful, but never stirring. And the reason for this is, he says, that in none of the group is there any emotional force.

> Having misled us into expecting arrows in the heart, they shoot pretty darts at the more sophisticated brain. They give us frail pictures—whiffs of windy beaches, marshes, meadows, city streets, disheveled leaves; pictures pleasant and suggestive enough. But seldom is any of them more than a nice description, coolly sensuous, a rustle to the ear, a ripple to the eye. Of organic movement there is practically none.

He then chooses Mr. Fletcher as the best poet of the group because he alone "betrays a feeling for movement, for flow and balance." The rest are "music-deaf." Imagist poetry as a whole he describes as "a gentle preciosity of sound and color which may please the jaded connoisseur," and he concludes his article with the opinion that there is a field for imagism, albeit a limited one: the field of "the semi-precious in experience."

There is nothing vitriolic in this criticism, though there is much damning with faint praise. Still, it brought forth a counter attack from W. S. Braithwaite, who, as a matter of fact, was from the beginning one of the most ardent defenders of imagism. In the *New Republic* for June 12, 1915, under the title, "Imagism: Another View," Mr. Braithwaite openly took issue with Mr. Aiken, and wrote as follows:

All really great poets have broken the traditional regularities of form handed on to them by their predecessors; they found their genius could not achieve within the restrictions, and instead of adding to the mediocrity of the art, imposed technical obligations on themselves which only the most rigorous and persistent labors could accomplish. This, it seems to me, is what the Imagists are doing. It is what Chaucer, Shakespeare, Coleridge, Blake, Poe and Henley have done . . . . Whether the poetry of this modern Imagist group is great poetry is a matter with which we ought to have but little concern at present; that it is good poetry can easily be proved.

Then taking an exact cue from Mr. Aiken, he declares:

The final test of poetry is not that it stirs one—for to be stirred is only a transitory experience, and this the merest jingle has often effected—but that it haunts one. It is not the feeling of contemplative anxiety aroused by the philosophical or moral imagination that gives to poetry its highest value, but the agitated wonder awakened in the spirit of the reader by the sudden evocation of magic. This is the haunting quality in poetry, a thing that has no web of reasoning, and whose elements are so unaccountably mixed that no man has yet learned its secret. Now I contend that this is what the contemporary Imagists are striving for. They do not always get it, but they get it, this subtle quality of magic, in a measure beyond the reach of all but a few poets of today.

I fear that Mr. Braithwaite's defense had in it more good

will than accuracy. Its generalities did not meet properly the specific charges made by Mr. Aiken, but it belongs in the record, if only because of its good will.

Before we go on to more elaborate and serious reviews, we may pause to inspect a typical example of many comments which appeared in American periodicals, particularly provincial newspapers, in which the attitude of the critic was plainly one of annoyance and bewilderment. In the Los Angeles *Times* of June 13, 1915, we discover the following notice:

> The Imagists as a class are obstreperously eccentric. They have nothing new in their verse. They are more concerned with saying something in an odd way than in saying something worth while. Almost every one of them now and then flashes out with a line that sparkles, but the bulk of their work is pure affectation, much of it is nonsensical, some of it is idiotic.

Occasionally there appeared a criticism which reflected a rather detached point of view. The following, with its note of humor, was written by J. B. Kerfoot, and was published in *Life* on June 10, 1915:

> Realism is the raw material of both "naturalism" and the Imagist art. "Naturalism" tries to extract the living kernel from the realistic husk. The Imagist tries to isolate the germ cell in the kernel. A whiffed odor can carry us half across the world. An Imagist poet deals in verbal perfumes. On occasion—like the little girl with the curl—they can be wonderful creatures. And this little book contains enough occasions to pay for thumbing it.

After all, it is reassuring to discover that the leading American journal of humor could react so sensibly to a new literary movement—could be amused without descending to guffaws, and could recognize what so many more pretentious periodicals seemingly could not, that there was a point to imagism.

It was in the autumn of this imagistic year that the enemy brought its big guns into position. The opening of the universities may have had something to do with it, for the atmosphere was charged with intellect. And on the 18th of September the storm broke. On that day the Chicago *Evening Post* published the first of a series of four articles entitled "The New Poetry — A Critique," by Professor William Ellery Leonard, of the University of Wisconsin. In recent years Professor Leonard has won a very important place for himself among American poets, particularly with his magnificent sonnet-sequence, *Two Lives*; but in 1915 he appears to have been more interested in slaughtering other poets than in proving himself one. The four parts of the essay referred to above appeared at weekly intervals (September 18 to October 9), and together formed the most scholarly, sarcastic, and seriously-considered attempt at the annihilation of imagism yet recorded. It is so entertaining in its frenzied passion, so striking in its illustrations and parodies, so brilliant even in its false moments, that I feel justified in quoting from it extensively. And I do not mean to imply that I consider it utterly wrong or ridiculous. It is merely not fair, for it is inspired by aesthetic hatred.

One of the most annoying things to Professor Leonard was the imagist tendency to refer to ancient literatures. He wrote:

Their manifestos are prettily adorned with occult references to Japanese poetry and criticism, with much expenditure of printer's ink in spelling out exotic-looking syllables in ki, ka, and ko. They are, indeed, very skilful in the artistic use of the exotic. Which seems strange. For what is the psychology of the exotic but the generation of a mood—wistful, far, romantic—and is this, is this a poetic effect induced in the delightful reader's mind by their one poetic cathartic, the image?

In passing, we may note that at the time the above criticism was printed, none of the six self-labeled imagists had shown any special interest in Oriental poetry. Ezra Pound was the one who had begun work in that field. Later, of course, Mr. Fletcher and Miss Lowell developed a similar interest and reflected it in their work. The above criticism, then, must be applied to Mr. Pound alone. We may also question the correctness of Professor Leonard's implication that the image is ill adapted to the creation of a poetic mood. Japanese poetry is often pure imagism, and above all other types of poetry it aims at the creation of mood. The criticism was hasty and was based on a misconception.

Much do they murmur no less of Sappho, Villon, and Catullus— an hexameter, by the way, but let it stand; the Imagists have already turned prose into verse; so why should their prophet not use verse for prose? But let me, at least, print it properly:

Much do they murmur no less of Sappho, Villon, and Catullus.

I don't see exactly why. Unless the names be to their ears somewhat unfamiliar and exotic. Unless, perhaps, because these poets are by literary tradition the conventional names in use among people who talk about lyric poetry and "the resonant hearts of exquisite moments." But, then, the imagists abhor the conventional, and all literary traditions.

Here again, I fear, the critic erred. Those members of the imagist group who made reference to Latin, Greek, and French poets had a reasonably good knowledge of the classic poets mentioned. Professor Leonard perhaps had no way of knowing that almost without exception the imagists specialized in classics—in Latin and Greek—and that they all read French. He may have had some reason for suspecting the Americans (knowing how few American writers are well grounded in classics), but certainly he had less reason to suspect the English.

In spite of his rage, Professor Leonard managed to organize his attack under four general propositions (a relief from the customary academic three, at least), and these he stated as follows:

1. The Imagists can't see straight.
2. The Imagists can't feel straight.
3. The Imagists can't think straight.
4. The Imagists can't talk straight.

These propositions, sufficient, if sustained, to annihilate utterly any body of writers, he then attempted to prove. The following excerpts illustrate his method:

Imagists, doubtless, hear things more wonderful than Beethoven's symphonies in the buzz of the mosquito on the flats back of Chicago, and they whiff more than all the perfumes of Arabia in the summer steam of a Jersey dunghill.

Their physical eye is abnormal. They are often myopic: little minutiae of life, the shadow on a half-leaf caused by the upcurling of the other half, the white lines between the bricks of a chimney, the fly-speck on the window-frame between you and the blue sky (I take my illustrations from what is before me as I look up from my desk), details which a de Maupassant or a Tennyson would perhaps weave harmoniously into a larger picture or situation, become for the Imagists the whole horizon.

Of all writers Imagists might be expected not to violate the two simplest maxims of making images—that the given image should be capable of actual visualization, and that its parts should hang together. Not in the pinchbeck ingenuities of Young's inflated "Night Thoughts" will one find more essential bombast. Young's big drum is lacking; but the Imagist accomplishes the same thing with a squeak.

> "The sky was green wine held up in the sun.
> The moon was a golden petal between—"[3]

says one. Says another (and I purposely name no names):

> "My thoughts
> Chink against my ribs
> And roll about like silver hailstones.
> I should like to spill them out . . . ."[4]

Dear lady, I wish you might; you would feel easier. But a member of parliament (I think it was Lord Castlereagh) unwittingly extemporized long ago what is in some respects the best Imagist poem:

> "My lords,
> I smell a rat.
> I see him floating in the air.
> But mark you.
> In a trice
> I will nip him
> In the bud."

Professor Leonard goes on to say that the imagery of the imagists, when it is inconsistent, "as in the first example, is as old as the first muddlehead, and may be paralleled by the examples listed from all second-rate literature in the old-fashioned 'Principles of Rhetoric'—useful books still, it would seem. In so far as it is consistent, as in the second example, consistent in its elaboration of an initial false note and crotchet of thought, it may be paralleled in the worst 'Elizabethan Conceits' of Joshua Sylvester, Dr. Donne, and Abraham Cowley. John Dryden, when still under the influence of this historic fad of the fantastic, writing an elegy on

---

[3] From "Green" by D. H. Lawrence. *Some Imagist Poets.* 1915.

[4] From "Bullion" by Amy Lowell. *Some Imagist Poets.* 1915.

a young nobleman, dead of smallpox, achieved this imagism:

> 'Each little pimple had a tear in it
> To wail the fault its rising did commit.'

This, as the Imagist ought to say, is perfect work; nor should the form, good old heroic couplets, blind us to its perfection —as a sample of imagism." He goes on:

They mistake the fervor of compositional zeal, ambition to bowl a big score on the Imagists' tally-board (for the Cult spends half its time and ink in reviewing its members' performances); they mistake, I repeat, scribbler's itch for the impulse of the living word. Hence their painful hunt for emotions and subject-matter—the bizarre, the sordid, the exotic, the Circassian tea-tray and the back-alley tomato can . . . . Far from being original, it is their helpless unoriginality, their commonplace dullness of feeling, that compels them to the outer theme, as well as to the outer form . . . .

"The secret of boring is to tell everything," said Hugo. The secret of charm, say the Imagists, is to seem to have something to tell and to avoid telling what it is. They are so archly allusive! . . . . It is the most conventional and hackneyed of literary tricks.

And finally, because they can't feel, arises their barbarous diction. Their words don't spring to life, as wisdom from power, Athena from the head of Zeus. Their words are sought for, hunted out; not prayed for, waited for. Thus with them thoughts chink; and thus, combined with their resolution to emphasize sense impressions, we get a rich assortment of pseudo-onomatopoetic words in -oggle and -uggle, -abble and -obble, in -ittle and -attle, in -ish and -ush.

Is there anything more to say about this quackery, except that in the wide interest it has aroused it seems to bear out P. T. Barnum's discovery that "the American public likes to be humbugged"?

I believe it is unnecessary for us to take up separately and evaluate the points made by Professor Leonard. That certain of them indicated the weak points in imagism cannot be denied, but their effectiveness was greatly reduced by the unconcealed prejudice of the critic, by his untempered sarcasm, and in some cases by his misconception of the imagist point of view. He was quite right in objecting to inconsistent imagery and to far-fetched trivial conceits. But he was surely quite wrong in implying that these false steps were typical of the major imagist poems, and he was wrong also in failing to recognize the value of concentration and suggestion in poetry. It is rather a cheap trick to expose a literary method by only bad examples of that method.

And before the reverberations from Professor Leonard's artillery had died away, another bombardment began. This one, too, was of the grand sort. The enemy was O. W. Firkins, and his medium was the *Nation* (New York) for October 14, 1915. The actual title of the article was, "The New Movement in Poetry." It was a long article, and dealt with various phases of modern poetry, including the technique of vers libre. We reproduce the paragraphs most pertinent to imagism:

The misadventure of the Imagists lies in the fact that in extending deviation they have annihilated the one point which makes deviation influential or even perceptible—the basis of defined expectation. The variations have consumed the standard; the transgressors have repealed the law. Where all expectation is vague, all unexpectedness is vapid,

This sounds well, and beneath its pomposity is an idea which, though reactionary, is pertinent. But Mr. Firkins should admit that in good free verse there is a basis of expectation, less clearly defined, of course, than in poems of conventional meter and stanza, but perceptible to the trained ear, and often more pleasurable on account of its subtlety of definition. He ignores balanced cadence, and the strophe as a unit of composition. He continues:

The theory of Imagism breeds forecasts of incisive and picturesque variety, of darts and sallies, of clashes perhaps and bickerings, such as one dramatizes in some Genoese or Florentine marketplace in the bright turbulence of the receding Middle Ages. But the truth is that a meter of this kind cannot be multiplex for the same reason that a liquid cannot be supple; it is not firm enough. The psychology of the transaction is pointed. The cautious reader is afraid of these disparate and dissentient lines. He interposes, therefore, the cushion of a long, ceremonious pause; the movement becomes leisurely and calm; and, by a curious and pungent paradox, the incarnation of the versatile is entrapped by a phase of monotony. An air of dissipation and evanescence is the fitting Nemesis of a rhythm in which repetition and climax make no provision for the storage of metrical effects. Take Mr. Aldington's:

> O blue flower of the evening
> You have touched my face
> With your leaves of silver.

Never was so quiet an innovation made the subject of so clamorous an outcry; the gong has advertised the reed.

One might at this point interrupt to suggest that the gong is being struck by Mr. Firkins rather than by the imagists. A very large and sonorous gong. Let him strike again:

Another point of interest is the extraordinary detachment and solitude of the beings subjected to this curious regimen. The loneliness in which they dwell is almost polar; they are exiles who have actually accomplished the traditionally impossible feat of fleeing from themselves. One feels the futility of ransacking city directories or parish registries or voting lists in quest of an evidence of sonship or fatherhood or citizenship or occupation on the part of these landless and homeless men. They are not substances in their own right; they are receivers of sensation, leaves of a scratch-blank torn out by Nature for the hasty jotting of a casual memorandum. The man has vanished; what is left is a retina.

The solitude above described is not restricted to the observer; the object likewise is a drifting, homeless, expatriated thing. It is destitute alike of a place in a charted globe and a function in a civilized order. It has no history, no prospects, no causes, no sequels, no associations, no cognates, no allies. As the man is abridged into mere vision, the object contracts into pure visibility.

The psychology of Imagism . . . . contains matter of undoubted interest. Not the least conspicuous of its traits is the supineness or passivity of the attitude which the faithful assume in relation to the overshadowing or incumbent universe. They have the air of patients, of people under treatment; they *undergo* the things which other men observe or contemplate.

I feel I must apologize for having quoted so extensively from such a pedantic discourse, but who would cut off Polonius in the midst of his speech? Moreover, there is a grain of truth in what Mr. Firkins has laboriously said. The imagists ran the risk, and occasionally were guilty, of mere jotting, of note-taking, without proper regard for human significance. Such a danger was inherent in their objective method. But Mr. Firkins does not mention the opposite evil, which hundreds of poets have succumbed to, namely, elaboration of the subjective mood, vague wandering in the cosmic realm. One is constrained to believe that Mr. Firkins wrote his essay after reading the imagist credo and perhaps two or three of the shorter poems. Irritated by the credo, he allowed himself to imagine what the poetry must be like. His conclusions formed the essay. It is certainly not true that *Some Imagist Poets*, read throughout, could leave a sane person with the idea that its authors had lost their humanity or their touch with life. And as for their "undergoing" the things which "other men observe or contemplate," well, that seems to me exactly what all lyric poets must do. Mr. Firkins should have thought of Keats, for example, before making such a statement. The "other men" may possibly be critics, but it is doubtful if they are poets.

Another sharply adverse criticism of the imagists was made by Padraic Colum in the *New Republic* for November 20, 1915, under the title, "Egoism in Poetry." The burden of this complaint was that the imagist poets had made themselves appear more important than the occasions of their poems, and "it seems right that the thing that inspired the poem should not be dwarfed by the poet's vision of himself." In expanding this theme he declared:

One of the several differences between the Imagist verse and the work of accepted poets is that in the new verse there are many such inversions. Burns writes about a mouse and the mouse is not diminished by a grain. Byron writes about things that are obviously big—mountains, the sea, battlefields—and he leaves them at least as big in our imaginations as they were before. Now we may look at the work of some of the Imagists. John Gould Fletcher writes ("London Excursion")[5] about a city and it becomes as small as a place bestridden by a Colossus. Richard Aldington writes ("Daisy")[6] about a girl and she becomes, not a living creature, but a shell. When one speaks of egoism in poetry there is always someone present who mentions Byron . . . . If you believe that Byron was a great egoist in poetry read "When We Two Parted," and then look at Mr. Aldington's "Daisy."

[5] *Some Imagist Poets.* 1915.
[6] *Ibid.*

He then quotes the two poems in full, and continues:

Now Byron's poem may be of the drawing-room while Mr. Aldington's is of the mountain; "When We Two Parted" may be nerveless and sentimental while "Daisy" is clean-cut and virile. But Byron's is certainly less egoistic than the poem in *Some Imagist Poets*. One poem shows concern for a life other than the poet's; the other is concerned with the writer's own moment.

Those whom we may call the accepted poets wrote with constant reference to something which they thought was outside themselves— something that was not dwarfed by their own proportions. With Burns this something was the life of a community. With Blake it was God. With Byron it was a blighting and destructive force in nature and in the heart of man. With Shelley it was made up of ideal systems.

Mr. Colum recognizes what he considers the probable reply to his charge: that conventional writers have concealed their egoism by writing conventionally. Whereupon he continues:

I do not do this, an Imagist might say; I give you at least the truth of my egoism. A student of literature might say in reply, you must then appeal to the tolerance of the generations; Heine appealed to it by being witty and by being unique. Some of the Imagists try to be witty. But the form they have adopted does not tend to make their verse unique.

My own opinion is that "the form they have adopted" does tend to make their verse unique, but that it is a poor form for wit. As for the main part of Mr. Colum's argument, I shall let it stand for what it is worth. It represents a legitimate point of view. The imagists were unashamed of their egoism; one of their chief organs of expression was called the *Egoist*. They cannot complain at being left to "the tolerance of the generations." What poet isn't?

We have now given the high-lights of the autumn campaign. Things were quieter along the front during the winter—Christmas charity playing its part, perhaps. But an interesting onslaught was made by Professor John Livingston Lowes, of Harvard University, in the *Nation* for February 24, 1916. Onslaught is too strong a word, however, for what was really only a whimsical sortie. Under the title, "An Unacknowledged Imagist," Professor Lowes first restates the imagist credo and distils it to the following statement:

> Hard, clear images embodied in unrimed cadence; precision of delineation linked with flexibility of rhythm.

Then, after some introductory comments to the effect that vers libre may not be so well adapted to the English language as to the French, and that Amy Lowell is "the most competent spokesman of the group," he comes to his main point, which is that he remembers having read in the *Little Review* for the previous August a remark of Witter Bynner's that "George Meredith has thousands of imagist poems incidental to each of his novels." Glancing through his own copies of Meredith, Professor Lowes finds many such passages marked, and some of these he arranges as imagist poems. Good examples are as follows:

> Her face
> Was like an Egyptian sky
> Fronting night.
> The strong old Eastern blood
> Put ruddy flame
> For the red color.
> When she laughed
> She illuminated you;

Where she stepped
She made the earth hers.

. . . .

Over the flowering hawthorn
The moon
Stood like a wind-blown
White rose
Of the heavens.

. . . .

Great red sunsets
With women kneeling under them.
Do you know those long low sunsets?
They look like blood spilt for love.

. . . .

Edged moments,
When life is poised
As a crystal pitcher on the head,
In peril of a step.

IMAGISTS[7]

I.

Men
Lying on their backs
And flying imagination
Like a kite.

2.

A species
Of mad metaphor,
Wriggling and tearing its passage
Through a thorn-bush,
With the furious urgency
Of a sheep in panic.

. . . .

[7] Professor Lowes' own title, of course.

My heart
Is like a bird
Caught in the hands of a cruel boy.

My misery now
Is gladness,
Is like raindrops
On rising wings,
If I say to myself
"Free! free!"

I fly like a seed
To Italy,
I lift my face to that prospect
As if I smelt new air.

.   .   .   .

Following these quotations, he prints as prose three passages from vers libre poems by Amy Lowell, and concludes:

Miss Lowell's free verse may be written as very beautiful prose; George Meredith's prose may be written as very beautiful free verse. Which is which?

Thus the familiar ghost was raised again. But I am not required to formulate the obvious answer to Professor Lowes' question. In an interview given by Miss Lowell to Joyce Kilmer, and published in the New York *Times* for March 26, 1916, the poet herself makes answer:

As to Professor Lowes' query as to what is the difference between Meredith's prose and Imagist verse, I might answer that there is no difference. Typography is not relevant to the discussion. Whether a thing is written as prose or as verse is immaterial. But if we would see the advantage which Meredith's imagination enjoyed in the freer forms of expression, we need only compare these lyrical passages from his prose works with his own metrical poetry.

In other words she considered the poems lifted by Professor Lowes out of Meredith's novels, extraordinarily good poems. And she was right. If a poet writes novels, why should he not fill them with poems? He does not cease to be a poet while he is writing fiction. And why should he break the continuity of his narrative by printing the poetic passages in short lines? And if an imagist poet wishes to write the poems without the narrative, why should he not print them any way he likes?

There remains but one considerable review which I wish to record in this chapter. It appeared in the *Atlantic Monthly* for April 1916 with the title, "The New Naïveté," and was written by Lewis Worthington Smith. In the estimation of this critic, the imagist movement, and in fact the whole modern free-verse movement, is no more nor less than an attempt to get back to nature. He questions why it is necessary to "go back" to get to nature, but says:

> That returning to nature is going back, however, and going back a long way, even to the naïveté of infancy, is very clearly the actual, if not the conscious, doctrine of the new movement in poetry. Poem after poem in this sort is full of the simple wonder of a child picking up pebbles on the beach and running to some other child with yellow hair, in happy wonder at finding the pebble and the hair of a like color. That big-eyed recognition of agreement between two sense-impressions is about as far toward correlation of their material as the Imagists or the writers of free verse ever get.

His next point is that although the vers librists pretend they are revolting against literary forms, they are doing nothing of the kind: they are minor poets who cannot stand the strain of the sophisticated and complex world in which they find themselves, and so relax and take their experiences one at a time. He continues:

It is an astonishing thing. Among a highly sophisticated people, at the heart of a more eagerly progressive civilization than the world has ever known before, there develops in the highest, most complex, and most intellectual of the arts, the art of literature, a movement which encourages the inexperienced, the untutored, the unthinking to participate in that art. When, after centuries of hard self-tutelage, man has come to realize that he carries life forward with any certitude only by relating a multitude of experiences as fully as possible, then suddenly he stops, refuses to burden his mind with the business of so relating them any longer, is content merely to look at things, like a child, open-eyed and open-mouthed, to report the retinal image to the brain, to transfer it to innocent blank paper, and lastly to impose it on a credulous world for poetry.

. . . . If we were all to do that, our human world would go back promptly to chaos—or to wondering babyhood clutching at the moon. Fortunately, the world is not made up of minor poets trying to justify themselves by a philosophy and an art-theory adapted to the range of their vision and their capabilities.

After a scornful jibe at Mr. Pound for having suggested "that poets be endowed so that they may escape the need of writing to please the public," the writer insists that great poets have never cut themselves off from an audience, and have never wanted to write merely to please themselves. He concludes that imagism is a "freakish and barren cult" and only one of the signs of a new romanticism which will be "ultimately fruitful in the way of a fuller and more vital poetry."

The main point in this criticism is the writer's contention that the imagists have shirked the responsibilities of modern life. His argument is consistent, and to a certain extent convincing. Some of the imagist poems were childish, but they served to illustrate a method. The imagist poets themselves were not childish, even in 1915. All of them have written complex and subtle poems. It may be true, and I believe it is, that a "fuller and more vital poetry" has already appeared. T. S. Eliot, for example, has dealt with the modern world in an intellectually complex manner, but then Mr. Eliot must surely have profited by the experimentation of the imagists. What Lewis Worthington Smith failed to see, in 1916, was that if a hard, clear, objective poetry were to be developed, a certain number of blackboard exercises were necessary before anything important should be done. The five poems of Hulme, for example, and the more trivial poems of all the imagists. No one of the imagist poets maintained for very long in his writing the simple, wide-eyed wonder which was so valuable to him in his early practice with images. It was not so much that he was dodging the world, as that he was planning a new approach to it—perfecting a technique with which to master it.

In the foregoing reviews may be seen what the early critical reaction to imagism was, more particularly in America. These reviews bring out practically all the major points of controversy, and suggest every weakness in the imagist program. Later reviews tend to become more and more favorable, owing to the continuous propaganda of the imagists themselves and to the natural decline of prejudice toward something new. The critical writings of Amy Lowell, Louis Untermeyer, Alfred Kreymborg, Harriet Monroe, Alice Corbin Henderson, Marguerite Wilkinson, and other anthologists and editors, clarified the issues for the general reader, and the wide circulation gained for modern anthologies of poetry soon established the best imagist poems in popular favor. There are still dissenting voices, but they are no longer noisy.

IV ≺ THE PROSE-POETRY
CONTROVERSY

IT HAS already been made clear, I think, that one of the inevitable results of the imagist movement was a revival of the ancient controversy over the distinction between poetry and prose. In tracing the early critical reaction to imagism we encountered several critics who raised the point, notably Professor Lowes, who plucked poems from Meredith's prose, and reduced to prose certain poems by Miss Lowell. It should have been noted, too, that the same critic pursued his quest farther, for in chapters vi and vii of his interesting volume, *Convention and Revolt in Poetry*,[1] he gives a thorough discussion of the whole complicated problem. At one point he asks the pertinent question, What *is* free verse? and he then expresses his belief that "Miss Amy Lowell has been at more pains than anybody else to define and to explain it." He selects, therefore, from Miss Lowell's expository articles a number of statements incorporating her theories, and uses them as a foundation for his own argument. Among these quotations appear the following:

[1] Boston: Houghton Mifflin. 1919.

The definition of *vers libre* is: a verse-form based on cadence.

To understand *vers libre*, one must abandon all desire to find in it the even rhythm of metrical feet. One must allow the lines to flow as they will when read aloud by an intelligent reader.

Free verse *within its own law of cadence* has no absolute rules; it would not be "free" if it had.

The unit of *vers libre* is not the foot, the number of the syllables, the quantity, or the line. The unit is the strophe, which may be the whole poem, or may be only a part. Each strophe is a complete circle.

After considering these and related statements in detail, and after applying them to specimens of free verse and of prose, Professor Lowes comes to the conclusion that there is reason in Miss Lowell's argument, in spite of the fact that "The rhythms of *vers libre* in English . . . . are in large degree the rhythms of a certain type of modern rhythmic prose." In short, we are not justified in asserting that free verse is prose, for:

There are differences which set the one off from the other. The prose from which I have culled my excerpts does not maintain unbrokenly the rhythms which I have shown it to possess. If it did, we should certainly hesitate to call it prose. The best free verse poems, on the other hand, do maintain these rhythms consistently. And that is an important difference: the rhythms which are occasional in one are persistent in the other.

Having gone thus far, however, in admitting the existence of a form of poetry which the traditional conceptions of verse cannot include, he warns its practitioners that they are treading dangerous ground, and that sooner or later they will be forced to sharper definitions. The fact that they are exploring the borderland between verse and prose leaves them in a "No Man's Land . . . . open to fire from two sides at once." He feels, though, that free verse "is an artistic medium of not yet fully developed possibilities," and that in spite of the dangers inherent in its liberty, it is "gradually being perfected as an instrument of delicate precision and rare flexibility for recording the impressions of observed phenomena."

In other words, the Lowes-Lowell contribution to the controversy ended amicably, with free verse legitimatized as the somewhat immature but none the less hopeful offspring of poetry and prose. This was not by any means the only American contribution, but it was one of the most important, and I should say one of the sanest. I believe, too, that its conclusions were typical of those reached or accepted by the majority of American readers. It is the logical one for us to record here, for it grew directly out of the imagist movement, and centered around the work of the most active imagist poet in America.

In England, as I have said previously, the prose-poetry controversy was easily the most visible effect of imagism. To limit the discussion, and to maintain connection with our main theme, I shall summarize the contentions of a very small group of writers—the imagist poets themselves, and two or three others of their generation, who possess particular qualifications for speaking on this subject. The suspicious reader may at this point suspect me of partiality, but the truth is that I consider it unnecessary to present the point of view of the strongly prejudiced, reactionary critic who refuses to admit as poetry anything but strictly metrical verse. The arbitrary position of these reactionaries may be borne in mind by the reader, but it offers such a simple solution of our central problem that it requires no elaboration or exposition. Yet so modern a poet as T. S. Eliot maintains a position almost as arbitrary. Writing in the *New States-man* (London) for March 3, 1917, he says:

> It is assumed that *vers libre* exists. It is assumed that *vers libre* is a school; that it consists of certain theories; that its group or groups of theorists will either revolutionize or demoralize poetry if their attack upon the iambic pentameter meets with any success. *Vers libre* does not exist, and it is time that this preposterous fiction followed the *élan vital* and the eighty thousand Russians into oblivion.

A little later he insists:

> *Vers libre* has not even the excuse of a polemic; it is a battle-cry of freedom, and there is no freedom in art. And as the so-called *vers libre* which is good is anything but "free," it can better be defended under some other label.

It seems to him that any genuine verse form must have a positive definition, and this he declares free verse has not. He advances the idea that most of the good so-called free verse secures charm by "the constant suggestion and the skilful evasion of iambic pentameter." He then cites John Webster as a master of that technique, and remarks on Webster's similarity to certain modern poets, taking care, meanwhile, to distinguish between Webster's merely careless lines and his premeditated irregularities. He concludes that:

> We may, therefore, formulate as follows: the ghost of some simple meter should lurk behind the arras in even the "freest" verse, to advance menacingly as we doze, and withdraw as we rouse. Or, freedom is only truly freedom when it appears against the background of an artificial limitation.

His final statement is to the effect: "*Vers libre* does not exist, for there is only good verse, bad verse, and chaos."

This article was sure to draw fire from the imagists, who

were very busy indeed at that time trying to convince the public of the validity of their poetic medium. John Gould Fletcher immediately addressed a letter to the editor of the *New Statesman,* and this letter was published in the issue of March 24, 1917. It says in part:

> It is all very well for Mr. Eliot to declare that the same thing has been done already by Webster and Blake and Matthew Arnold, and that nothing was said about *vers libre* by these men. Does that affect the fact that once a thing is deliberately and constantly practised a new name has to be found for it? Can Mr. Eliot suggest a more appropriate name than *vers libre?*

Mr. Fletcher then denies Mr. Eliot's statement that iambic pentameter is the only basis for vers libre, and asks:

> What then becomes of the heptameters of Blake or the rough hexameters of Whitman? . . . . Mr. Eliot should remember that it is only in the last few years that any considerable body of poets have attempted to write in *vers libre* at all.

But Mr. Eliot was not won over, for two months later, writing again in the *New Statesman* (May 19, 1917), under the title, "The Borderline of Prose," he reiterates his position as regards vers libre, and makes interesting comments on that other disputed form, the prose-poem. He speaks of the growing popularity of the prose-poem, mentions its modern French origins, and declares that no one has come forward with any theory to disprove that the only distinction between poetry and prose is that "poetry is written in verse, and prose is written in prose; or, in other words, that there is prose rhythm and verse rhythm."

As an example of a modern writer part of whose work has failed through being neither poetry nor prose, he mentions Richard Aldington, who, he admits, "has done interesting work in what is unfairly called *vers libre*." Discussing this writer's prose-poems (not his vers libre), he says:

> Mr. Aldington seems to me to be avoiding the limitations of either poetry or prose; to use either when he wishes; and so to lose the necessary articulation of rhythm.
>
> And so one finds oneself constantly *trying* to read the prose poem as prose or as verse—and failing in both attempts. And then one goes on to imagine how it would have been done in verse or in prose—which is what a writer ought never to allow us to do. He should never let us question for a moment that his form is the inevitable form for his content. This inevitableness is the important thing. The moment we think of poetry as prose, or of prose as poetry, the artist's success is lost.
>
> The distinction between poetry and prose must be a technical distinction; and future refinement of both poetry and prose can only draw the distinction more clearly. And I cannot help thinking that Mr. Aldington's prose-poems (and I allow them great merit) fail exactly because they seek to evade the technical distinction between two forms. Both verse and prose still conceal unexplored possibilities, but whatever one writes must be definitely and by inner necessity either one or the other.

But Mr. Aldington defended his conception of the prose-poem as something independent and valid, and when pressed for a definition, he asserted that "The prose-poem is poetic content expressed in prose form." This definition Mr. Eliot seized upon and made the starting-point for a rather lengthy essay entitled "Prose and Verse," which was published in conjunction with two other essays on the same subject (by Frederic Manning and by Richard Aldington) in *The Chapbook: A Monthly Miscellany* for April 1921.[2] Needless to say, Mr. Eliot was acute enough to detect the insufficiency of

[2] London: Poetry Bookshop.

the definition (an insufficiency of which its author was fully aware), and his comment was as follows:

> Poetic content must be either the sort of thing that *is usually*, or the sort of thing that *ought to be*, expressed in verse. But if you say the latter, the prose poem is ruled out; if you say the former, you have said only that certain things can be said in either prose or verse. I am not disposed to contest either of these conclusions, as they stand, but they do not appear to bring us any nearer to a definition of the prose-poem. I do not assume the identification of poetry with verse; good poetry is obviously something else besides good verse; and good verse may be very indifferent poetry.

He then goes on to say that "The distinction between 'verse' and 'prose' is clear; the distinction between 'poetry' and 'prose' is very obscure." He considers at some length the sort of prose which is called "poetic" (that of Sir Thomas Browne, for example), and he also reminds us that in many long poems (Milton and Wordsworth offer examples), where intensity is not sustained throughout the poem, there is much which is prosaic. And although this lack of sustained poetic intensity has led some writers (Poe, among others) to declare that all poems ought to be short, Mr. Eliot sees no reason why, when we allow prose works (novels, histories, etc.) to be in part poetic, we should deny long poems the right to be in part prosaic. Nor does he see why, if we admit the long poem, we should not admit the short prose. And this brings him to the assertion that: "The short prose is, I believe, what most people have in mind when they speak of 'poems in prose.'" He continues:

> I object to the term "prose-poetry" because it seems to imply a sharp distinction between "poetry" and "prose" which I do not admit, and if it does not imply this distinction, the term is meaningless and otiose, as there can be no combination of what is not distinguished.

He cautions us, however, to remember that "verse is always struggling, while remaining verse, to take up to itself more and more of what is prose, to take something more from life and turn it into 'play,' " while, on the other hand, "prose, not being cut off by the barrier of verse which must at the same time be affirmed and diminished, can transmute life in its own way by raising it to the condition of 'play,' precisely because it is not verse." The conclusion is, therefore:

> We must be very tolerant of any attempt in verse that appears to trespass upon prose, or of any attempt in prose that appears to strive toward the condition of "poetry."

Mr. Aldington's attitude differs from Mr. Eliot's chiefly in the former's willingness to accept the term, "prose-poem," and to recognize it as standing for a definite art form. Both writers agree that there is no defined frontier between poetry and prose, but whereas Mr. Aldington feels justified in choosing a poetic passage from a novel and calling it a "poem in prose," Mr. Eliot balks and will admit merely that it is prose striving toward the "condition of poetry." Mr. Eliot is a stickler for exactness, and will tolerate neither loose generalizations nor merely convenient terms.

A quite different attitude, a more genial one, was advanced by F. S. Flint in the preface to his volume of poems, *Otherworld*.[3] This writer, one of the original imagists, and the inventor of the term "unrimed cadence," is untroubled by fine distinctions. His interest is in enlarging the field of poetry, in breaking down the boundaries of conventional versification. Poetry is to him a very inclusive term—embracing all writing wherein "you feel the warmth of human

[3] London: Poetry Bookshop. 1920.

experience and imagination." This quality may exist in prose, in verse, or in "unrimed cadence." But inasmuch as the possibilities of verse have been exhausted, and its artifices have brought the word poetry into contempt, the new poets must strive for "clarity and sincerity of speech," and must work in either prose or unrimed cadence. These two forms, he admits, are not entirely distinct from each other:

> The one merges into the other; there is no boundary line between them; but prose, generally, will be used for the more objective branches of writing—for novels, plays, essays and so on—and poetry in this form is accepted with so much good-will that I have some misgivings in applying to it its rightful name; cadence will be used for personal, emotional, lyric utterances, in which the phrasing goes with a stronger beat and the words live together with an intenser flame. If you ask why cadence should not be printed as prose, the reply is that the unequal lines mark the movement of the cadence and its tempo . . . .

A fairly similar view was, of course, held by most of the imagists. The idea that cadence should be substituted for meter, and that the result could be distinguished from prose, was at the very heart of the imagist credo. It was Amy Lowell's slogan in America; it was John Gould Fletcher's constant cry on both sides of the Atlantic; Richard Aldington propounded it in the *Egoist* and other English periodicals; it was implicit in all of H. D.'s lyrics. In the preface to his *Irradiations: Sand and Spray*,[4] Mr. Fletcher had argued:

> To begin with, the basis of English poetry is rhythm, or, as some would prefer to call it, cadence. This rhythm is obtained by mingling stressed and unstressed syllables. Stress may be produced

---

[4] Boston: Houghton Mifflin; London: Constable. 1915.

by accent. It may—and often is—produced by what is known as quantity, the breath required to pronounce certain syllables being more than is required on certain others. However it be produced, it is precisely this insistence upon cadence, upon the rhythm of the line when spoken, which sets poetry apart from prose, and not—be it said at the outset—a certain way of printing, with a capital letter at the beginning of each line, or an insistence upon end-rimes.

The rhythm may be the same in every line of the poem, as in most poems written during the eighteenth and nineteenth centuries, or it may vary according to the emotions of the writer:

I maintain that poetry is capable of as many gradations in cadence as music is in time. We can have a rapid group of syllables —what is called a line—succeeded by a slow, heavy one; like the swift scurrying-up of the wave, and the sullen dragging of itself away. Or we can gradually increase or decrease our *tempo*, creating *accelerando* and *rallentando* effects. Or we can follow a group of rapid lines with a group of slow ones, or a single slow, or *vice versa*. Finally, we can have a perfectly even and unaltered movement throughout if we desire to be monotonous.

The good poem is that in which all these effects are properly used to convey the underlying emotions of its author, and that which welds all these emotions into a work of art by the use of dominant *motif*, subordinate themes, proportionate treatment, repetition, variation—what in music is called development, reversal of rôles, and return. In short, the good poem fixes a free emotion, or a free range of emotions, into an inevitable and artistic whole.

And a year later Mr. Fletcher in the preface to another volume of his poems[5] attacked the problem again, this time demonstrating his conception of the psychological distinctions between prose and free verse:

[5] *Goblins and Pagodas*. Boston: Houghton Mifflin. 1916.

In prose, the emotions expressed are those that are capable of development in a straight line. In so far as prose is pure, it confines itself to the direct orderly progression of a thought or conception or situation from point to point of a flat surface. The sentences, as they develop this conception from its beginning to conclusion, move on, and do not return upon themselves. The grouping of these sentences into paragraphs gives the breadth of the thought. The paragraphs, sections, and chapters are each a square, in that they represent a division of the main thought into parallel units, or blocks of subsidiary ideas. The sensation of depth is finally obtained by arranging these blocks in a rising climacteric progression, or in parallel lines, or in a sort of zigzag figure.

Continuing this geometrical analysis he finds that:

In poetry we have a succession of curves. The direction of the thought is not in straight lines, but wavy and spiral. It rises and falls on gusts of strong emotion. Most often it creates strongly marked loops and circles. The structure of the stanza or strophe always tends to the spherical. Depth is obtained by making one sphere contain a number of concentric or overlapping spheres.

Regular rime and meter, Mr. Fletcher explains, are merely devices for making these loops and circles more accentuated, but they are not essential, for:

. . . . poetic circles can be constructed out of subtler and more musical curves than that which painstakingly follows the selfsame progression of beats, and catches itself up on the same point of rime for line after line.

Following this picturesque exposition, the writer subscribes to the belief that many excellent poems exist in pages of good prose, and that many long poems contain "whole pages of prose." He concludes:

The fact is, that prose and poetry are to literature as composition and color are to painting, or as light and shadow to the day, or male and female to mankind. There are no absolutely perfect poets and no absolutely perfect prose-writers. Each partakes of some of the characteristics of the other. The difference between poetry and prose is, therefore, a difference between a general roundness and a general squareness of outline.

Neither Mr. Fletcher nor his colleagues maintained that these theories of cadence, of vers libre, were new. Over and over they maintained that they were very old indeed, and had been forgotten or neglected. In *Some Imagist Poets, 1916*[6] considerable space is taken in the preface to emphasize this point, and the references go all the way back to Aristotle. In English poetry the imagists hail as fellow vers librists Dryden, Milton, Matthew Arnold, and Henley. Their complaint is that the public objects not to the thing itself but to the name, which, they admit, is new. In the same preface may be found a full reiteration of the theories of vers libre, with careful definitions of cadence and strophe. Quotation of these is unnecessary, for they have already appeared in this chapter in the excerpts from the expositions of Miss Lowell and Mr. Fletcher.

Before we leave this subject I should like to present the opinions of Herbert Read, an English critic and poet who has been a close observer of imagism and other contemporary poetic movements, and whose judgments are dictated by extraordinarily acute intelligence. In the introduction to his recent study, *English Prose Style*,[7] he finds it necessary to state what he believes to be the distinctions between prose and poetry. First he reminds us that verse is not necessarily

[6] Boston: Houghton Mifflin; London: Constable.
[7] London: G. Bell & Sons; New York: Holt. 1928.

poetry; after that he insists that there is not and never can be any formal distinction between poetry and prose. Classification of meter, theories of cadence, quantity, etc., cannot resolve the problem exactly. The real distinction is a psychological one. Poetry and prose are expressions of different forms of mental activity. He says:

> Poetry is creative expression; Prose is constructive expression. . . . . By creative I mean *original*. In Poetry the words are born or reborn in the act of thinking. The words are, in Bergsonian phraseology, a becoming; they develop in the mind *pari passu* with the development of the thought. There is no time interval between the words and the thought. The thought is the word and the word is thought, and both the thought and the word are Poetry.
>
> "Constructive" implies ready-made materials; words stacked round the builder, ready for use. Prose is a structure of ready-made words. Its "creative" function is confined to plan and elevation— functions these, too, of Poetry, but in Poetry subsidiary to the creative function.

Mr. Read foresees the question that will arise: "How are we to recognize originality when we see it?" In other words, how are we to recognize the poetic? His reply is that it is an instinctive matter, and, inevitably, an individual matter. Few people recognize any art, but those few do so instinctively. If this leaves the majority groping and uncertain, well, it cannot be helped; for "All art is difficult, remote, subtle . . . ."

PART II
THE IMAGISTS

RICHARD ALDINGTON
PHOTOGRAPH BY MAN RAY

V ⇜ RICHARD ALDINGTON:
The Rebel

RICHARD ALDINGTON was born at Portsmouth, Hampshire, in 1892, the son of a solicitor. His childhood was spent in and around Dover; he attended preparatory schools at Walmar and St. Margaret's Bay; he studied four years at Dover College and one year at the University of London. Like most English boys he began the study of Latin and Greek at a very early age and continued it throughout his formal education. French, too, he learned early—he could read it well by the time he was sixteen; and when he was nineteen he visited Italy and acquired a reasonable knowledge of Italian. In addition to the influences of a typical English school and college education, however, must be mentioned in connection with Aldington's literary development the many volumes of English poetry in his father's library. Among these the boy ran wild. At the age of sixteen he had read practically all the poets from Chaucer to Francis Thompson. And it was largely due to this precocious acquaintance with the English classics that he was prepared and inclined at the age of eighteen to launch a creative attack upon poetic tradition. Satiated with rime and meter, with rhetoric and romantics, he fell back on Hellen-ism—on imagery and unrimed cadence.

He had reached this stage when Ezra Pound met him in London. Pound recognized the authenticity of Aldington's poems, and succeeded in getting them published. It was also through Pound that Aldington met Hilda Doolittle, whose poetic inclinations harmonized with his own and who in 1913 became his wife. In the early poems of Aldington and H. D., published in *Poetry* and in *Des Imagistes*, the similarity be-tween the two poets was marked; readers even complained that they could not tell the work of one from that of the other. But gradually the two personalities emerged and de-veloped along quite distinct lines. Today they are very far apart indeed. The divergence, however, has been chiefly on Aldington's side. H. D. has remained remarkably true to the spirit and the form of her first Hellenistic poems; Ald-ington has wooed more than one Muse. H. D. built herself a Greek temple, and has remained within it, hidden from the noise and swirl of modern life; Aldington built a like temple, and though he returns to it now and again for votive offer-ings, he has become a part of his time, an unhappy, rebellious, but conscientious citizen.

The essence of Aldington's character, the key to his poetry, is rebellion. He cannot tolerate the status quo. That is why he admires Pound and Lawrence and Wyndham Lewis, and why his god is Voltaire. The youngest of the imagists, he proved one of the staunchest defenders of the faith, a warrior eager for battle, and armed with much learn-ing, tremendous mental energy, and a mocking, biting wit. His headstrong enthusiasms result sometimes in inconsistency and exaggeration, but generally he is a sound and penetrating thinker. He has been a professional critic almost as long as he has been a poet, and his reputation is as considerable in the field of prose as it is in that of verse.

In the days of the *Egoist* he not only served for some time as actual editor of that propagandist organ but also contributed to its pages a great number of articles, translations, and original poems. We find in these contributions an irrepressible spirit of artistic and intellectual rebellion, an impertinence almost Gallic in its gaiety, and an irreverence which could have been born only in the midst of a stodgy orthodoxy. In a racy, personal, provocative style he runs the gamut of his aversions and affections, pulling the leg of the unwary reader, and indulging in no end of *blague*. It is not only an exhibition of arrogant youth; it is an exhibition of youth conscious and proud of its arrogance. In a review of the then young American periodicals, *Poetry* and the *Little Review*, Aldington expresses himself with characteristic vigor.[1] Granting that American writing is generally slipshod and often incorrect, and that English periodicals are stylistically superior, he cries out:

. . . . for heaven's sake let us ask ourselves honestly whether this ingenuous energy is not fifty times more valuable than those "correct" manifestations of bourgeois mediocrity. Let us yield to the electric impulse of this "incorrect" and youthful exuberance! Youth is the great excuse, better than charity it hides, it decorates, it makes adorable its multitudinous sins. If youth were correct it might as well be middle-age and give up the game. It is youth, its generosities and injustices, its head-over-heels errors and dashing impulses that make one hurl the flatulent *Fortnightly* and the constipated *Contemporary* into the fire, which make one read the *Little Reviews* of the world from end to end and carefully preserve them in one's attic.

[1] "Young America," the *Egoist* (London), November 1, 1915, p. 177.

With the traditional prerogative of the Englishman, Aldington curses his countrymen (en masse) and chants his praise of foreigners—Americans occasionally, Frenchmen more often. He is forever kneeling in adoration before French poets and philosophers, and from this kneeling posture he thumbs his nose like a schoolboy at British saints. It was this devilish and perverse patriotism which prompted him to subscribe to the manifestoes designed by Ezra Pound and Wyndham Lewis and published in *Blast*, wherein, as Aldington himself once said, "the distressing and cow-like qualities of this nation are successfully blasted, and the admirable, unique and dominating characteristics piously blessed."

His own articles in the *Egoist* are full of blasts and blessings. Blasts for "cosmic" poetry, Irish sentimentality, Marinetti and futurism, Puritanism, British sports, British solemnity, and the pre-Raphaelites; blessings for the Greek poets, Remy de Gourmont, F. M. Hueffer, the imagists, and artistic liberty.

His early poems, written between 1910 and 1915, were published under the title, *Images.*[2] Some of them had appeared first, of course, in the 1914 and 1915 imagist anthologies, and in periodicals. They are nearly all in unrimed free verse, beautifully cadenced.

The book opens with "Choricos," a poem of studied and perhaps affected gravity, but one of Aldington's most effective efforts to recapture the Hellenic mood. The opening lines are typical of the austere grace which permeates the entire poem:

---

[2] London: Poetry Bookshop. 1915. As *Images, Old and New*, Boston: Four Seas. 1916.

The ancient songs
Pass deathward mournfully.

Cold lips that sing no more, and withered wreaths,
Regretful eyes, and drooping breasts and wings—
Symbols of ancient songs,
Mournfully passing
Down to the great white surges,
Watched of none
Save the frail sea-birds
And the lithe pale girls,
Daughters of Oceanus.

The salutation to death is magnificent in its coloring and movement:

For silently
Brushing the fields with red-shod feet,
With purple robe
Searing the grass as with a sudden flame,
Death,
Thou hast come upon us.
And of all the ancient songs
Passing to the swallow-blue halls
By the dark streams of Persephone,
This only remains—
That in the end we turn to thee,
Death,
We turn to thee, singing
One last song.

There are other lyrics in the collection which echo this classic mood, this coolness and dignity as of an Attic temple. But ere we have turned many pages we find ourselves in a more familiar world, with a poetry less archaic:

EVENING

The chimneys, rank on rank,
Cut the clear sky;
The moon
With a rag of gauze about her loins
Poses among them, an awkward Venus—
And here am I looking wantonly at her
Over the kitchen sink.

And presently we leave the kitchen sink for the streets of London, the underground trains, the cinemas, the iron and smoke of Whitechapel, a procession of cripples in Kensington. The flowery ways and glamorous gods of ancient Greece are almost forgotten; the poet glimpses them only now and then as welcome visions in a world of ugliness and pain. Since he cannot escape the life about him, he reviles it. Not only does he find the London of his young manhood awful; he comes to realize with terrible clarity that his childhood was spent in an atmosphere even worse. The horror of Dover in retrospect is too much for him. He does all that he can do now by way of getting even: he writes a rebellious poem in which the dreariness of an English town is etched in poison. This poem, "Childhood," is unfortunately too long to quote in its entirety, but an idea of its style can be obtained from a few lines:

I hate that town;
I hate the town I lived in when I was little;
I hate to think of it.
There were always clouds, smoke, rain
In that dingy little valley.
It rained; it always rained.
I think I never saw the sun until I was nine—

And then it was too late;
Everything's too late after the first seven years.

The long street we lived in
Was duller than a drain
And nearly as dingy.
There were the big College
And the pseudo-Gothic town-hall.
There were the sordid provincial shops—
The grocer's, and the shops for women,
The shop where I bought transfers,
And the piano and gramophone shop
Where I used to stand
Staring at the huge shiny pianos and at the pictures
Of a white dog staring into a gramophone.
. . . .

And there was a grey museum
Full of dead birds and dead insects and dead animals
And a few relics of the Romans—dead also.
. . . .

I was like a moth—
Like one of those grey Emperor moths
Which flutter through the vines at Capri.
And that damned little town was my match-box,
Against whose sides I beat and beat
Until my wings were torn and faded, and dingy
As that damned little town.

The school was dull, the public park was dull, the church was
dull, home was dull. Everything was gray, greasy, and
sordid. The result:

I don't believe in God.
I do believe in avenging gods

Who plague us for sins we never sinned,
But who avenge us.

That's why I'll never have a child,
Never shut up a chrysalis in a match-box,
For the moth to spoil and crush its bright colors,
Beating its wings against the dingy prison wall.

Of course, if he had a child he wouldn't have to raise it in Dover—but he hasn't, so the point is irrelevant. And he may have felt that his wings were torn and faded, but they weren't really. British wings are good and firm; they sail right over the chimney-pots and the rain. Aldington knows that as well as anyone. Still, he couldn't resist striking with all his might at something which he recognized as ugly, and which *might* have ruined him, even though it didn't. The poem brought a good deal of ridicule from critics, and it must be admitted that its self-commiseration is annoying, but its objective passages are vivid and of sufficient consequence to justify the whole.

Not Greek and not English, but merely imagistic, are many of the shorter poems in this volume. To them one may turn with absolute assurance of pleasure. Although their author denies any Oriental influence on his poetry, some of these excellent images might well have been inspired by the Japanese:

Like a gondola of green-scented fruits
Drifting along the dank canals of Venice,
You, O exquisite one,
Have entered into my desolate city.

. . . .

The red deer are high on the mountain,
They are beyond the last pine trees,
And my desires have run with them.

There are many more almost as charming and as skilfully wrought. They stand, with the short poems of H. D.,
as the best expression in miniature of the imagist ideal.

What would have happened to Aldington as a poet had
it not been for the War is a vain but inevitable query. It is
safe to assume that he would have changed, for it is in him to
change, but how no one can say. It is possible that without
the experience of war he would have become as bitter and as
cynical as he did with the experience. At any rate, his two
and a half years of service, with fifteen months spent at the
actual front, left him a quite different poet. Yet the change
was not immediate. His poems written during the War
period are a recognizable continuation of his early work, even
though their tone is sterner and their details are more vivid.
Images of War[3] contains certainly some of the truest and
most beautiful poems written by any soldier in modern times.
In the opinion of Harold Monro, "Except Siegfried Sassoon,
no 'war-poet' has represented the torments of military life
with such candor and so entirely without bombastic rhetoric."[4]

We sit in the trenches with this soldier-poet, contemplat-
ing death and the dead; we hear his thoughts:

SOLILOQUY—I

No, I'm not afraid of death
(Not very much afraid, that is)
Either for others or myself;

[3] London: Allen & Unwin. 1919. Included in *War and Love*, Boston: Four Seas. 1919.

[4] *Some Contemporary Poets*, p. 99.

Can watch them coming from the line
On the wheeled silent stretchers
And not shrink,
But munch my sandwich stoically
And make a joke, when "it" has passed.
But—the way they wobble!—
God! that makes one sick.
Dead men should be so still, austere,
And beautiful,
Not wobbling carrion roped upon a cart . . . .

Well, thank God for rum.

SOLILOQUY—II

I was wrong, quite wrong;
The dead men are not always carrion.
After the advance,
As we went through the shattered trenches
Which the enemy had left,
We found, lying upon the fire-step,
A dead English soldier,
His head bloodily bandaged
And his closed left hand touching the earth,
More beautiful than one can tell,
More subtly colored than a perfect Goya,
And more austere and lovely in repose
Than Angelo's hand could ever carve in stone.

In other poems we see and feel the cataclysm of bombardment, the loneliness of ruined fields and villages; we lean against a trench in the frosty night, making wisps of poems to the moon; we march wearily through the night and to the dawn; again and again we hear the whispers of death, the imminent lover. Almost never in these poems does the author allow self-pity to master him, and never does he indulge in heroics. He is consistently honest, and consistently an artist.

To the same period as *Images of War* belong the love poems called *Images of Desire*.[5] This small collection contains a surprising variety of manners. Indeed, it is as though the author had sought deliberately to celebrate his love in various ways—to weave a garland of diverse flowers, thus making the tribute as rich as possible. There are many short pieces, true images, of the Oriental type:

> Like a dark princess whose beauty
> Many have sung, you wear me,
> The one jewel that is warmed by your breast.

There are others in which passion awakens echoes of Swinburne:

> The naked pale limbs of the dawn lie sheathed in
>   dove-white folds of lawn,
> But from one scarlet breast I see the cloudy cover
>   slowly drawn.
> .   .   .   .
> Ah! slay me with your lips, ah! kill my body's
>   strength and spirit's will
> So that at dawn I need not go but lie between your
>   breast-flowers still.

Even the naïveté of the Middle Ages is invoked in "An Old Song":

---

[5] London: Elkin Mathews. 1919. (Reissued by Allen & Unwin, 1922). Also included in *War and Love*, Boston: Four Seas. 1919.

I have no lust or care
To sing of Mary,
I praise the quaint sweet air
Of a mortal lady.

In these and other modes appear the inevitable affirmations of love: the ecstasy of possession, the dread of loss, the agony of separation. Apart from their emotional content these poems are interesting to us because they indicate Aldington's transition from pure imagism to a less prescribed technique. They illustrate his rebellion against a method which at one time had satisfied him but which he now employs only on occasion.

To the same general period belongs *Myrrhine and Konallis*,[6] a series of poems celebrating the love of two Greek maidens. The first of these were written between 1913 and 1915, the remainder in 1919. In style they are akin to Mr. Aldington's translations from Anyte of Tegea, Anacreon, and Meleager.[7] They are rhetorical, archaic, and richly colored. The cadences are long and voluptuous; the imagery weighted with ornament:

Hierocleia, bring hither my silver vine-leaf-carved
    armlet and the mirror graven with two Maenads,
For my heart is burned to dust with longing for Konallis;
And this is the silver armlet which pressed into her side when I
    held her,
And before this mirror she bound up her golden-hyacinth-curled
    hair, sitting in the noon sunlight.

[6] *The Love of Myrrhine and Konallis, followed by Nineteen Prose Poems*, Chicago: Covici. 1926.

[7] See *Medallions in Clay*, New York: Knopf. 1921.

In the course of a eulogistic article published in the *English Review* (London) for May 1921 Miss May Sinclair pays particular tribute to these poems and rates them above Aldington's more modern and realistic work. She calls them "a sequence of the most exquisite love poems in the language, poems that, if he had never written another line ought to be enough to secure for him a high and permanent place in literature." She adds, "To be sure the love is Lesbian, but Mr. Aldington has kept for us its pagan innocence and candor, its mortal pathos, and left us no image that is not beautiful. The figures, exquisite and fragile, pass shining as in some processional frieze of marble overlaid by gold, washed clean by the light of a world too remote, too long dead to excite our repulsion or our blame: a world not quite real." She admires his translations from the Greek poets, but she feels that "*Myrrhine and Konallis* will remain as his highest tribute to the genius of Greek love, of Greek poetry."

I have spoken of the bitterness which the War brought to this poet. For its first violent expression we must turn to *Exile and Other Poems*.[8] This book, though small, contains three sections. The first is composed of poems chiefly in free verse and blank verse, all of them voicing the disillusionment and despair which besieged the poet in the post-war days, when memories of horror were still fresh, and when it seemed impossible to make a readjustment of life along the lines of peace. He cannot sleep for the nightmare of the past, and in his spiritual pain he questions fate:

> What is it I agonize for?
> The dead? They are quiet;
> They can have no complaint.

[8] London: Allen & Unwin; New York: Dial Press. 1923.

No, it is my own murdered self—
A self which had its passion for beauty,
Some moment's touch with immortality—
Violently slain, which rises up like a ghost
To torment my nights,
To pain me.
It is myself that is the Eumenides,
That will not be appeased, about my bed;
It is the wrong that has been done me
Which none has atoned for, none repented of,
Which rises before me, demanding atonement.
Tell me, what answer shall I give my murdered self?

Not all the moods are as black as this one; some are colored by laughter. But the laughter is not pure; it is stained
with mockery. It is the age-old laughter of the unhappy
clown who laughs because he must. The poet has lost his
dreams and must get new ones. The old ones he bartered
for reality, but he has had enough of that:

O Satan! You've disguised yourself as Truth
And make a solemn fool of more than me;
But by these presents, firmly weighed and penned,
I here renounce you and your verminous tricks.
Come, happy Falsehood,
Once again,
Make me a merry fool.

The second section of the book is composed of fourteen
songs, titled explicitly "Words for Music." Ten of them are
dedicated to Puritans and four to sensualists. As might be
expected, the Puritans are invited to participate in the joys
of the flesh, and the sensualists are treated to the purity of
star and blossom. All these poems are exquisitely modeled

upon seventeenth-century patterns, and one hears in them the scarcely disguised accents of Herrick and Carew. They contain little originality, but they testify to the virtuosity of their author.

The third section, called "Metrical Exercises," consists of only two poems: "The Berkshire Kennet" and "A Winter Night." Both are written in rimed couplets, in rather an eighteenth-century manner, and both are in praise of country life. Apart from their intrinsic beauty they are interesting because of their biographical and psychological significance. After the War Mr. Aldington settled down to live in a little cottage in the heart of Berkshire, at Padworth, a parish not far from Reading. There among the marvelously green fields, through which winds the river Kennet, he found the quiet, the solitude, which his heart required. There he escaped the turmoil of modern life, and there he found the healing balm for bitter memories of hate and death:

> Here where the osiers barely sigh
> Hour upon hour still let me lie,
> Where neither cannon roar nor noise
> Of heavy wheels my ear annoys,
> And there is none my face to scan
> Save some incurious countryman;
> And in my cool and hushed nook
> I read some old and gentle book
> Until in thought I lift my eyes
> To rest on dappled English skies,
> And hear the stream go murmuring by
> And watch the bubbling eddies fly
> As Kennet's waters glide forever
> To wed the elder, nobler river.....

The pastoral mood was authentic, but it was not permanent. How could it be, when it was only a phase of convalescence? The poet was still young and still rebellious. His spirit here waxed strong within him and produced *A Fool i' the Forest*,[9] a long, phantasmagoric poem, an autobiographical harlequinade, in which three characters (who symbolize three aspects of the author's personality) dance their way madly through the spinning world of consciousness and memory, until two of them are dead and the other is ignominiously submerged in conventional society. Taking the author's own description of the characters,

"I" is intended to be typical of a man of our own time, one who is by temperament more fitted for an art than a scientific civilization. He is shown at a moment of crisis, and the phantasmagoria is the mirror of his mind's turmoil as he struggles to attain a harmony between himself and the exterior world. Mezzetin comes from the *Commedia dell' Arte*. He symbolizes here the imaginative faculties —art, youth, satire, irresponsible gaiety, liberty. He is one or several of these by turns and all together. In a similar manner the Conjuror symbolizes the intellectual faculties—age, science, righteous cant, solemnity, authority—which is why I make him so malicious.

Although Aldington is not the first man in the world to suffer such an inner conflict and to face such a crisis, he is, I should think, one of the best modern examples of the type. And certainly he is one of the most articulate. Another excellent example is T. S. Eliot. In fact, it has already been remarked by critics that *A Fool i' the Forest* owes much to *The Waste Land*. Humbert Wolfe's comment is that "Aldington . . . . could only see life darkly in T. S. Eliot's looking-glass." But he adds that "that half-glimpse was worth the whole of the Imagist philanderings with verse

[9] London: Allen & Unwin; New York: Dial Press. 1925.

which was only free in the sense that a bolting horse is free."
His point is that in this work the poet has allowed life itself
to dictate form, whereas in the early imagist poems an attempt was made to impose order upon a living organism. I
cannot agree entirely with this generalization, but I do agree
that *A Fool i' the Forest* is Aldington's finest poetic achievement.

The whole poem has extraordinary pace, and a great
variety of rhythms. The narrative passages are in unrimed
verse, irregular, but hovering about the norm of a four-beat
line. Interpolated are many snatches of song, some of them
rimed and metrical—some of them satirically doggerel—
others in unrimed cadence. Moods alternate swiftly, thought
flashes and disappears, scenes shift as in a dream—a method
of presentation now common in fiction and drama as well as
in poetry. The settings are Venice, Athens, the battlefields
of France, and London. The time is the simultaneous past
and present, for consciousness and memory are blended.
Aldington the man is dragged from place to place by Aldington the poet and Aldington the scholar. The soul of the man
is fought for by the poet and the scholar. First one gains it,
then the other. They picnic in the shadow of the Parthenon.
They all get drunk, and argue about life and art and science.
The Conjuror falls asleep, and Mezzetin starts clowning:

> Mezzetin played ragtime on a banjo,
> Clog-danced round the sleeping Conjuror;
> Then he nasally orated:
> "Ladies and gentlemen, fellow-citizens,
> This is the famous Parthenon,
> The greatest temple in the World,
> Built five thousand years B.C.
> By Marcus Aurelius and Pericles

In honor of the heathen idol, Pallas Athene.
Although considerably out-of-date and dilapidated
It has been bought for ten million dollars
By a syndicate of our most cultured business men.
Repairs and alterations will be rushed
And in three weeks this old building
Will be as large and weatherproof
As the Capitol at Washington, D.C.
This, ladies and gentlemen, fellow-citizens,
Is another proof of the hearty co-operation
And good will of the New World to old Europe."

O Pall Athena
Amurica lo-oves you,
O Pall Athena
Here's a han' to you-ou
Hoodle-hoo, hoodle-hoo,

Our biggest high-brows
Are nuts on culture,
An' our Co-eds are
Readin' Homer through,
Toodle-oo, toodle-oo,
Our millionaires are buyin' Euri-pydes too,
Hoodle-hoo, hoodle-hoo,

And down in Boston where they bake the beans
They know what Happapappazouglos means,
So Pall Athena
Here's a han' to you
Hoo-hoo-hoo-hoo.

The shadow of the god passes between the pillars of the temple. Their levity rebuked, Mezzetin and "I" crouch

silently in awe. The Conjuror awakes and scoffs at their
superstitious fear. He leads them into the depths of the
temple, into the darkness smelling of dust and violets, and
shows them that there is nothing there:

> The Conjuror broke the silence
> And his voice grated in the gloom:
> "What are these myths but half-truths, quarter-truths,
> Dreams of semi-barbarous children
> With an exquisite aesthetic tact?
> Art is primitive and precedes true knowledge;
> The Cro-Magnon, the Cretan, the Ionian
> Possessed a subtle art-sense,
> But their minds stumbled through crude cosmogonies.
> The glory of Hellas is her thinkers,
> Not her poets and her artists;
> Other races have produced as great an art—"
>
> *(Mezzetin dropped his mandolin with a crash.)*
>
> "—But Hellas is the mother of science,
> Praise then to Pheidias and Sophocles,
> But glory, immortal glory, reverence,
> To Thales and Pythagoras, Empedocles,
> Parmenides and Heraclitus, Aristotle!"
> Then he panted, out of breath with shouting.
>
> Mezzetin whispered in my ear:
> "Not a word, you note, of Plato;
> Ask him what he thinks of Phaedrus."

The wild talk continues through the night, until the
Greek dream has melted away. Then the three renew their
wandering.

When my arm was held by Mezzetin
I heard sounds of distant singing,
Monotonous and poignant,
White-veiled women walked beside me
And I was touched to tears by a strange suavity
Compact of resignation, hushed desire,
And eager hope for some unknown good.

But when the Conjuror led me
The gloom raged with contending voices
And the clash of steel,
Dull flames glowed in the distance;
All was misery and confusion.

They come at last to the battlefields of France, and "I"
discovers that he and Mezzetin are privates, while the Conjuror is Sergeant-Major. The Conjuror orders them into
battle, and Mezzetin is killed. The poet is dead, and the
scholar is master. The triangle is broken. "I" weeps for
Mezzetin, and calls the Conjuror murderer, but the latter is
unmoved:

He kicked the passive body, muttering:
"I'm glad he's dead;
I always hated and despised him,
With his eternal jangling mandolin
And stupid jokes at high and serious things;
Now he's gone we'll make a man of you."

"I" knows that he in turn should kill the Conjuror, but
at the moment he lacks the necessary courage. For a time he
submits to the tyranny of his intellectual guide, but his patience breaks at last, and in London, whither they have
drifted after the War, he finds the courage to free himself.
"One morning about three o'clock," as he stands on Water-

loo Bridge, gazing moodily into the water, he seizes the
Conjuror firmly by the ankles and pitches him overboard.

He is now free. But without poetry and without "bright
intellect" what is he to do? Nothing, of course, but become
a respectable clerk, a typical citizen, with a family, a routine, a pride in pettiness, and only an occasional pang of re-
gret for his other slain selves.

> Every morning now at half-past seven
> Ethel thumps me in the back;
> Up I leap, a loyal English husband,
> —Whistle in the bathroom, gulp my bacon,
> Kiss the children—John and James and Mary;
> There's another coming, name not settled—
> Buy the morning paper as I hasten to the tube
> And read of all the wonders of the age.
>
> . . . .
>
> At the office I am diligent and punctual,
> Courteous, well bred, and much respected;
>
> . . . .
>
> Everything I do is wise and orderly;
> My will is made, my life's insured,
> The house is being slowly purchased;
> Yesterday I bought a family grave.

This ending holds the bitterest mockery of the whole
poem. It represents the sort of thing which Aldington most
despises; the hell which he has spent his life escaping. In
that sense it is an autobiographical conclusion, but in that
sense only, for actually the poet and the scholar both sur-
vived, and are still contending for the soul of man.[10]

[10] For a powerful development in prose of Mr. Aldington's main
themes, see his novel, *Death of a Hero*, New York: Covici, Friede. London: Chatto & Windus. 1929.

Something of this triangular struggle is reflected in Aldington's more recent poem, *The Eaten Heart*,[11] a single piece of some three hundred lines of free verse, with a theme drawn from the medieval legend of the beautiful lady who is tricked by her husband into eating the heart of her slain troubadour lover. The contemplation of this romantic story, with its tragic end, leads the modern poet to an analysis of love, to a contrast between old and new ideals, and thence to a semi-autobiographical rhapsody in which the recurrent motif is the struggle of a romantic nature to adapt itself to the hardness and disillusionment of a deflowered age, a post-war, machine-governed world. The conclusion, reached by a tortuous and sometimes prosaic road, is that the soul of the poet survives. It hardens itself and tunes itself to the machines. The tragic suffering attendant upon the metamorphosis is but another poetic experience in a life which is always and inevitably tragic. One kind of beauty is lost, but another is gained. Sweetness goes, but with it goes falsehood; and bitterness brings honesty, a virtue compatible with our age.

An astute psychoanalyst (or a lucky fortune-teller) could have predicted from reading *A Fool i' the Forest* that its author was soon to "make a journey" and experience a change of life. The pastoral interlude was drawing to a close; it had served its purpose. Convalescence threatened to become stagnation and atrophy. The horror of such a fate as overtook the "I" of the poem haunted the actual man like a nightmare. So in the summer of 1928 Richard Aldington forsook the green meadows of Berkshire for the cafés of Montparnasse. He doubts that he will reside again in England,

[11] Chapelle-Réanville, Eure, France: Hours Press. 1929. (Limited edition.) Also included in *Imagist Anthology, 1930.*

for intellectually and emotionally he is more at home on the Continent. The Conjuror continues to make excellent translations (from French, Italian, Latin, and Greek), and to contribute sane, authoritative articles to the English press; Mezzetin, having published his collected poems,[12] is more impish and irresponsible than ever. At times he is much taken with the ultra-modern (post-war) fashions in verse, and threatens to beat the clever Americans at their own game. In "Sepads: A Modern Poem,"[13] for example, he constructs an amusing poem from *Saturday Evening Post* advertisements. Again he is seriously rhapsodic in the old imagist manner, for it is distinctly the pre-war Aldington who writes these beautiful lines in "Passages toward a Long Poem":[14]

> Here is cyclamen
> That stands so stiff and pink
> And has such honey at its heart,
> And wild narcissus
> Soft and scented like your little breasts,
> And one carnation like an open jewel.
>
> . . . .
>
> Gold, sun-scented clusters,
> Black, violet-bloomed clusters,
> exquisite fruition
> of the mysterious vine
> rooted in the dark red flesh of men,
> in the aching ardent bodies of men—
> what wine, what wine shall be poured from you
> when you are crushed

[12] *Collected Poems of Richard Aldington.* New York: Covici, Friede. 1928. London: Allen & Unwin. 1929.

[13] *Imagist Anthology, 1930.*

[14] *Ibid.*

(for you must be crushed,
the exquisite grape clusters
golden and black must be crushed,
give up their perfume and their strength)
when you are crushed in the hot wine-press?

. . . .

And in another (most recent) mood, Mezzetin has permitted himself an excursion into sentimental narrative.
Under the title, *A Dream in the Luxembourg*[15] (published
in America as *Love and the Luxembourg*[16]), he recounts to
the music of a fountain, and in the melancholy accents of
reminiscence, the details of an amour. Biographically the
poem is interesting, because it chronicles the poet's flight
from England to the Continent. Artistically, I should say,
it is lacking in the merit belonging to *The Eaten Heart*
and "Passages toward a Long Poem." Here and there a
line flashes fire, but many passages are dull prose, and the
intensity of emotion which evidently inspired the poem is by
no means communicated to the reader. At best it exhales the
perfume of a long-pressed flower.

Thus much for the Conjuror and Mezzetin. As for "I"
—he is very much what he has been all along: a robust, clear-
eyed, impetuous, generous young Englishman, who Harriet
Monroe said looked like a football player, and whom Amy
Lowell described as a "dyed-in-the-wool Britisher." How
furious both these remarks made Mr. Aldington can be sur-
mised by those who know his attitude toward sports and
toward his typical countrymen. But then, he must be given
things to rebel at, for rebellion is the mainspring of his life.

[15] London: Chatto & Windus. 1930. (Limited and popular editions.)
[16] New York: Covici, Friede. 1930. (Limited edition.)

H. D.
PHOTOGRAPH BY MAN RAY

VI ⪻ H. D.:
The Perfect Imagist

HILDA DOOLITTLE was born at Bethlehem, Pennsylvania, in 1886. When she was still a child her father became director of the Flower Astronomical Observatory at the University of Pennsylvania, and the family moved to a suburb of Philadelphia, where Hilda entered public school. Later she attended a private school in West Philadelphia. In the autumn of 1904 she was admitted to Bryn Mawr College, where she studied for a little more than a year, until a complete breakdown in health compelled her to withdraw. The next few years she spent at home, slowly regaining her health, and indulging her already felt desire for literary expression by writing stories and poems.

In the summer of 1911 she sailed for Europe, and after some time in Italy and France arrived in London, where she renewed her acquaintance with Ezra Pound, whom she had known in Philadelphia. From Pound she received the encouragement which resulted in her adopting poetry as a career, and through him too she met Richard Aldington, whose fanatical devotion to Greek culture harmonized so perfectly with her own inclinations. The two young Hellenists set out together to recapture the beauties of an ancient world, and to create in modern English a poetry which in spirit and form would convey the Greek ideal. To this aesthetic bond was added another, for in the autumn of 1913 H. D. and Aldington were married.

As I have recorded in another chapter, the first poems of H. D.'s to be published appeared in *Poetry* (Chicago) for January 1913 through the efforts of Ezra Pound. Her poetic development from that point on is well portrayed in her various books, which we shall consider presently. But for information regarding her first efforts in verse, the trial flights necessary to every poet, we must go to H. D. herself. In response to a recent query of mine as to whether she had written poems before going abroad in 1911, she has been kind enough to comment informally as follows:

.... of course, I scribbled a bit, adolescent stuff. My first real serious (and I think, in a way, successful) verses were some translations I did of Heine (before I was seriously dubbed "Imagist"). I think they were probably very lyrical in their small way, but of course I destroyed everything. I did a little verse-translation of the lyric Latin poets at Bryn Mawr, vaguely, but nothing came of them. I do not think I even submitted them to the college paper. I do recall, however, how somewhat shocked I was at Bryn Mawr to be flunked quite frankly in English. I don't know how or why this shocked me. I really *did* love the things even when they were rather depleted of their beauty, *Beowulf* and such like. I suppose that was one of the spurs toward a determination to self-expression. I do know that in some way I was rather stunned at the time.

I scribbled later, just before coming "abroad," a half dozen rather free verses that might have been *vers libre*, but I had never heard of *vers libre* till I was "discovered" later by Ezra Pound. Ezra Pound was very kind and used to bring me (literally) armfuls of books to read. Among others, there were some old rather de luxe volumes of Renaissance Latin poets. I was happy with those because the Latin was easy yet held the authentic (though diluted) flavor of the overworked and sometimes slavishly copied Latin and Greek originals. I did a few poems that I don't think Ezra liked . . . . but later he was beautiful about my first authentic verses, "Hermes" and "Spare Us from Loveliness," and "Acon" (a transposition from that Renaissance Latin book) and sent my poems in for me to Miss Monroe. He signed them for me "H. D., Imagiste." The name seems to have stuck somehow . . . .

The extraordinary thing about H. D.'s poetry is that it has altered so little in the last seventeen years. It is somewhat astonishing that she should have arrived so quickly at the mastery of a difficult technique, but it is even more astonishing that a poet of her abilities should have been satisfied during so many years to labor within the bounds of one so narrow. Her development has been chiefly from the short lyric to the long, or rather, from the lyric to the narrative and the dramatic poem. Certainly she has not perceptibly widened her art, and it is questionable how much she has deepened it; what she has done is to lengthen it. For this reason it is not essential that we discuss her poems chronologically, though it may be useful to indicate the order of her published books.

H. D.'s first collection of poems was *Sea Garden*,[1] published in 1916. This was followed in 1919 by a set of translations, *Choruses from the Iphigeneia in Aulis and the Hippolytus of Euripides*.[2] In 1921 appeared *Hymen*,[3] a

[1] London: Constable; Boston: Houghton Mifflin.
[2] London: Egoist Press.
[3] London: Egoist Press; New York: Holt.

small volume of lyrics; and in 1924 a larger collection entitled *Heliodora and Other Poems*.[4] All these were gathered together and published in 1925 as the *Collected Poems of H. D.*[5] In 1927 appeared a complete play in verse, *Hippolytus Temporizes*,[6] which represents H. D.'s most sustained poetic effort, and marks the fulfilment of her long-presaged desire to approximate the achievements of the Greek dramatic poets. It seems doubtful, however, that her drama will count for more than a series of lyrics or at most a symphony of lyric themes.

From the beginning, critics recognized in H. D. a phenomenon—a modern poet who was able to recover and communicate the peculiar sensibilities of an ancient race. English poetry since the Renaissance has leaned heavily on the Greeks, in both form and spirit, but seldom has it given evidence of such authentic kinship as in the poems of H. D. With her it is much more than a mere employment of themes culled from the inexhaustible Greek mythology; it is more than a following of Greek unities or an acceptance of the Greek conception of tragedy. It is rather something suggestive of a mystical affinity, or, to the fanciful mind, a reincarnation. To her much more justly than to other moderns who have asserted their Hellenistic paganism may be applied the familiar phrase, "a Greek born out of her time."

Those who admire the isolated image, and who are willing to accept it as a poem, cannot but be delighted with such a vivid and clearly-wrought miniature as H. D.'s "Oread," which in its entirety is only six short lines:

[4] London: Cape; Boston: Houghton Mifflin.
[5] New York: Boni & Liveright.
[6] Boston: Houghton Mifflin.

Whirl up, sea—
whirl your pointed pines,
splash your great pines
on our rocks,
hurl your green over us,
cover us with your pools of fir.

And the least that other intelligent readers can admit is that this is a perfect fragment of a long poem never written. To me it seems complete as it stands. The personal emotion behind it is clear, and there is a kind of force gained from the expression of this emotion once and once only through an appropriate image, just as in other poems there is another kind of force gained from repetition and elaboration.

Even sharper intensity is obtained in the oft-quoted second part of "Garden," where the poet's sensation of summer heat is perfectly communicated:

O wind, rend open the heat,
cut apart the heat,
rend it to tatters.

Fruit cannot drop
through this thick air—
fruit cannot fall into heat
that presses up and blunts
the points of pears
and rounds the grapes.

Cut the heat—
plough through it,
turning it on either side
of your path.

It is this sort of accomplishment that has led critics to refer
to H. D. as the perfect, and as the only true, imagist. And
certainly it would be difficult to find a poem better qualified
than the one just quoted to represent the principles of
imagism as stated in the official credo.

Although the concentrated objectivity of much of H. D.'s
work has brought upon her the accusation of coldness and
inhumanity, it is a fact that few lyric poets of today have
succeeded so well as she in voicing pure ecstasy. Edna
St. Vincent Millay is perhaps her nearest rival in this respect.
Miss Millay wrote:

> Lord, I do fear
> Thou'st made the world too beautiful this year.
> My soul is all but out of me—let fall
> No burning leaf; prithee, let no bird call.

With purer diction and less obvious music, H. D. has con-
veyed a similar emotion in her poem "Orchard," of which
the opening lines are these:

> I saw the first pear
> as it fell—
> the honey-seeking, golden-banded,
> the yellow swarm
> was not more fleet than I,
> (spare us from loveliness)
> and I fell prostrate
> crying:
> you have flayed us
> with your blossoms,
> spare us the beauty
> of fruit trees.

H. D.'s cadences are her own. The movement is usually staccato, and is less varied than in the work of the other imagists. That it sometimes leads to monotony cannot be denied, yet few of the poems are so long as to become musically fatiguing, and the succession of short lines creates a breathlessness which is peculiarly effective. We are never allowed to "settle down" to H. D.'s poetry; we are never carried smoothly along on rolling billows of music; instead, we are always on tiptoe, strained and alert, while our fancy darts and flashes after the gleaming images. Yet in spite of the predominance of a bird-like quickness of style, we find in these poems movements which are extraordinarily legato, in which the short lines are so softened by word-music and by carefully modulated cadences that all abruptness disappears. An example of this is the second part of "Sea Gods":

> But we bring violets,
> great masses—single, sweet,
> wood-violets, stream-violets
> violets from a wet marsh.
>
> Violets in clumps from hills,
> tufts with earth at the roots,
> violets tugged from rocks,
> blue violets, moss, cliff, river-violets.
>
> Yellow violets' gold,
> burnt with a rare tint—
> violets like red ash
> among tufts of grass.
>
> We bring deep-purple
> bird-foot violets.

We bring the hyacinth-violet,
sweet, bare, chill to the touch—
and violets whiter than the inrush
of your own white surf.

Ordinarily H. D. does not employ rime, and when she does, it is carefully subordinated, almost concealed. She prefers assonance, and on occasion uses it strongly, with marked effect, as, for instance, in the poem "At Ithaca," the first stanza of which is as follows:

Over and back
the long waves crawl
and track the sand with foam;
night darkens and the sea
takes on that desperate tone
of dark that wives put on
when all their love is done.

Here the one pure rime is concealed, whereas the triple assonance (or quadruple, if we include "foam") is emphasized. Swinburne would have approved this stanza.

Only once in her *Collected Poems* does H. D. allow herself complete symmetry of form and a conventional rime-scheme. This is in "Lethe." And even here she succeeds in retaining by subtle means her individual qualities:

LETHE

Nor skin nor hide nor fleece
Shall cover you,
Nor curtain of crimson nor fine
Shelter of cedar-wood be over you,
Nor the fir tree
Nor the pine.

Nor sight of whin nor gorse
    Nor river-yew,
Nor fragrance of flowering bush,
Nor wailing of reed-bird to waken you,
    Nor of linnet,
    Nor of thrush.

Nor word nor touch nor sight
    Of lover, you
Shall long through the night but for this:
The roll of the full tide to cover you
    Without question,
    Without kiss.

It requires careful attention, as well as a considerable knowledge of H. D.'s sources of inspiration, to distinguish where the Greek poets leave off and the modern poet begins. Not that H. D. purposely conceals the line of demarcation, but merely that her work fuses so readily with that of her ancient models. In her most original poems the Greek spirit is dominant, and in her translations there is much that is purely herself. This fusion is, of course, best exemplified in the poems which she has constructed upon Greek fragments, particularly those of Sappho. In these she has woven a whole design from a single bright thread of song, and the design is approved even by those who know best the character of ancient Greek art. Recently an eminent American classical scholar, Professor Henry Rushton Fairclough, of Stanford University, in the course of his presidential address before the American Philological Association,[7] devoted considerable time to the poetry of H. D. and its Greek affinities.

[7] Published as *The Classics and Our Twentieth-Century Poets*. Stanford University, California: Stanford University Press. 1927.

Professor Fairclough has only admiration for H. D.'s work —such profound admiration, indeed, that he classifies her as one of the two greatest living American poets, the other being Edwin Arlington Robinson. H. D. is authentic, he says, for:

> . . . . a Greek scholar, after a perusal of her work, cannot but conclude that in Greek poetry and art H. D. lives and moves and has her being. So completely is she suffused with the Greek spirit that only the use of the vernacular will often remind the cultivated reader that he is not reading a Greek poet.

He goes on then to specify the ancient poets to whom she is particularly indebted and to indicate the characteristics of her technique. In his opinion the sort of free verse which she employs is admirably suited to the rendering of Greek lyrics, and is not, in her skilful hands, inappropriate to the dramatic odes and the epic. "Least peculiarly Greek," he says, "will seem the poems of *Sea Garden,* in which the flowers, shrubs, and trees growing near the sea, as well as the rocky cliffs, the beach, and the seaweed are all described with a minuteness of detail that we never find in Greek poetry." He calls "Hymen," her choral epithalamium, "supremely beautiful," and agrees that "she has made ancient Hellas live again in the present."

Elsewhere in the same address Professor Fairclough discusses the imagists as a group, and finds no serious quarrel with their principles or their practice, except in regard to their limitation of diction to the colloquial and their rejection of certain old rhythms merely because they are old. It seems to him that they have unnecessarily cramped themselves and that as a result their accomplishments have not, taken together, measured up to the potentialities of their imaginative powers. The great Greek poets, he points out, did not thus limit themselves, but made full use of all the richness of tradition, at the same time allowing themselves the freedom of innovation. H. D., he implies, is the only one of the imagists who has, in spite of a confining credo, achieved poetic greatness.

Having witnessed the placing of academic laurels on this poet's brow, let us examine briefly some of the tributes paid her by professional critics and by fellow poets. In this connection it may be remarked that no other imagist, and few non-imagist poets of today, have received so much intelligent admiration as H. D. Cut off, by its subtleties and by its esoteric sources, from the possibility of appealing to the uneducated, her work delights inevitably the connoisseur. The other imagists recognize and freely admit that H. D. surpassed them all in the field of pure imagism; whereas those critics who are inclined to damn imagism in general, frequently except H. D.'s poems from their denunciation.

Amy Lowell devotes some thirty pages of her *Tendencies in Modern American Poetry* to H. D.'s life and art, and although she makes many reservations as to the importance of this art, her discourse overflows with superlatives of praise for its excellence. It is too narrow an art, she maintains, and "it also bears with it the seeds of over-care, of something bordering on preciosity." Yet "These poems are fragile as shells . . . . and their modeling is as carefully done as that of a statue of Parian marble." Again, "H. D.'s poems achieve a beauty of cadence which has been surpassed by no other *vers libriste*. Indeed, her subtly changing rhythms are almost without an equal."

F. S. Flint, writing in the *Egoist* for May 1, 1915, says:

The poetry of H. D. has been described as a kind of "accurate mystery." I could not find a better phrase, for in detail it has the precision of goldsmith's work, in ultimate effect it is mysterious and only to be comprehended by the imagination. . . . . It must work on you as an evocation.

Louis Untermeyer, whose anthologies and critical essays have done so much to interpret and popularize the new poetry in America, has made some very apt and penetrating comments on H. D. "Her poems," he says, "capturing the firm delicacy of the Greek models, are like a set of Tanagra figurines. Here, at first glance, the effect is chilling—beauty seems held in a frozen gesture. But it is in this very fixation of light, color, and emotion that she achieves intensity. What at first seemed static becomes fluent; the arrested moment glows with a quivering tension."[8]

Herbert S. Gorman, writing in the New York *Times Book Review* for August 31, 1924, says: "H. D. stands quite alone among the new poets . . . . even the most conservative reader never doubts the actual poetry that illuminates all of her work. She is the most crystal-like of poets." Later, discussing her indebtedness to Greece, he remarks that "she is never classical in the accepted meaning of that term. Her work is never a cold revivification, a deliberate resuscitation of archaic impulses. It is always impregnated with a beating life and ecstasy that is as sweeping and beautiful as the wings of a bird. Above all things she realizes the intense humanity of the ancient Greeks."

We could go on almost indefinitely recording similarly enthusiastic appreciations from men and women whose knowledge of poetic values is expert. Still, there have been a good many dissenters. The most recent, as well as the most drastic, attempt to discredit H. D.'s poetry appears in

---

[8] *Modern American Poetry* (Third, revised edition), p. 405.

A Survey of Modernist Poetry,[9] by Laura Riding and Robert Graves. These two rampant and rather impertinent critics have no use for imagism, which they classify as a "dead movement," and they take special pains to abuse H. D. because of the imagists she was "the most publicly applauded." Here is an excerpt from their diatribe:

> The only excuse to be made for those who once found H. D. "incomprehensible" is that her work was so thin, so poor, that its emptiness seemed "perfection," its insipidity to be concealing a "secret," its superficiality so "glacial" that it created a false "classical" atmosphere. She was never able, in her temporary immortality, to reach a real climax in any of her poems. All that they told was a story of feeble personal indecision; and her immortality came to an end so soon that her bluff was never called.

It would not be difficult, it seems to me, to formulate a reply to these charges; but to take up only those which can be met briefly and without a tedious definition of terms, let us note that (1) H. D. has never been called incomprehensible by any except the uneducated, and certainly not by her admirers; (2) the classical atmosphere created by her poems has been approved as authentic by both English and American scholars of the highest standing; and (3) her popularity, if that is what is meant by the excessive word "immortality," has not come to an end, or her *Collected Poems* would not be selling as well as I happen to know it is selling. In respect of this matter I can but refer Miss Riding and Mr. Graves to H. D.'s publisher, who will supply them with rather astonishing figures.

More interesting, however, and certainly more amusing than attacks of this sort are the parodies which H. D.'s poems

[9] London: Heinemann. 1927. New York: Dutton. 1928. Pages 121–123.

have inspired. A good parody, as everyone knows, is in many ways the best form of criticism, for it must light upon the essential weakness of its model, and its satire must be based upon fundamental sympathy.

In *The Chapbook, A Monthly Miscellany*[10] for May 1921 appeared a group of parodies entitled "Pathology des Dommagistes." A sub-title explained that these poems were "Specimens for a Projected Anthology to Be Issued in the U.S.A." The victims were, of course, the imagists in general and H. D. in particular, for the reworking and imitation of Greek fragments was taken as the principal theme. Some of the best specimens were as follows:

PALAEOLITH

Bring now
Chryso-phrases two words long
Sprinkle the marble steps
White as her neck
Twice . . . .

ANOTHER

I

Hoi
The wet milk lashes me
A lank seaweed
Sheared the salt water
Long, long ago.
Wait for me
Where daisies twine round
Papuan mandragora.

II

Hoi . . . .

[10] London: Poetry Bookshop.

EPIGRAM

(After the Cretan)
Little Caligulala
Has tied one golden sandal
Round her pink ankle
Too tightly.
Heu! The discomfort
The varicose veins . . . .

Silver dust falls
Over the tepidarium . . . .

No one will deny that the anonymous author of these parodies understood and even appreciated the virtues of his models. Nor did he work harm to H. D.'s art by demonstrating the dangers of exotic mannerism and preciosity which inevitably surround her.

The comic aspect of the poetic fragment was fully realized by some of the imagists themselves. We find Ezra Pound, for example, mixing burlesque with his serious poems, trusting to a super-acute reader to distinguish between the two. One of his most amusing stunts is the following:

PAPYRUS

Spring . . . .
Too long . . . .
Gongula . . . .

This cryptic bit was, as a matter of fact, composed as a satire on H. D. and her Sapphics, but inasmuch as Pound scorns labeling it, and allows it to be printed without warning in his *Collected Poems*, it is only natural that it should prove bait to critics. Only recently I found it reprinted in the London *Observer* as a horrible illustration of what modern poetry had come to, and, in *A Survey of Modernist Poetry*,

Miss Riding and Mr. Graves, who do not by any means consider themselves gullible, devote a page of worried inquiry to the significance of this four-word joke of Pound's.

H. D. herself may possibly suffer as a poet from a lack of sufficient humor, but I think it extremely doubtful that many of her poems lend themselves to comic interpretation. She does not aim at the cryptic, and she seldom permits a fragment to stand alone. A handful of Greek dust may seem more precious to her than it does to most of us, but that is because in her hands it turns to something more than dust —to flowers or to flame.

H. D. is a lonely figure, and her loneliness cries out from her poems. She is not of this world, but of one long past, and we must not look to her for an interpretation of modern life. All that she brings to the twentieth century is a vision of beauty which has not altered since the days of Homer, and which may be perceived only by those who have within themselves something likewise fixed and immutable. Her shyness and her incapacity to assimilate the life of today have caused her much pain, but this has been made to serve the purpose of her art. During recent years she has spent most of her time at a quiet retreat in Switzerland, though occasionally she pays a visit to London. Only once since her arrival in Europe in 1911 has she returned to America. That was in 1920, and her stay was not for long.

She is still the elusive pagan spirit who woke to life in London under the magic incantation of the Greeks. What Amy Lowell once said of her is still true: "H. D. has a strange, faun-like, dryad-like quality; she seems always as though just startled from a brake of fern." There is no living poet who resembles her, though there may be one or two long dead. There was one of Lesbos . . . .

JOHN GOULD FLETCHER

VII ⪻ JOHN GOULD FLETCHER:
Pictorialist and Mystic

JOHN GOULD FLETCHER was born at Little Rock, Arkansas, in 1886, of Scotch and German ancestry. As a child he was encouraged to read widely, and also to study foreign languages. Under the influence of the traditional poets, he began composing verses at the age of eleven. It was at this age, too, that he was first sent to school, his education until then having been conducted by tutors. He finished high school in 1902 and was sent East to enter Phillips Academy, Andover, where he prepared for Harvard.

He spent the years 1904–1907 studying at Harvard, but left the University during his Senior year without taking a degree. He left because he could not stand any more academic training. He had not been a model student—his individualism was too strong; and he had often cut classes in order to read things he was attracted to instead of the things that were assigned. But while at Harvard he learned to read French (his earlier language studies had been in Latin and German), and developed a passion for French poetry. This interest proved of great importance in his own career as a poet.

In 1906, on his father's death, he inherited an income sufficient for his needs and on the strength of this he determined to devote his life to literature. On quitting the University he settled for a time in Boston, but, still dissatisfied, he sailed for Europe in August 1908. Chiefly because of his love for Kèats and Shelley he went straight to Italy and there (in Venice and Rome) steeped himself in history, in scenery, and in poetry. During this time he wrote a good many poems of his own, but most of them were too strongly derivative to possess any distinction. They were the practice-work of a college boy.

In May 1909 Mr. Fletcher left Italy and went to London, where, except during visits to America and the Continent, he has lived ever since. His early years in London were rather lonely. He read and wrote voluminously, but his human contacts were few. He lived practically the life of a recluse. During this time, however, he developed two new poetic interests. One was the new French poetry, particularly in its wilder manifestations; the other was Whitman, whom he had completely ignored during his student days in America but whom he now discovered through his association with certain London radicals. He became an ardent Whitmanite, and his own writing reflected this devotion. Miss Lowell was quite wrong in declaring that "the one poet who seems never to have affected his work in the slightest degree is Whitman."[1] The influence is not only apparent; it is admitted by Mr. Fletcher himself.

These new interests, combined with other events, brought about a complete revolution in his habits of thought and his methods of expression; but before entering on the new phase

---

[1] *Tendencies in Modern American Poetry*, p. 296.

he determined to settle accounts with his past. He had accumulated a great number of his own poems, and he had been unable to find a publisher willing to risk the expense of their publication. With the desperation felt by so many young writers, he threw his pride to the winds and paid for their publication himself. They were issued in five separate volumes (rather small volumes), with the imprints of four different London publishers.[2] All of them appeared in 1913. During the War, Mr. Fletcher withdrew from the hands of his publishers the remaining copies of these "poetic wild oats," and contributed the whole lot, as so much pulp, toward the alleviation of the paper shortage. Many worse poets might take note of this courageous gesture.

By no means all the poems in these volumes were capable of embarrassing their author in his years of discretion. Some of them were puerile; many of them were weak imitations of old masters; and many of them were ruined by barbarisms of diction and clumsiness of phrase. Most of them, too, were dominated by adolescent melancholy and melodramatic bitterness. But in spite of their undeniable faults, they showed a genuine poetic personality—a poet whose growing pains were excessively acute but who nevertheless was growing. The English reviewers, a number of whom took note of this extraordinary début, did not hesitate to poke fun at Mr. Fletcher's weaknesses, but nearly all of them recognized poetic talent and strength beneath the surface. A writer in the *New Age*, for example, commented on *Fire and Wine* as follows:

---

[2] *Fire and Wine.* London: Grant Richards. *Fool's Gold.* London: Max Goschen. *The Dominant City.* London: Max Goschen. *The Book of Nature.* London: Constable. *Visions of the Evening.* London: Erskine McDonald.

There are many ridiculous outbursts in this volume, yet sometimes appear suggestions of truer moods, though few persons will
care to seek for these amongst so much nonsense.

Of the same book the *Academy* reviewer wrote: "It is
sultry and filled often with lightning flashes." But the poet
is suspected of posing and of trying to "stagger his reader"
with extravagant outbursts of sorrow and disillusion. This
leads to an expression of the hope "that he may find healthier
topics for the exercise of his undoubted ability."

T. P.'s Weekly was very harsh:

The author seems to have lashed himself into the belief that
he is a poet, and he is constantly telling us so, sometimes in obscure,
sometimes in pretentious, and sometimes in merely bad verse.

But there was compensation in the friendly words of the
Athenaeum concerning *The Dominant City*:

Apart from an occasional tendency to verbal exaggeration, Mr.
Fletcher's work is deserving of unstinted praise. He has a rugged
strength and a fine imagination which go to lift his verse high above
the ordinary level of his contemporaries.

The *Daily Chronicle* could not find much to say in favor
of *Visions of the Evening*, except that:

John G. Fletcher is bold and a bit precious. He carefully cul-
tivates the gloomy mind . . . . he sees his own life as a long Via
Dolorosa; he has, in brief, that ultra-modern spirit which ties his
wreath of bays with mourning-bands.

In reviewing *Fool's Gold*, much the same criticism is
made by the *New Age*, with the difference that confidence is
here expressed in the author's ability to survive his sufferings:

This very gloomy author seems to have a genuine hatred of this planet. . . . . However, he has the manliness not to blame God, but himself and his fellows, for all bitterness. . . . . There is to be heard the howl, the curse, the groan of an indignant soul, but no whining. In fact Mr. Fletcher's language is so gritty that we should not wonder if he fought through to the calm which certainly awaits long-lived men of spirit.

But the most interesting criticism of these juvenilia—the most discriminating, and one of the most encouraging to Mr. Fletcher—was one written by Ezra Pound and published in the *New Freewoman*.[3] At the time the review was written Pound and Fletcher had but recently become acquainted, although they had both been in London several years. Pound, with his unusual perception, saw more clearly than anyone else what his fellow-American was driving at; he saw in him the poet that he was to become. He wrote:

Mr. Fletcher's music is more comparable to that made by a truck-load of iron rails crossing a cobbled pavement than to the wailful sound of violins. Mr. Fletcher has not the faults of the mellifluous versifier, of the great horde of publishing authors whose product reminds one more of perfumed suet than of any other nameable commodity. Mr. Fletcher has a fine crop of faults— mostly his own. He has such distinction as belongs to a man who dares to have his own faults, who prefers his own to those of anyone else.

He then went on to mention the French influence on Fletcher's verse, and to commend it. He lauded the poet's "determination to fight out his own rhythms," and his courage in daring "to go to the dust-bin for his subjects."

But although a discriminating mind could perceive in this

[3] Issue of September 15, 1913.

early work the tentative manifestations of a new and vital technique, it was not until these five books were published and out of mind that Mr. Fletcher really took hold of himself and, casting all conventions aside, announced himself a poet of the new age. Without abandoning set verse-forms (he has never done that), he concluded, nevertheless, that modern life demanded new rhythms, new patterns, new diction, and new subject-matter in poetry. He determined to extend the horizons of poetry as far as possible. He became one of the strongest and most convincing agitators for vers libre, as well as one of its ablest exponents. In the preface to his next published collection of poems, *Irradiations: Sand and Spray,*[4] he proclaimed exultantly his own vision of freedom, and exhorted his fellow-poets to join the adventure of experimentation:

> It is time to create something new. It is time to strip poetry of meaningless tatters of form, and to clothe her in new, suitable garments..... Never was life lived more richly, more fully, with more terrible blind intensity than it is being lived at this instant. Never was the noble language which is ours surpassed either in richness or in concision. We have the material with which to work, and the tools to do the work with. It is America's opportunity to lay the foundations for a new flowering of English verse, and to lay them as broad as they are strong.

The poems called "Irradiations" were all written between March and July, 1913. "Sand and Spray (A Sea-Symphony)," was written in October of the same year. When Amy Lowell visited London in June 1913, she and Mr. Fletcher met for the first time. They found much in common, for they were both enamored of modern French poetry

---

[4] Boston: Houghton Mifflin; London: Constable. 1915.

and were both interested in the trend of modern English poetry. Fletcher showed her the portions of "Irradiations" which were then completed. He explained his conception of free verse. Miss Lowell was greatly impressed by both the theory and its results. From that time forward she was an ardent believer in the principles advanced by Fletcher, and she consistently employed them in her own poetry. On her next visit to London, in the summer of 1914, she learned that no English publisher had been found willing to undertake the publication of *Irradiations: Sand and Spray;* so, with the enterprise which was characteristic of her, she borrowed the manuscript, took it with her to America along with *Some Imagist Poets,* and arranged for its publication the following spring.

These poems received a great deal of praise. They were refreshing, vigorous, filled with new imagery, and surprising in their variety of musical effects. In brief, they overflowed with creative energy. The chief objection raised against them was that they lacked human emotion—that they were compounded of magic but empty phrases. Such a criticism is understandable, though unjust. It merely shows a lack of sympathy with the objective method which Mr. Fletcher and the other imagists adopted. A few poems in the volume may be deficient in emotion, and may be little more than conscious exercises, but these are surely in the minority. Take one of the best and most-quoted examples from this collection:

VII

Flickering of incessant rain
On flashing pavements:
Sudden scurry of umbrellas:
Bending, recurved blossoms of the storm.

The winds came clanging and clattering
From long white highroads whipping in ribbons
    up summits:
They strew upon the city gusty wafts of
    apple-blossoms,
And the rustling of innumerable translucent
    leaves.

Uneven tinkling, the lazy rain
Dripping from the eaves.[5]

To say that such a poem is unemotional is nonsense. What is true is that in this poem the poet does not talk about himself. Nor does he talk about his emotions. He presents, objectively and artistically, the materials of life which have aroused his emotions, and if we are sufficiently poetic to be readers of poetry, we will feel an emotion closely akin to his own. Such a poem cannot be labeled mere description, for it is description in terms of personal feeling. It is the portrait of a mood. It is very good imagism.

There is no doubt that much of Mr. Fletcher's poetry suggests the art of painting (he has long been a student of this art, and has even done a little painting on his own account), but then, so does much of it suggest the art of music. There is nothing reprehensible in this fact. All the arts learn from one another, and it is only occasionally that one goes too far in its imitation of another, thus losing its own identity. Mr. Fletcher's poems are unusually rich in their associations with the other arts, but primarily they are always poems.

What gives even his most objective compositions a lyric,

[5] From *Preludes and Symphonies*. By permission of The Macmillan Company, publishers.

an emotional, strength is Mr. Fletcher's intensely personal and unique approach to the external world. He not only sees things in his own way; he lets himself into things, into the very core of their being; and from this inner dwelling-place his images arise. First to possess, then to create—that is the true process of the artist. See how this poet enters into the essentials of a hot summer afternoon:

VI

The balancing of gaudy broad pavilions
Of summer against an insolent breeze:
The bellying of the sides of striped tents,
Swelling taut, shuddering in quick collapse,
Silent under the silence of the sky.

Earth is streaked and spotted
With great splashes and dapples of sunlight:
The sun throws an immense circle of hot light
    upon the world,
Rolling slowly in ponderous rhythm
Darkly, musically forward.

All is silent under the steep cone of
    afternoon:
The sky is imperturbably profound.
The ultimate divine union seems about to be
    accomplished,
All is troubled at the attainment
Of the inexhaustible infinite.

The rolling and the tossing of the sides of
    immense pavilions
Under the whirling wind that screams up the
    cloudless sky.[6]

[6] From *Preludes and Symphonies*. By permission of The Macmillan Company, publishers.

The severest critics of "Irradiations" admitted the brilliance of Fletcher's imagery and the power of his fancy. They admitted, too, the impressive music of his cadenced lines. It would be hard not to appreciate the movement in:

> Over the roof-tops race the shadows of clouds;
> Like horses the shadows of clouds charge down the street.

It must not be inferred from these quotations that all the poems in the volume are without rime, for a good many of them are strongly rimed. Conventional stanza forms, however, are employed rarely, and in most instances the lines vary considerably in length. Regularity appears only when monotony is essential to the mood behind the poem. Miss Lowell's admiration for these shifting cadences caused her to declare that "No one is more absolute master of the rhythms of *vers libre* than is Mr. Fletcher."[7] And later in the same critical essay she remarks with justice that in his vers libre his rimes (casual and capricious) are more felicitous than they are in his regular metrical verse. "Where it is not imperative, it is often most cunningly accomplished." But whether his lines are rimed or not, their sound values are carefully considered, too carefully, sometimes, for those who are chary of word-music. In this connection we must remember Mr. Fletcher's intensive study of modern French poetry, in which the musical value of a word or a phrase is often an end in itself.

This same emphasis on music, combined with a stronger emphasis on color, dominates Fletcher's next published collection of poems, *Goblins and Pagodas.*[8] The book is in two parts: the first, called "The Ghosts of an Old House," comprises twenty-four lyrics written from impressions of the

[7] *Tendencies in Modern American Poetry*, p. 304.
[8] Boston: Houghton Mifflin. 1916. London: Constable. 1918.

author's old home in America; the second, "The Symphonies," represents an ambitious attempt to arrange the intellectual and emotional life of an artist in eleven separate movements, each movement being dominated by a color-harmony. But before we discuss these poems we should note that in the autumn of 1914 Mr. Fletcher left England for America, and that he did not return to London until May 1916, the month following the publication of *Goblins and Pagodas*. During this long visit to his native country he spent some time in Little Rock, Arkansas, renewing acquaintance with the house in which his childhood had been spent.

"The Ghosts of an Old House" was all written in February 1915. It is not a great performance, though it contains bits of poignant writing. It is human, it is simple, it is sincere, it avoids the maudlin—even that is a good deal to say for poems of reminiscence. The total effect of this group of lyrics is, I think, rather powerful—more powerful than one would suspect from reading certain ones separately. It is the mosaic of childhood which impresses us, and it is only when the mosaic is complete that we realize the force of its reality. Over the whole scene plays a somber fancy, the fancy of a poet who has known much grief and who sees about him the symbols of that grief—the bed where his father died; the disused, tainted well; the dark, empty room in the cellar; the dust and the broken chairs in the attic; the owls and rats in the ancient barn; and ghosts, ghosts everywhere. For this mood we are not unprepared; it is established in the prologue, which begins:

> The house that I write of, faces the north:
> No sun ever seeks
> Its six white columns,
> The nine great windows of its face.

The picture grows more and more somber as we progress:

> The windows rattle as if someone were in
>   them wishing to get out
> And ride upon the wind.
>
> Doors lead to nowhere:
> Squirrels burrow between the walls.
> Closets in every room hang open,
> Windows are stared into by uncivil, ancient
>   trees.

And finally we are told:

> All over the house there is a sense of
>   futility;
> Of minutes dragging slowly
> And repeating
> Some worn-out story of broken effort and
>   desire.[9]

It is all very convincing. The pathos is communicated; we suffer—not grandly, to be sure, but legitimately. We are not asked to bathe in sickly sentiment; the tone is too austere for that. It is a human document recorded in imagery.

The "Symphonies" were written during 1914 and the early part of 1915. The "Blue Symphony," to me the most successful of the series, was composed in one day, January 30, 1914. It was first printed in *Some Imagist Poets* (1915). In these long and complicated poems Mr. Fletcher is shown at the height of his powers as an imagist. One cannot pretend that he succeeds at every point; the eleven poems are not equally good. But each includes passages of remarkable

[9] From *Preludes and Symphonies*. By permission of The Macmillan Company, publishers.

beauty and mastery of form, and several are consistently excellent.

In a long and studious preface to the volume which contains them, the author gives us the clue to the technique which underlies them, discusses "the emotional relations that exist between form, color and sound," and finally gives a brief synopsis of the themes of which the "Symphonies" are the elaboration. That this was dangerous ground he must have been well aware, for there have been many abortive attempts to express one art in terms of another, but he was undaunted by the specter of confusion. He was determined to create a literary work in which colors should serve as musical motifs. Lacking a universally accepted law of relationship between color, sound, and form, he was forced, naturally, to an arbitrary system based on his own perceptions. The poems, therefore, appeal most strongly to those readers whose perceptions correspond closely to Mr. Fletcher's. It is partly a question of temperament and partly a question of training. In the case of some colors, the symbolism is readily accepted — the emotional values and the associated qualities are more or less conventionalized. For example, few persons would find themselves disturbed by Mr. Fletcher's statement that "blue suggests to me depth, mystery, and distance." Our experience of the external world has prepared us for such an idea. Nor is one startled by the poet's choice of green as the symbol for the pagan worship of nature. But one ponders over the selection of white-and-blue as a motif for the struggle between the spiritual and the sensual; and one is not instantly convinced that orange is the color of war.

There was no way to avoid these debatable points, except by abandoning the plan and leaving the poems unwritten, in

which case no one would have had any fun. Mr. Fletcher
did the right thing—he wrote the poems, and let those enjoy
them who could.

Among anthologists the "Green Symphony" has perhaps
proved the most popular, and it is certainly one of the best;
but to me the "Blue Symphony" is finer. And when recently
I mentioned this prejudice to Mr. Fletcher, I found that his
opinion coincided with my own. The "Blue Symphony" is
a subtly modulated and exquisitely suggestive allegory (I
use this word hesitantly) of the pursuit of beauty, the beauty
which is never to be found. It is the vision of the young man
as artist who realizes the futility of the search but who knows
that nevertheless his life must be devoted to it.

The setting of the poem, its atmosphere and detail, is
Oriental—an arbitrary choice on the author's part, but an
appropriate one for a theme verging on the mystical, in which
elusiveness is the keynote. It is a fact worth noting that at
the time he composed the "Blue Symphony" Mr. Fletcher
was decidedly under the influence of Chinese poetry—first
discovered by him in French translation and afterward in
the work of Ezra Pound, when the latter was preparing his
very beautiful "Cathay" poems from the notes of Ernest
Fenollosa.

The "Blue Symphony" opens with a passage of master-
ful imagery, in which the mood is strongly impressed. The
artist, entering upon a new phase of his life, contemplates
the past, and faces the uncertain future.

I

The darkness rolls upward.
The thick darkness carries with it
Rain and a ravel of cloud.
The sun comes forth upon earth.

Palely the dawn
Leaves me facing timidly
Old gardens sunken:
And in the gardens is water.

Somber wreck—autumnal leaves;
Shadowy roofs
In the blue mist,
And a willow branch that is broken.

Oh, old pagodas of my soul, how you glittered across
    green trees!

Blue and cool:
Blue, tremulously,
Blow faint puffs of smoke
Across somber pools.
The damp green smell of rotted wood;
And a heron that cries from out the water.

In the second part he sees himself starting on the long
search. His path leads him through meadows, where he asks
of the flowers and the rocks if they know aught of her
(Beauty) whom he seeks. He is answered only by silence.
In the third part he comes to a brook, where the water-
sprites mock him with their whispers, and where

    The vast dark trees
    Flow like blue veils
    Of tears
    Into the water.

But here there is no answer either. Only the wind rattling
in the reeds, and "A faint shiver in the grasses." In the
fourth part the pilgrim has ceased his wandering. Weary of

an unyielding quest, he reclines at ease in the city, watching the stream of life and dreaming listlessly. In the fifth and final part he accepts the inevitable and prepares graciously for death.

v

And now the lowest pine branch
Is drawn across the disk of the sun.
Old friends who will forget me soon,
I must go on,
Towards those blue death-mountains
I have forgot so long.

In the marsh grasses
There lies forever
My last treasure,
With the hopes of my heart.

The ice is glazing over,
Torn lanterns flutter,
On the leaves is snow.

In the frosty evening
Toll the old bell for me
Once, in the sleepy temple.

Perhaps my soul will hear.

Afterglow:
Before the stars peep
I shall creep out into darkness.[10]

Because of its almost flawless imagery, its subtle cadence, and its remarkable unity of effect, this poem will very likely

[10] From *Preludes and Symphonies*. By permission of The Macmillan Company, publishers.

stand, along with two or three of the other "Symphonies," as one of the finest examples of sustained imagistic writing.

Mr. Fletcher's next book of verse, *The Tree of Life*,[11] is in quite a different vein. Because of this difference, and because the author's reticence over its intensely personal note prevented its publication until 1918, it is generally thought of as belonging to the post-imagist period. But as a matter of fact its composition covers the whole time of Mr. Fletcher's most imagistic writing. The first section was written in the autumn of 1913, the second during the summer of 1914, while he was at work on the "Symphonies," the third during the winter of 1914–1915, and the fourth and fifth during the following summer and autumn. The epilogue belongs to the early part of 1916.

The Tree of Life was not well received by the public. In America it was almost completely ignored, and in England it was "torn to pieces" by reviewers. This reaction wounded Fletcher deeply, for he felt, and still feels, that the book contains some of his best work. His point of view is easily comprehended, for into these lyrics he poured his whole soul. They form the record of a long-drawn-out and heart-searing experience with love, in which despair, frustration, loneliness, and the rest of love's attendant evils lash the poet into frenzied rhapsodies. That out of this mass of passionate writing may be gathered precious bits of poetry, no one, I think, will deny. Nor can it be denied that the book as a whole creates a powerful effect, if only because of the profound sincerity, the human reality, which underlies it. But personal suffering (particularly from love) is always difficult material to transmute into pure art: to do so requires more

[11] London: Chatto & Windus; New York: Macmillan. 1918.

detachment, a sterner aesthetic conscience, than Mr. Fletcher exhibited in *The Tree of Life*. Nearly all his critics have agreed that his weakness is the lack of a selective faculty, and in none of his books is this deficiency more apparent than in the volume under discussion. Many of the poems are marred by awkward spontaneities; occasionally an entire poem could be dispensed with advantageously. The fact that brilliant figures leap from the melancholy pages, or that rich music rises from the tortured lines, cannot entirely compensate for the impurities. The artist too often was mastered by the man.

Still, it is easy enough to choose from among these lyrics one which is successful. The following, for example:

THE RETURN TO LIFE

We lay on the beach again together,
We who had passed through so many sunless hours
With clutched hands, impotently striving
For a happiness unattainable in this world;
Having leapt from the white peaks of longing,
Having shot the green rapids of passion,
Having swept down the broad stream boiling and curdling
About our bannered prows day after day,
Having come to the sluggish deltas of parting,
And from thence having found the open sea,
All land departed and the scream of the gulls in our ears;
We came at last to that lonely beach
And lay down on it, together, saying no word,
Having lost all desire but for sunlight,
And the clash of the breakers boiling up on the white cliff
above us.[12]

[12] From *The Tree of Life*. By permission of The Macmillan Company, publishers.

This poem carries conviction, and at the same time it has the repose which is so valuable in a work of art. Its music is not exceptional (there are many poems in the volume which are more interesting musically), but its movement is in accord with the theme. The central idea is good, and the treatment is mature. It does not strike us, as do some of the lyrics which accompany it, as being slightly adolescent. Whatever else may be said of these emotional poems, one thing is clear: the author of the cold, objective imagist pieces in *Irradiations* and *Goblins and Pagodas* was not, even in his most imagistic days, without a heart.

Less personal, less pretentious, and certainly less important than either of his previous collections of poetry, was *Japanese Prints*,[13] published in the same year as *The Tree of Life*. This book was the outgrowth of Mr. Fletcher's interest in and admiration for Japanese poetry and painting. A poet of his wide interests and experimental tendencies could hardly be expected to escape the influence of the Japanese. Ezra Pound felt this influence, and so did Amy Lowell. So have many of their contemporaries and followers. The tiny, clear-cut, suggestive *tanka* and *hokku*, the essence of refined imagery and concentration, appeal inevitably to the imagistic poet.

In the preface to *Japanese Prints* Mr. Fletcher treats of Japanese prosody (a subject on which much has been written since 1918) and discusses in detail the merits of the poem in miniature. He urges that the spirit rather than the form of Japanese poetry be followed by Occidental poets, and states definitely that his own poems (i.e., the poems to which these comments are prefaced) do not pretend to be Japanese,

[13] Boston: Four Seas. 1918.

but merely "illustrate something of the charm" which the author has found in the literature and pictorial art of Japan. A typical specimen is the following:

THE YOUNG DAIMYO

When he first came out to meet me,
He had just been girt with the two swords;
And I found he was far more interested in the glitter of the hilts
And did not even compare my kiss to a cherry blossom.

This little poem, like others in the same collection, is pleasantly suggestive of Oriental atmosphere. It is not, however, based on any profound knowledge of the Japanese, as Professor William Leonard Schwartz has pointed out in an essay dealing with Amy Lowell's Far Eastern verse.[14] Miss Lowell had praised this poem of Fletcher's.[15] Professor Schwartz says this proves that in 1917, at least, her acquaintance with Oriental matters was rather superficial, for "Young daimyo in feudal Japan were first girt with two swords at a much more tender age, nor was kissing practised at that time. Fletcher's cherry-blossom simile is incorrect and foreign to Japanese thought." Under the circumstances it is rather fortunate that Mr. Fletcher protected himself by saying that his poems did not pretend to be the genuine Japanese article. Many of them, indeed, are more Chinese than Japanese; others are purely Occidental in thought and feeling. Their chief resemblance to Japanese poems lies in their brevity and in their "stage properties," that is, their paraphernalia of swords, cherry blossoms, palace gardens, jewel trees, and the

[14] *Modern Language Notes* (Baltimore), March 1928, p. 147.
[15] *Tendencies in Modern American Poetry*, p. 339.

like. This does not mean, of course, that they are without charm.

In *Breakers and Granite*[16] we have something entirely different. This volume represents Mr. Fletcher's salutation to America—a richly imaginative interpretation of his native land as it appeared to him after years of residence in Europe. Most of the poems were written during his 1914–1916 visit, the remainder in 1920. Vers libre is the predominant form, though a number of pieces are in "polyphonic prose." Curiously enough, it was Fletcher who invented this term to describe some poetic experiments of Amy Lowell, which had been inspired by her reading of Paul Fort. Whether it is a just, a legitimate, name for this type of composition need not concern us here. Miss Lowell liked it and used it, and her polyphonic prose was sufficiently striking to cause some of her contemporaries to essay the same form. Mr. Fletcher, for example, frankly admits that his own attempts in this direction were due primarily to his admiration for her achievements. Polyphonic prose is a kind of free verse, except that it is still freer. An absurd statement, but one which we are forced to make if we take at its face value Miss Lowell's own definition.[17] According to its inventor, polyphonic prose is the most elastic of all poetic forms. It makes full use of all the "voices" of poetic expression—cadence, rime, alliteration, assonance, return, and so on—hence the name, "polyphonic," which means "many-voiced." The only rule which governs it is the taste and feeling of its author. It is printed as prose, but it is not prose. Rather confusing, but . . . .

Mr. Fletcher does some very interesting things in this

[16] New York: Macmillan. 1921.
[17] See preface to *Can Grande's Castle*.

hybrid form. He finds it particularly suited to colorful action, as he demonstrates in "Clipper-Ships," the opening paragraph of which runs as follows:

Beautiful as a tiered cloud, skysails set and shrouds twanging, she emerges from the surges that keep running away before day on the low Pacific shore. With the roar of the wind blowing half a gale after, she heels and lunges, and buries her bows in the smother, lifting them swiftly, and scattering the glistening spray-drops from her jibsails with laughter. Her spars are cracking, her royals are half splitting, her lower stunsail booms are bent aside, like bowstrings ready to loose, and the water is roaring into her scuppers, but she still staggers out under a full press of sail, her upper trucks enkindled by the sun into shafts of rosy flame.[18]

The poem in its entirety creates a very beautiful effect, and offers a stirring description of the almost forgotten Yankee sailing ships which used to round the Horn.

For the most part, of course, the book gives us pictures of the land rather than of the sea. We view the canyons of Manhattan as well as the Grand Canyon of the Colorado, the quiet fields of New England, and the vast sweep of the Mississippi. We taste deeply the spirit of the Old South; we join the festival dances of the Arizona Indians. It is a Whitmanesque book, overflowing with rich impressions, welling up from deep springs of feeling. It is a patriotic book, though it is not sentimental. It is not the product of an exiled mind, for Mr. Fletcher has never ceased to think as an American; nor is it the nostalgic cry of the prodigal son—its author is too sane for that. Its vision is clear and its emotions are balanced. It reaches a magnificent climax in the final

[18] From *Breakers and Granite*. By permission of The Macmillan Company, publishers.

poem, "Lincoln," which has already taken its place beside Whitman's "When Lilacs Last in the Dooryard Bloom'd," as one of the greatest eulogies inspired by the best-loved American.

With the publication of *Parables*[19] in 1925 this fecund and ever-dissatisfied poet made manifest an aspect of his personality which could scarcely have been perceived by a reader of his previous volumes. In *Parables* Mr. Fletcher appears before us suddenly as a militant Christian—as a modern crusader, whose sword, like the sword of Blake, is poetry. And indeed the spirit of the book is such that we are obliged to think of its author as having sworn Blake's oath:

> I will not cease from mental fight,
> Nor shall my sword sleep in my hand
> Till we have built Jerusalem
> In England's green and pleasant land.

There are seventy-eight separate compositions, some in prose, some in free verse, and others in conventional verse forms. The three modes are freely intermingled. Half the book is devoted to Parables of Christ, half to Parables of Antichrist—Christ and Antichrist being defined by the author as states of the soul. The prose pieces are now rhetorical, with a suggestion of Biblical style; again they are sharp and epigrammatical; occasionally they become merely colloquial —to their detriment, I fear. The poems are on the average superior to the prose pieces. They are less imagistic than most of Mr. Fletcher's poetic work, but they are patently the creation of a poet who has served his apprenticeship and whose knowledge of rhythm, rime, and imagery has become

[19] London: Kegan Paul.

instinctive. That religious fervor sometimes overshadows art in the pages of this book cannot be denied. The wonder is that it does so with such infrequency.

The more mystical themes are, naturally enough, the most poetic; and there is a considerable amount of mysticism here set forth. But there is a very great dramatic strength in the rhetorical prose passages, wherein the evils of the modern world are arraigned. Europe is seen to be dying, refusing the light of salvation even as she dies; Asia is slowly wakening from a long, drugged sleep, and fate hangs above her, hazily, a question-mark writ in smoke; America rushes and plunges in a darkness of physical life— yet she alone gives promise of a faith to save the world. These themes are elaborated with a deal of skill, and with a hard directness which gives them power. The following lines will serve as an example:

> Christ dances on a thousand graves. Out of them all He is risen. Out of Greece, the grave of the past. Out of France, the grave of the Middle Ages. Out of Italy, the grave of the Renaissance. Out of Russia, the grave of the Nineteenth Century. In England the grave is made and open, but mankind will not descend.

It is a very rugged and masculine Christianity which animates this book. It is bold, it is bitter, it is a challenge and an indictment. What peace it mirrors resides not in the world, but in the depths of the poet's heart. This peace is reflected clearly in the following lyric:

THE ATTAINMENT

> Daring in my humility
> I tore the veil aside and there lay truth
> Outstretched and shining like a sleeping bride,
> Beyond the grasp of genius or of youth.

Long I gazed lovingly on her; she slept still;
And in her naked glory all the earth
Dwindled down to a narrow speck, until
I rose and, ere I passed through gates of birth,
I prayed that as Isaiah's lips with fire
Were purged, so on my lips the fire might be.
And then I merged with that eternity
Which is beyond the world and its desire.

This is certainly "cosmic" poetry—the very sort that most of the imagists inveighed so heavily against in the days of their propaganda. But then, as I have indicated previously, Fletcher has never, even in those days, allowed himself to be circumscribed by any set of artistic principles. His inner needs are always forcing him along new paths.

Branches of Adam,[20] which followed close upon *Parables*, is a further development of the religious theme. It is a single long poem, in four parts, recounting the myth of Creation, the Fall of Man, the Flood, etc.; in short, another "Paradise Lost," with a hint of "Paradise Regained." In the preface the author says:

The object of this poem is to show that good and evil exist in this world simultaneously; that good in fact depends upon evil and evil on good; that this world could not exist if it were altogether good, or if it were altogether evil. . . . .

I prefer not to discuss here the theological aspects of the poem. As to the form in which it is cast, it is in irregular blank verse, unrimed lines of five, six, and seven beats, with iambic units predominant. The style is rugged, and occasionally compelling, but on the whole is undistinguished. Certainly it falls short of the grandeur necessary to such a

[20] London: Faber & Gwyer. 1926.

theme; and it lacks the brilliance and originality which alone could recommend it to the majority of modern readers. In other words, its appeal must be almost exclusively to a few persons whose appetite for Christian myth is extraordinary and whose attitude toward poetry is not primarily aesthetic.

But whatever judgments may be passed on the books of which we have spoken, or whatever place in modern poetry may be assigned to Mr. Fletcher, one thing is sure: that in the twenty years which have passed since he settled down in London to become a poet, he has steadily, persistently, developed in depth of thought and, with a few relapses, in power of expression. Very few modern poets can exhibit anything like the same progress. And to realize how true this is, one need only compare one of Fletcher's early volumes with his latest, *The Black Rock*,[21] which is filled with pure poetic gold. Although there is no finality in this book —its author is too young and too alert for that—there is, nevertheless, a remarkable maturity, and a kind of gathering together of all his best themes and poetic styles. In the main, though, these later lyrics tend toward the symmetrical in form, and their music is strongly enhanced by rime. There is very little that could possibly be called experiment for its own sake. There is nothing that seems wilfully wayward. The freest of the poems is steady and sure of its direction.

The Black Rock gives us, as I have implied, an excellent balance of themes. The imaginative reading of nature, with images as symbols, is present; there are autobiographical poems, with America as a background; there are religious poems, radiant with mystical fervor. Over all and through

[21] London: Faber & Gwyer; New York: Macmillan. 1928.

all there is a many-sided and mellow personality, unwearied
of the eternal quest for the beauty and the meaning of life.
Always, too, there is humility, not unlike the humility of
the greatest English mystic, of whom Fletcher has written:

BLAKE

`Blake saw
Angels in a London street;
God the Father on a hill,
Christ before a tavern door.
Blake saw
All these shapes and more.

Blake knew
Other men saw not as he;
So he tried to give his sight
To that beggarman, the world.
"You are mad,"
Was all the blind world said.

Blake died
Singing songs of praise to God.
"They are not mine," he told his wife,
"I may praise them, they are not mine."
Then he died,
And the world called Blake divine.[22]

A good deal of the melancholy which dominated his
youth has dropped away from Fletcher's life. Today he is
an energetic, genial man of many friends and many interests.
He lives at Sydenham, a London suburb, with his wife,

---

[22] From *The Black Rock*. By permission of The Macmillan Company, publishers.

whom he married in 1916, and her two children by a former marriage. Fletcher has no children of his own. He is excessively fond of London, except for its winter climate, which he detests. He knows the great city from one end to the other, and is a marvelous guide to its wonders. He is fairly tall, his shoulders are slightly rounded, and he walks with a long stride that leaves his companions lost behind him in the traffic. He has a high forehead, a long face, and dreamy gray eyes. His voice is pleasant and low-toned, with strong American inflections. He talks easily on any subject, and when he talks he does nothing else. If he is dining with you, he forgets to eat, particularly if the conversation is on poetry or painting. His pockets always bulge with books.

When Fletcher is not writing poetry he is writing criticism or biography. He is an authority on modern painting and on the art of the motion picture. When he is bored with writing he can wander in London streets, or, if the weather is nasty, he can go down into the basement of his house, where his wife keeps fifty canary birds. As a final resort, he can cross the Channel or the Atlantic—each of which he does from time to time. In spite of his long residence abroad, he is in no sense an expatriate. He believes in affirming and remaining true to one's inheritance. So, in spite of his English wife and his love of the English people and the English scene, he remains an American citizen. This fidelity should be appreciated by a country which in recent years has lost more than one of its poets. It is surely something to have retained the affection of a man whom Paul Fort has called "One of the great figures of contemporary literature," and whom another eminent Frenchman, Jean Catel, has justly characterized as: "Le grand rêveur de la poésie contemporaire d'Amérique."

F. S. FLINT

VIII ⪻ F. S. FLINT:

The Londoner

F. S. FLINT was born in London, December 19, 1885, the son of a commercial traveler. The family was in poor financial circumstances, and the boy's early years were spent amid actual squalor. He attended common school until he was thirteen and one-half years of age, when, by virtue of passing special examinations, he was allowed to terminate his "official" education six months ahead of the legal requirement. He then went to work for his living, and for several years took any odd job that came his way. Part of the time he worked in a warehouse.

When he was about seventeen he began buying cheap books from the street stalls, and one day he happened to acquire along with other bargains a volume of Keats's poems. Immediately a new world was opened to him—a world as thrilling as the one which Keats himself beheld in Chapman's *Homer*. His life, which till then had been so dirty and, as he says, so "fleabitten," came now under the spell of beauty, and it was in this first lyric intoxication that he began composing poems of his own.

At the age of nineteen he entered the Civil Service, and

obtained employment as a typist. At the same time he en-
rolled in a workingmen's night school, and there, among
other subjects, he studied Latin and French. Finding that
his talent for languages was extraordinary, he began doing
some translations. Later, without instruction and purely on
his own initiative, he broadened his linguistic studies, and
today he is capable of reading at least ten foreign languages.
His knowledge of French (which he can write fluently in
either prose or verse) is probably unsurpassed by anyone in
England.

In 1909, when he was twenty-four, he married and the
struggle for existence began in earnest. The next year a
daughter was born, and five years later a son. His wife died
in 1920. Shortly afterward Flint married again.

Coincident with his first marriage came the publication
of his early poems in a volume called *In the Net of the
Stars*.[1] Most of them are love lyrics. They are youthful,
romantic, and derivative; yet in spite of their indebtedness
to Keats, Shelley, and Swinburne, they hold for the careful
reader certain presages of their author's later style and attitude, certain hints as to his poetic personality. It is interesting to note that at this early date, before there was a
free-verse movement in England, Flint was feeling his way
toward freer rhythms and truer diction. In the brief note
with which he prefaced the volume, he said:

> I have, as the mood dictated, filled a form or created one. I
> have used assonance for the charm of it, and not rimed where there
> was no need to. In all, I have followed my ear and my heart, which
> may be false. I hope not.

This warning would prepare the average reader for

---

[1] London: Elkin Mathews. 1909.

poems much more radical than those which actually followed. Few of the forms were "created," and seldom was
conventional rime discarded. Not more than three or four
poems in the book contain sufficient irregularities to justify
the application of the term, free verse, and even these do not
wander far from the familiar pattern of English blank verse,
or the rhythms of the Old Testament. The freest of them
all begins thus:

> This is a rose of burning wine—
> This is a star.
>
> This is a rose that grew on a star—
> This is a star in a battle line
> Of whirring worlds,
> Chanting a hymn of flight
> In the fight
> With Night—
> This is a rose of burning wine—
> Our love.

An amateurish mixture of unfelicitous music and inex-
cusable imagery, capable of inducing in a reader the wish that
the author had stayed faithful to Keats. But so it is always
with innovators; many blunders must be forgiven them. In
the crude experiment quoted above we can at least see a
young man striving toward a personal technique; in the following excerpt (from a sonnet in the same book) we can
see only the ghosts of the nineteenth century guiding his
hand:

> Red poppies wanton in the golden corn
> That aureoles the green, dividing lane;
> Intent, a linnet pecks the tender grain,
> Unmindful of the lark, or, all forlorn,

The cuckoo's mournful voice; wind-tossed and worn,
Purple and gold with cloud and sun, complain
The white-flecked waves, chanting an old refrain;
Afar is heard the winding of a horn.

As we have indicated in an earlier chapter, Flint was one
of the associates of T. E. Hulme during the days when
imagism was only a theory. The two men were drawn together by their interest in modern French poetry, that of
the symbolists in particular, and by their common belief that
a new technique should be adopted in English poetry. Hulme
made philosophical notes, and composed a few poems by way
of illustrations; Flint wrote a number of critical essays on
the new French poetry—essays which did more than anything else to awaken interest in this subject in England—and
at the same time underwent a complete metamorphosis as a
poet. He dropped his Keats-Shelley-Swinburne romanticism,
and emerged a modern classicist—in brief, an imagist. By
the time Ezra Pound was ready to edit *Des Imagistes*, Flint
was ready to make some of the finest contributions to that
collection. By way of illustrating the evolution of his poetic
manner, we may take the opening portion of a poem which
appeared in his first book, *In the Net of the Stars* (1909),
and compare it with the imagist poem which he constructed
from it. The revised version appeared in *Des Imagistes*
(1914). The early poem was called "A Swan Song," and
began thus:

Among the lily leaves the swan,
The pale, cold lily leaves, the swan,
With mirrored neck, a silver streak,
Tipped with a tarnished copper beak,
Toward the dark arch floats slowly on;
The water is deep and black beneath the arches.

The fishes quiver in the pool
Under the lily shadow cool,
And ripples gilded by the whin,
Painted, too, with a gloom of green,
Mingled with lilac blue and mauve,
Dropped from an overhanging grove;
White rose of flame the swan beneath the arches.

After this descriptive passage, the poem continues at length in a personal, subjective vein, an emotional rhapsody in which the swan returns as a symbol of human sorrow. The author, looking back with an imagistic eye, saw that, unlike most of his early work, this poem contained materials which could successfully be recast in the new manner. First, the elaboration of personal emotion must be entirely cut away; the explanation of the symbol must be barely suggested; the objective presentation of the symbol must be shortened and hardened; and finally, meter must be supplanted by cadence. The result follows:

THE SWAN

Under the lily shadow
and the gold
and the blue and mauve
that the whin and the lilac
pour down on the water
the fishes quiver.

Over the green cold leaves
and the rippled silver
and the tarnished copper
of its neck and beak,
toward the deep black water
beneath the arches,
the swan floats slowly.

Into the dark of the arch the swan floats
and into the black depth of my sorrow
it bears a white rose of flame.

This, from the imagist point of view, and from the point
of view of all who cherish conciseness and suggestiveness
more than rime and meter, is a very good poem. It attains
that perfect chiseled beauty which is the essence of classical
art. It is devoid of superfluities and of clichés. As in the
case of the best Japanese poems, its emotional force reaches
its climax after rather than during its development—thus
allowing the reader to participate in the act of poetic creation
by completing the analogy.

The five poems which Flint contributed to *Des Imagistes*
were included in his next book, *Cadences*,[2] a slim volume
containing only twenty-two lyrics in all. One of these is
written in metrical form with regular rime; the rest are in
free verse. It was with the appearance of *Cadences* that Flint
emerged not only as a full-fledged imagist, but as an interpreter of London. He had not only cast aside the patterns
and diction of the nineteenth century; he had discarded also
the nightingale and the "magic casement." In other words,
he had become a poet of his own time and place.

Many poets, ancient and modern, have sung of London;
few have sung more honestly or more touchingly than F. S.
Flint. A child of her myriad streets and yellow fogs, his
ear is tuned to her music, his eye trained to her color and her
form. The crowded streets, the tired faces of swarming
workers, the open markets, the traffic of the Thames, the
sudden glimpse and odor of trees and flowers in the park—
these things course in his blood and are transmuted to poetry.

[2] London: Poetry Bookshop. 1915.

His love of the city is extended to all its inhabitants, or, if not his love, at least his sympathy. More than any other of the imagist poets, he stresses the human note, and for that very reason his work sometimes grows softer than imagist poetry should be. Not only does he pity the sufferers about him; he also submits to the temptation to pity himself. Very human, but very dangerous artistically, this weakness, fortunately, does not appear often, nor is it tolerated for long. Before it can alienate the reader, it is corrected by the poet's geniality or by his return to an objectively realistic attitude.

Often he feels that the city is crushing him, and that another day's routine cannot be borne; but night, with its dreams, and morning, with its cool scent, restore him and give him the courage for which he prays:

> Each day I hope for courage to bear
> and not to whine;
> to take my lot as bravely as the bees
> and as unbroodingly.
>
> Each day I creep a little nearer,
> let me hope;
> soon may the morning leaves
> remain as green about my heart all day,
> and I, no longer taking myself to heart,
> may laugh and love and dream and think of death
> without this yearning poison.

Thus he concludes the poem called "Courage," an honest and noble expression of his belief in acceptance as a means of salvation. But he cannot always reconcile himself to this philosophy. There are many times when escape seems absolutely the only way. That this vacillation is the key to Flint's poetry was pointed out many years ago by one of the men who know him best, Richard Aldington.[3] And Mr. Aldington's contention is that even though Flint's poems of acceptance (of modern life, of sordid surroundings, of soul-crushing routine) are "bitter and angry," they are nevertheless capable of affording greater artistic pleasure than his poems of escape, which lead us into a romantic past or else into charming rural scenes. At least we must agree with Mr. Aldington that if Flint "succeeds in reconciling us with a forced existence in this gloomy market-prison-metropolis he will have accomplished a very difficult and admirable task."

As a matter of fact, in spite of courageous efforts, he does not accomplish this task. As we read his later poems we are forced to the conclusion that it was only the man who accepted (perforce), and that the poet escaped. In his third and most recent published collection of poetry, *Otherworld*,[4] Flint exposes, with the touching sincerity and naïveté that are so characteristic of him, the inevitable duality of his life. In the long title poem he pictures himself sitting in a garden, "beneath a cherry tree in bloom," meditating in the carefree manner of the poet upon the beauties of the world, the love of wife and children, the goodness of friendship, the joyousness of a happy household on a spring morning; and then he has a vision of his other self, his real self, inhabiting not the "Otherworld," but this world:

Tomorrow I shall wake up tired and heavy-minded
With a bitter mouth and bleared eyes.
Sluggishly, reluctantly, I shall pull myself from my bed.
I shall thrust on my shabby clothes and wash my face and hands;

[3] See "The Poetry of F. S. Flint," the *Egoist* (London), May 1, 1915.
[4] London: Poetry Bookshop. 1920.

Put on a collar and tie, a waistcoat, all in haste,
Drink a cup of hot tea, eat a few mouthfuls of bread and butter;
Then, with a hurried kiss to wife and children,
Run down the stairs into the miserable street.
All I meet are shabby, all go one way,
Drawn on by the same magnet, urged by the same demon.
We are the respectable; and behind us, though we do not see him,
Driving us with his goad, is hunger—the first law of our land.

The poem continues, and pictures the deadening routine of the day and the return of the worker at night to his home, weak and disheartened, his memory choked with impressions of bitterness, of cruelty, of jealousy, of futile struggle, of human misery. Again he must escape "on the viewless wings of poesy," to that star

the light of whose sun
Has not yet reached the earth, and may never reach it.

Once more he dwells in his "Otherworld," where

I come into breakfast clean of body and rich of mind,
And hungry with the morning air.
My boy sits before a bowl of purple wild pansies,
And my girl has a slender green jar of red poppies,
Whose hairy stalks spring from a blue cluster of speedwells.
They have been out in the fields, barefoot in the long wet grass,
The meadow foxtails brushing their legs with a silky touch;
And they shook the jewels from the heart of the clover,
As they passed and sang with the birds.

He sees his wife at the breakfast table, serving "Fruit and milk and eggs and bread and butter and honey"; his love for her wells up afresh, and he goes into the garden to pluck her a rose. In the afternoon, when the children are at their studies, and he is sitting in the garden, with coffee and a

cigarette, his dearest friend arrives. The two men go swing-
ing off on a long walk through woods and over hills to the
sea, and to the poet comes the recollection of another time
when they marched side by side to war. His friend did not
come back. So reality intrudes and reminds us that we are
still following the poet's dream. But the dream must, for
him at least, have a reality of its own, or life is intolerable:

> You may not believe in my other world; but it is no dream.
> It can be proved with compass and scales and a plus b.
> Who will integrate space and time and prove that the sum
> Does not contain the quantity I describe?

If there can be no convincing denial, then he will affirm the
existence of his other self; and, furthermore:

> He is sitting beneath a cherry tree in bloom,
> Watching the afterglow of sunset and the evening stars,
> He is sitting in the quiet and peace of the evening
> And the peace of the winds;
> The darkness is creeping up behind him from the hills;
> He does not stir; the first cold shiver of evening has not come.
> Perhaps in this calm and the calm of his mind he thinks of me.

This is, of course, soft poetry. It is much softer than
most poems written by the imagists. But it is absolutely human, and it is of the pattern of its author's life.

But if the title poem of the volume is diffuse and romantic, not all the accompanying pieces are. A sterner and
more rigid art underlies the short poems of London life.
Here is one, for example:

EAU-FORTE

> On black bare trees a stale cream moon
> Hangs dead, and sours the unborn buds.

Two gaunt old hacks, knees bent, heads low,
Tug, tired and spent, an old horse tram.
Damp smoke, rank mist fill the dark square;
And round the bend six bullocks come.

A hobbling, dirt-grimed drover guides
Their clattering feet—
                    their clattering feet!
                to the slaughterhouse.

Yet even here the note of pity forms the climax of the poem.
Unlike most of his fellow-imagists, Flint finds it impossible
to conceal his tenderness in even his most objective writing.
According to the point of view of the reader, this difference
is a superiority or an inferiority.

Toward the end of *Otherworld* appears a poem which
has some anecdotal interest, and which also affords us another
opportunity of looking for a moment into the poet's work-
shop, of seeing what may happen to a theme when it is subjected to two different techniques, applied by the same
writer. The title of the poem is "To a Young Lady Who
Moved Shyly among Men of Reputed Worth," and it was
written one evening at a literary party in London, when
H. D. and Flint, finding themselves sitting in a corner, both
rather shy and "out of it," challenged each other to write a
sonnet. H. D. did not complete hers, but Flint's was as
follows:

The olive sky shone through the birch's lace
Of hanging leaves. The silken air was still.
London was beautiful. A tender thrill
Of sunset shook throughout the evening's grace.

Under an apple tree I stood a space,
And watched the birds hop on the lawn, until

Darkness had bent all image to his will,
When, oh!, upon the rapt sky dawned your face!

Be brave, O Moon, lonely among the stars.
Be unrebuked and radiant, they will pale;
And Earth will love you for your loveliness.

My brain beats madly at the golden bars
That stay it, and my heart would have me scale
The moonlit branches where the night winds press.

For a "party poem" this certainly is not bad. From the imagist point of view, however, it is padded with phrases which do little more than meet the requirements of the sonnet pattern. Reworked, it became one of Flint's most admired and most frequently quoted poems. It appeared originally in *Des Imagistes,* and later in *Cadences:*

LONDON

London, my beautiful,
it is not the sunset
nor the pale green sky
shimmering through the curtain
of the silver birch,
nor the quietness;
it is not the hopping
of the birds
upon the lawn,
nor the darkness
stealing over all things
that moves me.

But as the moon creeps slowly
over the tree-tops

among the stars,
I think of her
and the glow her passing
sheds on men.

London, my beautiful,
I will climb
into the branches
to the moonlit tree-tops
that my blood may be cooled
by the wind.

It is, I believe, one of the most successful of the early imagist poems and an unusually good example of unrimed cadence. We may note, in passing, that it was Flint who invented the phrase "unrimed cadence," though Amy Lowell popularized its usage.

The question will arise: what has Flint been doing these last ten years, that he has not produced more poetry? The answer is that the poet in him was defeated—partly by the difficulty of earning a living for himself and his family; partly by a peculiarity of his own nature, a tendency toward self-disparagement, which not only cuts off his creative powers, but which also prevents him from impressing his work on the public. Had it not been for Amy Lowell's imagist anthologies, Flint's work would be unknown in America and much less known in England than it is. Richard Aldington, with the license of friendship, declares that Flint is possessed of "an almost imbecile modesty."

As for his occupation, he is still in the Civil Service, though he is no longer a mere typist. On his discharge from the army in 1919 (he served eleven months in England, but was never at the front) he was taken into the Ministry of

Labor, where, after several promotions, he is now Chief of the Overseas Section, Statistics Division. In this capacity he employs to the government's advantage his expert knowledge of foreign languages, as well as his talent in statistical compilation. His literary activities are confined largely to translations and reviews. His translations include several important books from the French and German, and his reviews appear regularly in the *Criterion,* the quarterly magazine edited in London by T. S. Eliot. As a poet he appears to have completed his work.

I have already indicated, I think, that Flint's poetry must, even more than in the average case, be considered in relation to his personality and the circumstances of his life. He is primarily a human being—a highly intelligent one, to be sure, but one in whom intellect has never superseded the natural qualities of friendliness and sincerity. To flavor his poems fully one must have walked by his side (as I, fortunately, have done) through the teeming streets of London or over the Berkshire meadows. Then one begins to understand this man who has been torn between reality and dreams, between this world and another world, and has wearied of trying to express in poetry this never-ending conflict. The poet is, of course, still present in the man, and dominates his friendships and his enthusiasms for life and literature, but he has forsaken the printed page. Possibly, for Flint is still young, there will be a revival of his creative zeal. If not, then we must treasure all the more carefully the poems from his past, for these are unique and precious—the heart and soul of a man whom Ford Madox Hueffer called "One of the greatest men and one of the most beautiful spirits of the country."

D. H. LAWRENCE

IX ⪻ D. H. LAWRENCE: *The*
Passionate Psychologist

AVID HERBERT LAWRENCE was born at Eastwood, Derbyshire, in 1885, the son of a coal-miner. The elder Lawrence was a common, rough, intemperate workman; his wife, the mother whom D. H. Lawrence celebrated in many of his poems, was a sensitive and rather refined woman, the victim of environment. The poet said of his boyhood, "I was a delicate, pale brat with a snuffy nose, whom most people treated quite gently as just an ordinary delicate little lad."[1]

When he was twelve years old he was granted a county council scholarship, and entered Nottingham High School. Shortly after leaving school at the age of sixteen, he fell victim to what he terms "a very serious pneumonia illness," which damaged his health for life. "A year later," he says, "I became a school-teacher, and after three years' savage teaching of collier lads I went to take the 'normal' course in Nottingham University.

"As I was glad to leave school, I was glad to leave

---

[1] "Autobiographical Sketch" in *Assorted Articles*. New York: Knopf; London: Secker. 1930.

college. It had meant mere disillusion, instead of the living contact of men."

From college he went to teach in an elementary school at Croydon, a suburb on the southern side of London. Here he remained for several years, earning a scanty living by his teaching, and working hard at poems, stories, and a novel. Some of the poems were sent surreptitiously by a friend, a girl whom Lawrence calls the chief friend of his youth, to the *English Review,* which Ford Madox Hueffer was then editing. Hueffer printed the poems, asked Lawrence to come to see him, read the manuscript of *The White Peacock,* the novel which had been in the process of composition for four or five years, and assured the young author that he had genius.

"When I was twenty-five," Lawrence tells us, "my mother died, and two months later *The White Peacock* was published, but it meant nothing to me. I went on teaching for another year, and then again a bad pneumonia illness intervened. When I got better I did not go back to school. I lived henceforward on my scanty literary earnings."

In 1914 he married Frieda von Richthofen, the former wife of a professor at Nottingham University and a sister of the famous German flying ace. Mrs. Lawrence had children by her first husband, but none by D. H. Lawrence. Her German name caused them considerable trouble during the War, and although Lawrence offered himself three times for military service and was refused each time, they were persecuted again and again as enemy sympathizers.

From the time that Lawrence abandoned routine work and threw himself on his own resources as a creative artist, he lived restlessly, moving from country to country, driven partly by his natural craving for experience, partly by the dictates of poor health. His frequent sojourns in southern climates—Italy, Southern France, Mexico, New Mexico— were of course conditioned by his chronic tuberculosis. Had he been willing to remain for a long time in one of the places where the climate agreed with him, it is likely his death would not have come so soon. But he wore himself out traveling, and died at Vence, France, March 2, 1930, longing desperately at the last moment for his ranch in New Mexico.

Lawrence is better known as a novelist than as a poet, yet there are those who affirm that his novels are great because of the poetry that permeates them. That his work should claim a chapter in this book is the result of sheer accident, for which a personal whim of Amy Lowell's must be held completely responsible. Lawrence took no real interest in imagism as a theory of poetry or as a movement. He happened to be in London when Miss Lowell was collecting the material for the imagist anthologies, and was asked by her to contribute to them. He replied that he was not an imagist. She insisted that he was, and by way of proof quoted the opening lines of one of his early poems:[2]

> The morning breaks like a pomegranate
> In a shining crack of red;

As though images could not be plucked from the work of any poet! Lawrence, of course, was not taken in by this frail argument, but having no conscientious objection to his poems appearing under the imagist banner he gave Miss Lowell what she wanted, and was ever after under the necessity of explaining how he got into such company. The whole thing amused him. During a conversation I had with him in May

[2] "Wedding Morn."

1929, he joked a good deal about it and declared there never had been such a thing as imagism. It was all an illusion of Ezra Pound's, he said, and was nonsense. "In the old London days Pound wasn't so literary as he is now. He was more of a mountebank then. He practiced more than he preached, for he had no audience. He was always amusing." Lawrence's blue eyes danced. For the professional imagists he had little praise. H. D. was an exception. He admired her poems, though he couldn't read many of them at once, and the longer ones, he thought, got rather boring. "She is like a person walking a tight-rope; you wonder if she'll get across."

I have been told by one of the imagists that Lawrence was included in the anthologies for the simple reason that in 1914 he was looked upon as a writer of genius who would certainly achieve fame and would therefore shed glory on the whole imagist movement. I am inclined to believe that some idea of this kind prompted Miss Lowell's invitation. I have also been told by one of the imagists that in spite of Lawrence's protestations to the contrary, he was influenced by the imagist credo, and composed certain poems in conscious conformity with the principles enunciated therein. This point cannot be proved or disproved. So far as I can determine, however, there was no radical change in Lawrence's poetry as a result of his association with the imagists. Even the poems by which he is represented in the anthologies are only occasionally imagistic—accidentally so, one would say. The strongest influence in his work—and this he himself admits —is Whitman. He derived little or nothing from the Greek poets, and nothing at all, he says, from the French, whose verse he has always considered "piffling, like lacy valentines." He began writing free verse not because of any theories, but because of an inner need. "It is so much easier to handle some themes without a regular pattern."

Lawrence began writing poems when he was nineteen. Of his first pieces he has said,[3] "Any young lady might have written them and been pleased with them; as I was pleased with them." When he was twenty he began to write what he considers his "real poems." These went toward the making of his first published collection, *Love Poems and Others*,[4] which, as I have already mentioned, appeared in 1913. Six other volumes of his verses were published between 1913 and 1923, and in 1928 appeared his *Collected Poems*,[5] in which one may find the sum of his poetic output for the years 1906 to 1923. In the collected edition, Volume One is designated as "Rhyming Poems," and includes the contents of *Love Poems and Others*, *Amores*,[6] *New Poems*,[7] and *Bay*.[8] Volume Two, called "Unrhyming Poems," includes *Look! We Have Come Through!*,[9] *Tortoises*,[10] and *Birds, Beasts, and Flowers*.[11] As readers will quickly notice, and as reviewers were amused to point out, Volume Two contains a considerable number of rimed poems. J. C. Squire, writing in the London *Observer* for October 7, 1928, takes this discrepancy as an example of Lawrence's logic, and concludes that "He did not arrange this as a feeble, practical joke . . . .

[3] See note prefixed to *Collected Poems*.

[4] London: Duckworth; New York: Mitchell Kennerley.

[5] London: Secker; New York: Cape & Smith. 1929. 2 vols.

[6] London: Duckworth; New York: Huebsch. 1916.

[7] London: Secker. 1918. New York: Huebsch. 1920.

[8] London: Beaumont Press. 1919. (Limited edition.)

[9] London: Chatto & Windus. 1917. New York: Huebsch. 1918.

[10] New York: Seltzer. 1921.

[11] London: Secker; New York: Seltzer. 1923.

he merely did not notice. He is too febrile, hectic, full of blood, and haunted by dreams to be precise about title-pages and the arrangement of books." Which is perhaps partially true, though it fails to take into account Lawrence's explanation in the prefatory note to the effect that in arranging the poems he "tried to establish a chronological order, because many of the poems are so personal that, in their fragmentary fashion, they make up a biography of an emotional and inner life." It so happened that practically all of his early poems were rimed, and that most of his later poems were unrimed. This led to the general designations, which, though not accurate, seemed true enough to Lawrence. What makes matters even worse is that he did not follow the chronological method either. He sacrificed it for his desire to keep intact the various collections of poems which had appeared together in separate volumes, and also for less obvious psychological reasons. Thus the contents of *Bay* (written chiefly in 1917 and 1918) appear at the end of Volume One, whereas, *Look! We Have Come Through!* (written between 1912 and 1917) forms the first part of Volume Two. This order is chronologically incorrect from the standpoint of either composition or publication. In other words the *Collected Poems* is arranged according to at least three conflicting plans —chronological, technical, and psychological—and is therefore annoying to those who prize neatness and consistency. This confusion is, of course, a purely superficial defect, and has nothing to do with the fundamental worth of the poetry. It would not even merit our attention were it not for the fact that Lawrence himself emphasizes the arrangement as being valuable to an understanding of his work.

The "Rhyming Poems" of Volume One are for the most part love poems. A few are poems of mood and circumstance, a few are descriptive nature pieces, and the rest are dramatic narratives or character studies in dialect. All but one of the poems are rimed, and most of them fall under the rules of metrical scansion. Only occasionally in this volume does Lawrence betray the Whitman influence; more often he suggests an English heritage—not from specific poets, but from late nineteenth-century poetry in general. In the love poems there is a suggestion, perhaps, of Meredith, and in the dialect pieces one is aware of Housman; otherwise the clues are vague. Even as a young man, Lawrence was remarkably himself. It is obvious that he always wrote from personal emotion and in an unusually personal way. His work is almost free from exercises, from conscious efforts toward the development of a poetic technique. For this reason his poems are authentic even when they are infelicitous.

For those who are familiar with Mr. Lawrence's novels and with his later poems it is interesting and significant that one of the first poems in Volume One should be concerned with the violence of sex, for this is a theme from which he never escaped. And as a matter of fact he seldom treated the theme more impressively than in this eight-line poem which he must have written when he was quite a young man:

DISCORD IN CHILDHOOD

Outside the house an ash tree hung its terrible whips,
And at night when the wind rose, the lash of the tree
Shrieked and slashed the wind, as a ship's
Weird rigging in a storm shrieks hideously.

Within the house two voices arose, a slender lash
Whistling she-delirious rage, and the dreadful sound
Of a male thong booming and bruising, until it had drowned
The other voice in a silence of blood, 'neath the noise of the ash.

We sense in this awful and yet beautiful recollection the morbid preoccupation which dominated a great deal of Lawrence's writing and which critics have been at some pains to explain. This one poem, taken by itself, would not, of course, indicate an abnormal interest in the male-female struggle; but taken in conjunction with the later poems it is prophetic. There are readers, undoubtedly, who look upon Lawrence as an embodiment of sexual energy, as a kind of superman who was driven by abundance of vitality to something that can perhaps be described as sophisticated savagery. There are others, more discriminating, I believe, who take an opposite view, and who look upon Lawrence's obsession as an indication of debility and frustrated desires. To these his amorous poems are attempts at compensation by imaginative means, and are not, like the pagan chants of Whitman, the exuberant expression of a healthy lover.

The most interesting exposition of this latter view is given by Joseph Collins in his volume of interpretative essays, *The Doctor Looks at Literature*.[12] Dr. Collins is not, I think, an impeccable critic, and to many he appears, no doubt, a Puritan. He is, nevertheless, a physician of experience and repute, one who has devoted his life, as he himself says, to the "study of aberrations, genesic and mental, as they display themselves in geniuses, psychopaths, and neuropaths, as well as in ordinary men." He has read with considerable care all of Lawrence's important works (up to 1923), and although he expresses admiration for their style, he is forced to unpleasant conclusions regarding their psychological and moral values. He disparages Lawrence's "scientific" writing, and deplores his attempt to foist upon modern

[12] New York: Doran. 1923.

life a barbarous mysticism based upon sexual ecstasy. He identifies Lawrence with certain characters in his novels, and implies that the weaknesses of the latter are inherent in the former. Particular identification is made between the author and those male characters who are "mother-sapped" and who progress from the love of woman to the love of man.

Dr. Collins declares that Lawrence as a youth read and was greatly influenced by the doctrines of two Austrian psychologists, Weininger and Freud, and that, like the former of these, he evolved a plan of life in which woman is eventually eliminated, "and the polarity is between man and man." To quote the physician:

Mr. Lawrence thinks there are three stages in the life of man: the stage of sexless relations between individuals, families, clans, and nations; the stage of sex relations with an all-embracing passional acceptance, culminating in the eternal orbit of marriage; and, finally, the love between comrades, the manly love which only can create a new era of life. One state does not annul the other; it fulfills the other. Such, in brief, is the strange venture in psychopathy Mr. Lawrence is making. . . . .

He gives many instances of Lawrence's abnormal preoccupation with sex-symbols, and points out that even the flowers which his characters look upon and the food which they eat are charged with sexual significance. Indeed, the very names of the characters are symbolic of their sex-characteristics. Following his analysis, he remarks that:

My experience as a psychologist and alienist has taught me that pornographic literature is created by individuals whose genesic endowment is subnormal *ab initio*, or exhausted from one cause or another before nature intended that it should be, and that those who would aid God and nature in the ordering of creation are sterile, or approximately so. This is a dispensation for which we cannot be too grateful.

His conclusion is that much of Lawrence's writing is obscene, in both the etymological and the legal senses of the word, and that society is justified in censoring it. That this opinion is shared by some others is evident from the experience which Lawrence had with government officials in England and in the United States. Several of his books have been banned, and in the spring of 1929 there was a furor in England over the seizure by Scotland Yard operatives of the manuscript of his new collection of poems, entitled *Pansies,* intercepted in the mails while on its way from Lawrence to his literary agent.

But although sex is the chief motive of Lawrence's work, it is not the only one. A less delicate aspect of the poet's life is presented in a series of schoolroom pieces, with himself as teacher. In "A Snowy Day in School" we are let into the dark, brooding mind of the unhappy man, and into the hushed, charged atmosphere of the room where he is prisoner. Falling snow muffles the outer world; tedium and the drone of the schoolroom muffle his mind. A sense of unreality comes over him:

But the faces of the boys, in the brooding, yellow light
Have been for me like a dazed constellation of stars.
Like half-blown flowers dimly shaking at the night,
Like half-seen froth on an ebbing shore in the moon.

Out of each face, strange, dark beams that disquiet;
In the open depths of each flower, dark, restless drops;
Twin-bubbling challenge and mystery, in the foam's whispering riot.
— How can I answer the challenge of so many eyes?

The thick snow is crumpled on the roof, it plunges down
Awfully! — Must I call back a hundred eyes? — A voice
Falters a statement about an abstract noun —
What was my question? — My God, must I break this hoarse

Silence that rustles beyond the stars? — There! —
I have startled a hundred eyes, and now I must look
Them an answer back; it is more than I can bear.

Less atmospheric, and less poetic, but no less unhappy in
its mood, is "Last Lesson of the Afternoon," where we find
the poet in open revolt against pedagogy:

I will not waste my soul and my strength for this.
What do I care for all that they do amiss!
What is the point of this teaching of mine, and of this
Learning of theirs? It all goes down the same abyss.

What does it matter to me, if they can write
A description of a dog, or if they can't?
What is the point? To us both, it is all my aunt!
And yet I'm supposed to care, with all my might.

I do not, and will not; they won't and they don't; and that's all!
I shall keep my strength for myself; they can keep theirs as well.
Why should we beat our heads against the wall
Of each other? I shall sit and wait for the bell.

No one else has ever, so far as I know, written so well of
the schoolroom and the emotions of the teacher. Even the
pleasant, one is inclined to say the "inspiring," side of the
profession finds perfect expression in "The Best of School":

This morning, sweet it is
To feel the lads' looks light on me,

Then back in a swift, bright flutter to work;
Each one darting away with his
Discovery, like birds that steal and flee.

Touch after touch I feel on me
As their eyes glance at me for the grain
Of rigor they taste delightedly.

As tendrils reach out yearningly,
Slowly rotate till they touch the tree
That they cleave unto, and up which they climb
Up to their lives—so they to me.

I feel them cling and cleave to me
As vines going eagerly up; they twine
My life with other leaves, my time
Is hidden in theirs, their thrills are mine.

No one who can write so beautifully can go on indefinitely teaching school.

The love poems which make up the bulk of this volume are no less autobiographical than the school poems. Several women appear in them, and the aspects of love which they show are diverse. Yet the dominant tone is melancholy and the sense of frustration is frequent. Even when the affection is reciprocal there is a cry of dissatisfaction and of mocking hatred. The pain of love invariably outweighs the joy —the dream is of bliss, but the fact is torture. When the trouble is not physical it is psychological, or else the two causes intertwine. And through all these sorrowful songs runs a gleaming vein of imagery, such pure poetry that no one can mistake it. The opening lines of "Repulsed" offer an illustration:

The last silk-floating thought has gone from the dandelion stem,
And the flesh of the stalk holds up for nothing a blank diadem.
So night's flood-winds have lifted my last desire from me,
And my hollow flesh stands up in the night like vanity.

And the concluding lines reiterate the striking simile:

The night is immense and awful, yet to me it is nothing at all.
Or rather 'tis I am nothing, here in the fur of the heather
Like an empty dandelion stalk, bereft of connection, small
And nakedly nothing 'twixt world and heaven, two creatures hostile
     together.

I in the fur of the world, alone: but this Helen close by!
How we hate one another tonight, hate, she and I
To numbness and nothingness; I dead, she refusing to die.
The female whose venom can more than kill, can numb and then
     nullify.

It is the woman, usually, who is blamed in Lawrence's
poems. Either she shuns and repulses the poet-lover, or she
proves her incapacity for perfect love. In both instances the
poet denounces her bitterly. Occasionally, as in "Release,"
there is a note of satisfaction, but at such times, one hears also
a plaintive protest against enslavement. There are no echoes
of mutual and equal joy.

Woven among the poems to Helen, to Miriam, and to
the unnamed woman of "Kisses in the Train" and "Hands
of the Betrothed," are the poems to the poet's mother. And
so strong is the affection they betray that it is necessary for
the reader to look twice at them to discern them from the
others; an interesting phenomenon, and one which holds
particular interest for those familiar with Lawrence's novels,
in which the mother-son relationship plays such an important

part. The poems form a sequence, beginning with the mother's illness and continuing for some time after her death. The idolatry which permeates them is religious in its solemnity and in its fervor. It verges on the mystical. The poems of anxiety and first grief are fairly natural: the opening stanzas of "The Virgin Mother" illustrate their tenderness:

> My little love, my darling,
> You were a doorway to me;
> You let me out of the confines
> Into this strange country
> Where people are crowded like thistles,
> Yet are shapely and comely to see.
>
> My little love, my dearest,
> Twice you have issued me,
> Once from your womb, sweet mother,
> Once from your soul, to be
> Free of all hearts, my darling,
> Of each heart's entrance free.

But the silence which surrounds the poet afterward, the brooding grief which envelops him, gives rise to more somber and imaginative reveries, in which symbols and strange forces appear. In "Troth with the Dead" the conception is grotesque:

> The moon is broken in twain, and half a moon
> Beyond me lies on the low, still floor of the sky;
> The other half of the broken coin of troth
> Is buried away in the dark, where the dead all lie.
>
> They buried her half in the grave when they laid her away;
> Pushed gently away and hidden in the thick of her hair

Where it gathered towards the plait, on that very last day;
And like a moon unshowing it must still shine there.

So half lies on the sky, for a general sign
Of the troth with the dead that we are pledged to keep;
Turning its broken edge to the dark, its shine
Ends like a broken love, that turns to the dark of sleep.

And half lies there in the dark where the dead all lie
Lost and yet still connected; and between the two
Strange beams must travel still, for I feel that I
Am lit beneath my heart with a half-moon, weird and blue.

As a relief from the subjectivity of the poems of which I have spoken, one may turn to the descriptive pieces or to those in dialect. The descriptions are not so coldly objective as some to be found in the work of the purer imagists, for Lawrence's introspective nature never permitted him to maintain for long a detached attitude; yet by comparison with his love poems they are strongly externalized. Superior, I think, are the character studies and narratives in Midland dialect. In this genre Lawrence equals any of his contemporaries. The directness and simplicity of his style suggests the older ballads, and his understanding of human motives is remarkably sure. Less ingratiating than Housman, a better craftsman than Masefield, he achieves a combination of reality and art which one must go far to match. "The Collier's Wife" and "Whether or Not," each too long to quote here, are dramatic lyrics of great power, and they represent a Lawrence too little known, a Lawrence free from his ego.

Volume One concludes with the war poems—in which subjectivity and objectivity alternate or combine to form an effective if not supreme expression of the moods and sensations of the soldier (though Lawrence was never a soldier) and the war-time citizen. Among them we find examples of this poet's most imagistic writing. The following, for instance, with its description of London during an air-raid:

BOMBARDMENT

The town has opened to the sun.
Like a flat lily with a million petals
She unfolds, she comes undone.

A sharp sky brushes upon
The myriad glittering chimney-tips
As she gently exhales to the sun.

Hurrying creatures run
Down the labyrinth of the sinister flower.
What is it they shun?

A dark bird falls from the sun.
It curves in a rush to the heart of the vast
Flower: the day has begun.

Volume Two of the *Collected Poems*, though by no means monotonous or even unified, presents less diversity than its predecessor. The first section, published originally as *Look! We Have Come Through!*, is a poignant record of the poet's major experience with love; the second, published as *Birds, Beasts, and Flowers*, consists of rhapsodies arising from the contemplation of the workings of love (or, should we say, the "sex"?) in all creatures and growing things. In the latter scheme man, and particularly Lawrence, is a part, for he feels himself blood-brother of the lower forms of life, and he partakes of their mysteries.

Prefaced to *Look! We Have Come Through!* (a perfect title, incidentally, for the poems of one who "goes through" as much as Lawrence did) is the following "Argument," which may be taken literally as an autobiographical statement:

> After much struggling and loss in love and in the world of man, the protagonist throws in his lot with a woman who is already married. Together they go into another country, she perforce leaving her children behind. The conflict of love and hate goes on between the man and the woman, and between these two and the world around them, till it reaches some sort of conclusion.

Please note that Lawrence is a realist; he does not say "till it reaches a happy conclusion." Still, the poems themselves indicate the attainment of much more happiness than is indicated by any of the earlier poems. The storms of hatred and struggle are more bitter, but so is the peace which follows, deeper. The psychology of Lawrence is like that of Strindberg. These poems are another "Dance of Death." The theme may be found in the opening lines of "Both Sides of the Medal":

> And because you love me,
> think you you do not hate me?
> Ha, since you love me
> to ecstasy
> it follows you hate me to ecstasy.

The marital dance is a mad one, and we follow it from England to Germany, and at last to Italy, where sunshine blesses the final conciliatory movement. In its course we run the gamut of male emotions, expressed in all the poetic modes, from lashing scorn and blind vituperation to dove-like wooing and mystic adoration. There is no good of reproducing fragments of this "Portrait of an Artist as Married Man." To do so would be to betray the effectiveness of the whole. The poems must be read completely, and in sequence; then the experience is revealed, an experience guaranteed to frighten into spinsterhood any but the most adventurous maid.

Under the stress of these emotions, Lawrence burst the bonds of meter and of rime; not regularly, but often enough to establish a free-verse style. In his next book, *Birds, Beasts, and Flowers,* he threw conventions overboard, and leaped up free, a very Whitman. His spirit, too, rose on new wings. Where before he had taunted himself, or the women he loved, he now taunted the whole wide world. The opening lines of the first poem in this group are:

> You tell me I am wrong.
> Who are you, who is anybody to tell me I am wrong?
> I am not wrong.

To be sure, this is only meant as a prelude to a discussion of pomegranates and their symbolic significance, yet it may be taken as an indication of the provocativeness of the poems which follow, provocative especially to those who dislike having their world turned into a museum of sex symbols. The pomegranate is interpreted, and after it the peach, the medlar, the fig, and the grape. And so beautiful is the performance that one forgets, or forgives, the obscenity. So rich an imagination falls over the humblest fruit, such symphonies of mystery are woven about its familiar form, that one yields perforce to the poet's magic, and becomes as sensuous as he. Hear how he chants of the peach:

Blood-red, deep;
Heaven knows how it came to pass.
Somebody's pound of flesh rendered up.

Wrinkled with secrets
And hard with the intention to keep them.

Why, from silvery peach-bloom,
From that shallow-silvery wine-glass on a short stem
This rolling, dropping, heavy globule?

I am thinking, of course, of the peach before I ate it.

Why so velvety, why so voluptuous heavy?
Why hanging with such inordinate weight?
Why so indented?

Why the groove?
Why the lovely bivalve roundnesses?
Why the ripple down the sphere?
Why the suggestion of incision?

Why was not my peach round and finished like a billiard ball?
It would have been if man had made it.
Though I've eaten it now.

But it wasn't round and finished like a billiard ball.
And because I say so, you would like to throw something at me.

Here, you can have my peach stone.

He is less whimsical, more ecstatic, over the medlars and
sorb-apples:

I love you, rotten,
Delicious rottenness.

I love to suck you out from your skins
So brown and soft and coming suave,
So morbid, as the Italians say.

. . . .

What is it?
What is it, in the grape turning raisin,
In the medlar, in the sorb-apple,
Wine skins of brown morbidity,
Autumnal excrementa;
What is it that reminds us of white gods?

Gods nude as blanched nut-kernels,
Strangely, half-sinisterly flesh-fragrant
As if with sweat,
And drenched with mystery.

Sorb-apples, medlars with dead crowns.

I say, wonderful are the hellish experiences,
Orphic, delicate
Dionysos of the Underworld.

The fig stirs him to even greater frenzy—to what may
be described only as a poetic orgy. It is above all others the
secretive fruit, the feminine fruit:

Folded upon itself, enclosed like any Mohammedan woman,
Its nakedness all within-walls, its flowering forever unseen,

and in its ripeness he sees the symbol of human fruition,
the uttering of the eternal secret of life. It is a long poem,
and a highly indelicate poem, but it is pure Lawrence. It is

the psychologist on a mystic spree, and at his rhapsodic best. Someone, William Lyon Phelps, I think it was, said recently that D. H. Lawrence grew inflamed at the sight of a feminine ending on a French adjective (I quote from memory and perhaps inaccurately). This witty exaggeration is true enough. And a fig is much more stimulating than an adjective.

Following the fruits, trees, flowers, birds, beasts, and reptiles pass in parade before the poet's inward-seeing eye. He questions them, and then supplies the answers. The old habit of the lyricist—identifying himself with his subject, feeling what he deems it must feel—is here exhibited fully, and with much success. Keats may have looked through his window at a sparrow pecking among the gravel and felt himself pecking among the gravel too; but Lawrence sucks blood with a mosquito, darts with a fish, swoops with a bat, wriggles over the desert floor with a snake, shuffles through the tropics with an elephant, hops with a kangaroo, and makes love with goats and tortoises. With the tortoises he remains the longest, recording their emotional life from babyhood until their crucifixion on the cross of love, which is always the real cross to Lawrence. Wonderful excursions, these, into dark realms of sense where the life-force stirs and urges, finding imperfect voice. Not sentimental excursions, either, but fanatically persistent probings after the secret, the germ, the soul—adventures of a passionate psychologist.

This preoccupation with the undercurrents of life, with the instincts and sensations of animals, and primitive men, and with the subconscious life of civilized man—this is the raison d'être of Lawrence's writing. In poetry and prose his method is the same. He explores. And the darker the cavern, the more feverish is his search. A very able English critic,

I. A. Richards, writing in the *Criterion* (London) for July
1925, discusses this point, and expresses the opinion that
Lawrence's attitude represents an attempt to escape from
modern civilization. He links him with two other poets,
Walter de la Mare and W. B. Yeats, both of whom seem to
him also poets desirous of escape, and he notes the various
means chosen by the three:

> Mr. de la Mare takes shelter in the dream-world of the child,
> Mr. Yeats retires into black velvet curtains and the visions of the
> Hermetist, and Mr. Lawrence makes a magnificent attempt to re-
> construct in himself the mentality of the Bushman.

Mr. Richards goes on to say that Lawrence appears to
have revolted against civilization purely because of experience—his beliefs were formulated afterward, to support the
attitudes which he adopted in place of the conventional attitudes of modern society. Since the attitudes themselves are
primitive, the beliefs must necessarily be so too. It is not
surprising, says the critic, that the world-picture worked out
by Lawrence should be similar to that described in *The
Golden Bough*.

> The mental process at work is schematically as follows: First,
> undergo an intense emotion, located with unusual definiteness in the
> body, which can be described as "a feeling as though the solar plexus
> were connected by a current of dark passional energy with another
> person." Those whose emotions tend to be localized will be familiar
> with such feelings. The next step is to say "I must trust my feel-
> ings." The next is to call the feeling an intuition. The last is to
> say "I *know* that my solar plexus, etc." By this means we arrive at
> the indubitable knowledge that the sun's energy is recruited from
> the life on the earth and that the astronomers are wrong in what
> they say about the moon, and so on.

Such a muddled basis for poetry is most unsatisfactory, says Mr. Richards. In the case of such gifted poets as Lawrence and Yeats it is calamitous. Both have discarded conventional beliefs; both have refused science as a substitute; they have reverted to beliefs which cannot form a basis for poetry of major significance to the modern world.

Lawrence was easy prey for critics. His armor was full of holes. But it is a fact that even his greatest detractors found him an admirable victim. He was something like the Irish rebel of whom I once heard Yeats tell. The rebel was stood against a wall and shot. Afterward his official slayers reported: "A brave man, a wonderful man—it was a pleasure to shoot him." What Lawrence's critics all agree on is that somehow, in spite of his egoism, his crudities of style, his sex-mania, and the rest, he was a great writer. Above all, he was a personality. Like Ezra Pound, he was hot-tempered, arrogant, insulting, and forever scornful of diplomacy. Like Pound, too, he was revered by those who had most reason to hate him. The best picture of him as a man and as a writer is to be found in Richard Aldington's essay, *D. H. Lawrence —An Indiscretion*.[13] Aldington knew Lawrence from the pre-war London days when imagism was just being born. He calls him "a great living example of the English Heretic," one of those rampant personalities whom the English persecute but love, "for somewhere, deep down, they know that their Heretics are the life of the race, the salt of the earth." He deplores Lawrence's mysticism, and finds him, when in that vein, "a crashing bore." He deplores his errors of style, but his virtues he finds so numerous that they crowd

[13] Number six, University of Washington Chapbooks, Seattle: University of Washington Bookstore. 1927. London: Chatto & Windus. 1930.

the pages of his essay. I cannot find space to reproduce them here.

Mr. Aldington, of course, is somewhat of a rebel himself, and his estimate of a fellow-rebel may be discounted. But no such reservation can be made in the case of J. C. Squire, who, in his review of Lawrence's *Collected Poems*,[14] asserted:

> The fact remains that Mr. Lawrence, passionate, brooding, glowering, worshipping man, is undoubtedly a man of genius and big and fiery enough to eat a dozen of his merely clever contemporaries.

Big and fiery in his writing, yes; but in the flesh he was a small man, quiet and incisive. Illness gave his figure an added slenderness and his manner an unusual delicacy. His head, which Aldington described as looking "moulded of some queer-colored stone," was long, and it narrowed as it descended. Dark red hair fell loosely over the forehead; a beard concluded the downward sweep of the face. The very blue eyes were sharp, alert, quizzical, and taunting. "And his voice—" (I am quoting again from Aldington) "such a pleasant devil's voice, with its shrill little titters and sharp mockeries and even more insulting flatteries. At any moment one expects to see him sprout horns and a tail and cloven hoofs and to run trotting about poking his dull or resentful guests with a neat little pitchfork."

Meeting him, one found it difficult to believe him the creator of the many powerful works which bear his name. There appeared to be no physical basis for such energy. The easiest explanation of the anomaly would be one suggested

[14] The *Observer* (London), October 7, 1928.

by his own semi-mystical beliefs—one which would make him the sensitive medium of great hidden forces. Any non-magical theory must certainly tax the resources of the analyst.

Two volumes of poetry by D. H. Lawrence have been published since the appearance of his *Collected Poems*. The first of these, *Pansies*,[15] is a rather large collection of work extremely varied in style and filled with brilliance and power. The second, *Nettles*,[16] is a thin book, containing only twenty-five short poems, most of which are inartistic rimes dashed off in petulant moods during the last year of his life, when his health was desperate and his temper was unusually aggravated by trouble with the censors. Not only was the manuscript of *Pansies* seized in the mails by order of the Home Secretary, certain poems being deleted before publication was permitted, but Lawrence's first public exhibition of paintings in London was raided by the police and certain paintings were forcibly unhung. His pride was severely wounded by these interferences, and he struck back with all the scorn of which he was capable. In *Nettles* he excoriates the censors in rime, and in an essay, *Pornography and Obscenity*,[17] published two days before his death, he contributes a courageous and sincere, if not entirely logical, argument to the prose literature on the vexed subject of artistic freedom versus morality.

I shall not concern myself here with the question of Lawrence's rightness or wrongness in his fight with the police. I wish only to emphasize his sincerity. Through his entire literary career, covering approximately twenty years,

[15] London: Secker; New York: Knopf. 1929.
[16] London: Faber & Faber. 1930.
[17] London: Faber & Faber. 1929. New York: Knopf. 1930.

he fought for certain standards of honesty and frankness in matters of sex relationship, and these standards he considered more wholesome than those generally in effect. That he scolded his adversaries in too shrill a voice and in too authentically Derbyshire profanity must be admitted. But though his technique was often at fault, his motives were always, I think, sincere and idealistic. He was too high-strung for strategical debate. He was a poet.

Pansies was a splendid work with which to crown his poetical career. It exhibits far more variety than any other single volume of his poems, and it contains many specimens of the sort of lyric which expresses Lawrence at his best— that is, the spontaneous, open-hearted rhapsody, with its highly personal music, its complete disregard of convention, its sensitive recording of external images, and its echoes of mystical depths. His old themes are here again: the mystery of animals, the complexity of the man-woman conflict, hatred of the bourgeoisie, etc. But there are others not so old with him. He chides the younger generation for its decadence, its lack of virility, its love of obscenity:

Beware, O my dear young men, of going rotten. It's so easy to
    follow suit;
people in their thirties, and the older ones, have gotten bad inside,
    like fruit
that nobody eats and nobody wants, so it rots, but is not forgotten.

His plea is for the sacredness of sex—a sacredness secured not by concealment but by wisdom and respect:

Sex isn't something you've got to play with; sex is you.
It's the flow of your life, it's your moving self, and you are due
to be true to the nature of it, its reserve, its sensitive pride
that it always has to begin with, and by which you ought to abide.

These are very moralistic poems to have come from the pen of one who constantly was accused of immoral writing.

Another major theme in *Pansies* is Lawrence's difficulty in finding his proper social class. This problem had always worried him, but toward the end of his life it became rather an obsession, due partly to the fact that as he grew more and more famous he became increasingly conscious of the discrepancy between his lowly birth and his final position in the literary aristocracy. The middle class he could not tolerate; their smugness and commercialism upset him dreadfully. The upper class he found generally rotten. For the lower class he felt some affection, but this affection flowered best at a distance. He could not really make himself at home among the workers. What he did, therefore, was to stay pretty close to his intellectual and artistic acquaintances, and to their amusement or boredom or horror, play up his Derbyshire origin for all it was worth. It was a very human solution of a class-complex. Recalling his boyhood and his early companions, he writes in a poem called "Up He Goes!——":

> Up I rose, my lads, an' I heard yer
> sayin': Up he goes!
>
> Up like a bloomin' little Excelsior
> in his Sunday clothes!
>
> Up he goes, up the bloomin' ladder
> about to the giddy top!
> Who'd ever have thought it of that lad, a
> pasty little snot! —
>
> Never you mind, my lads, I left you
> a long, long way behind.

You'll none of you rise in the world like I did;
an' if you did, you'd find
it damn well wasn't worth it,
goin' up an' bein' refined;
it was nowt but a dirty sell, that's all,
a *damn fraud,* underlined.

The rest of the poem is devoted to a denunciation of the upper classes.

There is a decidedly dominant note of sadness, almost of despair, running through the book. This may be explained partially, no doubt, by Lawrence's physical condition; but it is based also upon an acute critical sense of the futility of much that is typical of modern civilization. Unnecessary noise and activity, superficial standards of life, money-grubbing, idiotic competition, mechanization, masculinity of women and effeminacy of men—these and other aspects of twentieth-century life drove Lawrence to the deepest spiritual depression. It led him to assert that we are approaching the end of a cycle—a tragic cycle. In "The Death of Our Era" he cries:

Our era is dying
yet who has killed it?
Have we, who are it?
In the middle of voluted space
its knell has struck.
And in the middle of every atom, which is the same thing,
a tiny bell of conclusion has sounded.
The curfew of our great day
the passing-bell of our way of knowing
the knell of our bald-headed consciousness
the tocsin of this our civilization.

In a whole series of poems he repeats with changing metaphors the impending calamity:

> For there are all sorts of flame:
> slow, creeping, cold ones
> that burn inwardly
> like flickering cancers.
> And the slow, cold flames
> may burn for long years
> before they've eaten through the joists and the girders
> and the house comes down, with a subsiding crash.
>
> . . . .
>
> The only thing to be done now,
> now that the waves of our undoing have begun to strike on us,
> is to contain ourselves.
> To keep still, and let the wreckage of ourselves go,
> let everything go, as the wave smashes us,
> yet keep still, and hold
> the tiny grain of something that no wave can wash away,
> not even the most massive wave of destiny.

Civilization is in the throes of dissolution, but the "tiny grain" will survive. There will be a Resurrection, though when and how are not vouchsafed. There is something infinitely touching in these slightly hysterical chants of doom and prophecies of salvation, coming as we know they did from a strong spirit on the verge of death. And most touching of all is the poem called "Sun in Me," where Lawrence invokes his old mystical power for the last time and sings beautifully of his peculiar pagan faith:

> A sun will rise in me
> I shall slowly resurrect
> already the whiteness of false dawn is on my inner ocean.

A sun in me.
And a sun in heaven.
And beyond that, the immense sun behind the sun,
the sun of immense distances, that fold themselves together
within the genitals of living space.
And further, the sun within the atom
which is god in the atom.

There was always a sun in D. H. Lawrence, and from its
light sprang flowers.

AMY LOWELL

X ⇜ AMY LOWELL:
The Success

Amy Lowell was born at Brookline, Massachusetts, February 9, 1874, the descendant of a long line of well-bred New Englanders, several of whom were men of letters. Her mother's father was Minister to England, and her paternal grandfather's cousin was the distinguished poet, James Russell Lowell. Her mother was a highly cultivated woman, a musician and a linguist, and it was from her that Miss Lowell derived much of her interest in the arts and her early knowledge of the French language and literature. She was educated privately, and spent a great deal of time, even as a child, traveling abroad. As a young woman she continued her travels, spending one winter on the Nile, another in California, and still another in Greece and Turkey, not to mention several summer trips to the principal European countries.

It is not at all strange that in this environment, and with such rich experiences, Miss Lowell should have tried her hand at literary expression. Yet the fact is that the creative impulse developed in her slowly. She is said to have begun writing poems at the age of thirteen (like most other girls), but it was not until she was twenty-eight that she decided to become a poet, and she was thirty-four when her first poems appeared in print. Two years later she gathered into a volume all her early poetic efforts which she considered worthy of preservation, and these were published as *A Dome of Many-Coloured Glass*.[1] This book did not startle anyone. It contained only conventional poems: uninspired lyrics on the usual themes, a group of sonnets, and some children's verses. It was exactly the sort of first book of poems to be expected from a young woman of Miss Lowell's social and intellectual class. Louis Untermeyer, in his *American Poetry Since 1900*, says it is so trite that one can hardly believe Amy Lowell the author of it. He thinks it showed no promise of the originality which distinguished much of her later work. Most critics, I believe, held the same view, though it has been suggested by one that in the poem which opens the volume, "Before the Altar," we have a definite indication of the author's tendency toward free verse and an individual technique.[2]

What we can say certainly is that in these trial verses Miss Lowell showed an authentic, if not extraordinary, poetic sensibility; that she proved herself a conscientious craftsman; and that she revealed several of her major passions: Keats being one, Japanese art another, and colorful gardens a third. These passions were lifelong with Miss Lowell, and recur regularly in her writing.

In *A Dome of Many-Coloured Glass* Amy Lowell paid her tribute to poetic convention. Never again was she to accept so complacently the patterns and the diction of popular English verse. Henceforth she was to play the part of chief

[1] Boston: Houghton Mifflin. 1912. Oxford: Blackwell. 1913.

[2] *Amy Lowell—Her Life and Work.* (Pamphlet) by Richard Hunt. New York: Macmillan. No date.

experimenter in the laboratory of Anglo-American poetry—
experimenter and interpreter both. She was always willing to
employ fixed forms, and to write in perfect meter with perfect rime, but after 1912 she strove for newer imagery and
diction, and her best energy went toward the making of vers
libre and the still more radical polyphonic prose.

Two things conspired to drive Miss Lowell from the
sanctuary presided over by Keats and his fellow romanticists.
One was her study of modern French poetry; the other was
her association in London with Ezra Pound and those who
were to become the imagists. She visited London during the
summer of 1913. She came in contact with poetic minds
more original than her own. She saw the stirrings of a new
force. What she had learned from reading the French poets
(the Parnassians and the symbolists) helped her to grasp
the theories advanced by the London group, and presently
she found herself an absolute convert to the principles of the
"new" poetry. Before leaving America she had written one
poem in free form, unrimed.[3] This she gave to Pound for
use in *Des Imagistes*, and at once set about writing others of
the same sort.

A year later she was in London again. This time she was
surer of herself and of her mission. She had been asked to
deliver in Boston a series of lectures on modern French poetry, and the summer trip to Europe was to provide her with
additional knowledge of the subject. Also she had been
thinking about the poets whom Pound had gathered around
him. Her typically American flair for organization and pro-
motion had set her imagination working, and she now had
plans for advancing the cause of imagism. How she put these
plans into effect has been described in chapter ii.

[3] "In a Garden."

In October 1914, shortly after Miss Lowell returned to America with the manuscript of *Some Imagist Poets* in her bag, a new volume of her own verse was published. This was *Sword Blades and Poppy Seed*,[4] an assortment of work which demonstrated clearly all the new interests and influences to which her poetic consciousness had been subjected during the preceding two years. In her preface to the book, she states her "immense debt" to the French—particularly in the matter of technique; and declares herself to be strongly under the spell of the Parnassians. She does not mention imagism, but she discusses briefly the principles of vers libre, and suggests that Flint's phrase, "unrimed cadence," is an appropriate English equivalent for the French term. She mentions also that three of the poems in the book are written in a form which, so far as she knows, "has never before been attempted in English." She means, of course, what later came to be known as "polyphonic prose." The invention of the form she ascribes to Paul Fort.[5] But no-

[4] New York: Macmillan. Oxford: Blackwell.

[5] Later, in an article entitled "A Consideration of Modern Poetry," published in the *North American Review* for January 1917, Miss Lowell amplifies these remarks on the origin and use of the new form. She says:

"In the late 'eighties and early 'nineties, a French Poet, M. Paul Roux, better known by his pen-name, Saint-Pol-Roux, started to experiment with poems irregularly rimed and printed as prose. His cadences were very regular, and his rimes were, as a rule, placed at the ends of them, but the poet varied them with skill, and succeeded in producing a verse which was clearly neither one of the usual forms of French prosody nor *vers libre*, then just coming into fashion.

"Contemporary with Saint-Pol-Roux, although a much younger man, came M. Paul Fort. Whether M. Fort was influenced by his *confrère*, or whether he arrived at his form independently, I do not know, but he began very early to write in this manner. He gave his form no name, merely stating that it admitted of both prose and verse in the same poem."

She then expresses the opinion that while Saint-Pol-Roux may have

where in the preface does she mention any of the London
poets—perhaps because no one of them was well known, perhaps because she was not quite conscious of her indebtedness
to them. Yet anyone who reads through the book can see
that she owed something to several of her fellow imagists.
Take an obvious example:

WHITE AND GREEN

Hey! My daffodil-crowned,
Slim and without sandals!
As the sudden spurt of flame upon darkness
So my eyeballs are startled with you,
Supple-limbed youth among the fruit trees,
Light runner through tasseled orchards.
You are an almond flower unsheathed
Leaping and flickering between the budded branches.

This is not derived from the French. Nor is it original
Amy Lowell. It is simply a poem in the manner of H. D.,
bungled slightly by the imitator's hand. "The Pike" is in
Flint's style:

In the brown water,
Thick and silver-sheened in the sunshine,
Liquid and cool in the shade of the reeds,
A pike dozed.
Lost among the shadows of stems
He lay unnoticed.

----

exhibited more subtlety in his use of the form, it was Paul Fort who gave
it vitality and demonstrated its dramatic possibilities. She concludes:

"It will be seen, therefore, that in taking over the form invented by
Saint-Pol-Roux and Paul Fort, I have had so to adapt and alter it as to
make it practically a new form. I owe its very descriptive name to my
friend, John Gould Fletcher, who has done some excellent work in this
medium."

> Suddenly he flicked his tail,
> And a green-and-copper brightness
> Ran under the water.

In other poems one may easily find traces of Pound and Aldington and Fletcher. It was natural for Amy Lowell to imitate—her curiosity was extraordinary, and her love of experiment amounted to a passion. What she admired she emulated, and she was not always scrupulous in the matter of acknowledgments. Catch any one of the other imagists off guard and he will confess that some time or other he has been startled to find Miss Lowell proudly exhibiting jewels filched from his own store. I do not mean to imply that the other imagists never borrowed methods—some of them even borrowed in return from Miss Lowell, but they were at great pains to say so; and besides, her indebtedness was always greater than theirs. Her most distinctive contribution to the imagist movement (in the opinion of her colleagues) was her business sense and her indefatigable enthusiasm for propaganda. She was their Barnum. They were amused by her flamboyant methods; they were content to profit from her success.

What impressed them most in her poetry was her polyphonic prose. Not that they all liked it, but they felt that in spite of what it owed to Saint-Pol-Roux and Paul Fort, it was an actual contribution to modern poetic technique. John Gould Fletcher was so struck by the effectiveness of this method that he adopted it in several of his own compositions (see *Breakers and Granite*), and Richard Aldington, writing in the *Egoist* for November 16, 1914, not only praises the polyphonic prose pieces included in *Sword Blades and Poppy Seed*, but advises "all young poets to study these poems attentively," and adds "I am not a bit ashamed to confess that

I have myself imitated Miss Lowell in this, and produced a couple of works in the same style."

It is easy to understand how any writer interested in new effects would be tempted to essay the polyphonic form, if for nothing more than his own amusement. No medium offers better opportunity for a display of virtuosity. Particularly arresting, and probably most successful of Miss Lowell's early examples of the method, is the melodramatic narrative, "In a Castle," wherein cadence and rime are cunningly interwoven. This is the opening movement:

Over the yawning chimney hangs the fog. Drip — hiss — drip — hiss — fall the raindrops on the oaken log which burns, and steams, and smokes the ceiling beams. Drip—hiss—the rain never stops.

The wide, state bed shivers beneath its velvet coverlet. Above, dim, in the smoke, a tarnished coronet gleams dully. Overhead hammers and chinks the rain. Fearfully wails the wind down distant corridors, and there comes the swish and sigh of rushes lifted off the floors. The arras blows sidewise out from the wall, and then falls back again.

It is my lady's key, confided with much nice cunning, whisperingly. He enters on a sob of wind, which gutters the candles almost to swaling. The fire flutters and drops. Drip — hiss — the rain never stops. He shuts the door. The rushes fall again to stillness along the floor. Outside, the wind goes wailing.

Even so brief an extract is enough to demonstrate the extraordinary scope of this "many-voiced" form, this omnibus capable of carrying at one time all the devices of poetic expression: meter, cadence, prose rhythms, assonance, alliteration, rime, and return. Amy Lowell was peculiarly fitted to do the pioneer work in English polyphonic prose, for she was nothing if not a virtuoso. Her pleasure was to make words dance surprisingly; to startle her readers with pyrotechnic displays of color and curious medleys of sound. Depth she sometimes attempted, but seldom attained. Brilliance was her forte. And so it was that although *Sword Blades and Poppy Seed* contained many varieties of verse, conventional and otherwise, its significance centered in these introductory specimens of a novel and exotic technique.

A year after the appearance of these poems, Miss Lowell brought out her valuable essays, *Six French Poets,*[6] which grew from the series of lectures she delivered in Boston during the winter of 1914–1915. In the brief preface she deplores the ignorance of Englishmen and Americans in the matter of contemporary French poetry and dedicates her own abilities to its correction. How enthusiastically she approached her subject may be judged from her statement that "France has just been passing through one of the great poetical epochs of her career — one of the great poetical epochs of the world." The six essays of the book deal in turn with Emile Verhaeren, Albert Samain, Remy de Gourmont, Henri de Régnier, Francis Jammes, and Paul Fort. Miss Lowell does not give her reasons for choosing these particular poets; she leaves us to assume that they are the best representatives of their period. With this choice F. S. Flint, for one, takes issue. In the *Egoist* for January 1, 1916, he writes reminiscently of a discussion he and Miss Lowell had on the subject, and restates his position.

When, in the summer of 1914, she told me of her intention to write this book and of the names of the poets she had chosen, I

[6] New York and London: Macmillan. 1915.

objected to Samain. Samain, I said, was exquisite, but not important; and he could only be read a few pages at a time without weariness. Stuart Merrill and Francis Vielé-Griffin, I went on, are both more considerable poets; both are Americans, and the public to which you make your first appeal is American; if you will not have them, Rimbaud and Laforgue are immensely more important than Samain; and since you insist on including Remy de Gourmont as one of your poets, you might increase your number to seven, in many ways an appropriate number where poets are concerned; and so on. But she would hear nothing of it.

Yet he thinks that the book is in the main excellent, and he bestows particular praise on the prose translations which Miss Lowell made from the work of the six poets and which she included as an appendix. "The best translations," he says, and in this field Flint's word must be considered authoritative, "the best translations into English that so far exist of the six poets in question, or, it might truly be said, of the French poets of the symbolist generation."

Elsewhere in the same article he speaks of Miss Lowell's devotion to the French poets, and takes the opportunity to describe the strong effect created upon him and other members of the London group by her informal readings of French poetry. He recalls the scenes at the Berkeley Hotel:

No one, I suppose, will have listened to Miss Lowell's causerie in so happy a setting as the sitting-room of her hotel, where she talked to us in the August of 1914. Through the long French window open in the corner could be seen the length of Piccadilly, its great electric globes, its shiny roadway, and, on the left, the tops of the trees of Green Park, dark grey in the moonlight; the noise of the motor-buses and of the taxis reached us in a muted murmur, and at the corner of the park opposite, beneath a street lamp, stood a newsboy, whose headlines we strained our eyes from time to time to catch. It was in this tenseness created by the expectation of news that Miss Lowell read Paul Fort or Henri de Régnier to us (she reads French beautifully); and it is the emotions of those evenings, more than anything else, that her book brings back to me.

The War shortened Miss Lowell's stay in London, but it did not interfere with her work. If anything it increased her productivity, for her next book of original verse, *Men, Women, and Ghosts,*[7] exhibited a tremendous amount of writing done in a relatively short space of time. Too much writing, probably, for the actual amount of legitimate emotion behind it. But Miss Lowell was always brimming over with energy, and at that stage of her career when she had just caught the public attention she was totally unrestrained. *Men, Women, and Ghosts* includes three hundred and sixty pages of verse, yet we are told in the preface that the author has excluded "all purely lyrical poems," leaving only "stories." But the "stories" are more varied than one would suppose. There are narratives in conventional form, others in free verse, and still others in polyphonic prose. There are short pieces, primarily descriptive, in which there is certainly no story, except by vague implication. There are historical romances (swiftly impressionistic), New England dialect tales (not-too-successful tours de force) and modern war episodes. In fact there is a vast array of miscellaneous subjects, strung on a thread of theory. Miss Lowell had dedicated herself to the task of exploring the possibilities of rhythm—particularly the rhythms of free verse—and she was therefore ranging far in search of material. One day she would attempt to reproduce "the circular movement of

[7] New York: Macmillan; Oxford: Blackwell. 1916.

a hoop bowling along the ground," again "the suave, continuous tone of a violin." From an effort to capture the grace of eighteenth-century Venice she would turn to the angularity of rustic New England, and thence to the Aquarium or a Boston drawing-room. It was certainly cold-blooded, this combination of note-taking and laboratory transcription. The surprising thing is that its results were so animated. Amy Lowell herself was so vital that she imparted warmth to the most mechanical exercise. When emotion was lacking she created the illusion of emotion—which is almost the same thing in a work of art.

There are, I think, many poems in *Men, Women, and Ghosts* which are mediocre or worse. They represent the inevitable failures of the prolific and experimental poet. But there are a few which "come off" excellently, and which represent minor triumphs in the field of modern poetry. "Patterns" is one of these, and "Malmaison" is another. Both are stories in the true sense, the former an outstanding example of Miss Lowell's skill in the manipulation of free-verse rhythms and of her effective use of color and form to convey emotion, the latter a proof of the adaptability of polyphonic prose to the requirements of dramatic narrative. Both are interesting, also, as specimens of sustained imagistic writing.

Never was Miss Lowell more deft than in "Patterns," where cadence follows the shifting mood as easily, as infallibly, as its shadow follows a bird; and the curves of the song are tipped with felicitous rime. The setting is a garden, the time is summer, and the speaker a maiden of an earlier century, whose lover is fighting in Flanders:

> I walk down the garden paths,
> And all the daffodils
> Are blowing, and the bright blue squills.

> I walk down the patterned garden paths
> In my stiff, brocaded gown.
> With my powdered hair and jeweled fan,
> I too am a rare
> Pattern. As I wander down
> The garden paths.

The fullness of summer, the beauty and softness of the flowers, waken her passion, which "wars against the stiff brocade," and listening to the "splashing of waterdrops in the marble fountain," she dreams of herself as a bather, spied upon by her lover:

> What is Summer in a fine brocaded gown!
> I should like to see it lying in a heap upon the ground.
> All the pink and silver crumpled up on the ground.
> I would be the pink and silver as I ran along the paths,
> And he would stumble after,
> Bewildered by my laughter.
> I should see the sun flashing from his sword-hilt and the
>   buckles on his shoes.
> I would choose
> To lead him in a maze along the patterned paths,
> A bright and laughing maze for my heavy-booted lover.
> Till he caught me in the shade,
> And the buttons of his waistcoat bruised my body as he
>   clasped me,
> Aching, melting, unafraid.
> With the shadows of the leaves and the sundrops,
> And the plopping of the waterdrops,
> All about us in the open afternoon—
> I am very like to swoon
> With the weight of this brocade,
> For the sun sifts through the shade.

But the dream is a pathetic one, for her lover has been killed
in action, and now her proud fidelity gives rise to a cruel
vision of the future:

> In Summer and in Winter I shall walk
> Up and down
> The patterned garden paths
> In my stiff, brocaded gown.
> The squills and daffodils
> Will give place to pillared roses, and to asters, and to
> snow.
> I shall go
> Up and down,
> In my gown.
> Gorgeously arrayed,
> Boned and stayed.
> And the softness of my body will be guarded from
> embrace
> By each button, hook, and lace.
> For the man who should loose me is dead,
> Fighting with the Duke in Flanders,
> In a pattern called a war.
> Christ! What are patterns for?

Apart from the technical expertness of this poem, and
its resultant emotional force, there are other reasons for considering it representative of Miss Lowell's best poetic vein.
First, it has a garden setting; second, it deals with persons
of refinement; third, its action is laid in the romantic past.
With such elements she was always happy, and always reasonably competent. Instinctively and by familiarity with
them, she understood them. With coarser and more typically
modern elements she was not at ease—in spite of much determination and good will.

After this third book of verse, which on the whole tended
to strengthen her literary position in America, Miss Lowell
published another volume of prose criticism, *Tendencies in
Modern American Poetry*,[8] by means of which she hoped to
clarify the confusion which existed in the public mind regarding the poets of the American renaissance. As in the case of
her treatment of French poetry, she here limits herself to six
representative figures, and devotes to each a combined biographical and critical analysis. Imagism she treats as the
third stage in the development of the new poetry, and after
giving considerable space to the imagist principles and something of the history of the movement, she examines in detail the lives and poetic works of H. D. and John Gould
Fletcher.

The book was found useful, and still is—although its
real mission was an ephemeral one. Its chief value today is
historical, for as a document it is important; as criticism it
has been superseded by more discriminating works. At the
time of writing this book, Miss Lowell was too much a part
of the general movement, and of the imagist movement in
particular, to be a thoroughly just interpreter of the new
American poetry. She strove for impartiality, but in vain.
Consequently, those critics who desired to do so, found it
comparatively easy to demonstrate her critical faults and to
show her in the rôle of propagandist.

Perhaps the most annoyed of the critics was Conrad
Aiken, who found the book intolerably egotistical, colloquial
to the point of vulgarity, malicious in its partisanship, and
fundamentally false in its logic.[9] After perusing it carefully

---

[8] New York: Macmillan. 1917.
[9] See his *Scepticisms*, pp. 22 and 251 ff.

he concluded that "a certain intellectual unripeness and sketchiness, a proneness to hasty and self-satisfying conclusions without careful or accurate survey of the facts, make of Miss Lowell an amateur rather than a serious critic. She is engaging, clever, an industrious assimilator of current ideas, and to some degree she sifts among them the bad from the good; but the instant she enters the psychological or philosophical or reflective spheres she proves herself a child, swayed very largely by her emotions and desires."

And T. S. Eliot, reviewing the book in the *Egoist* for April 1918, greatly deplored its bad taste and its nationalism. It strikes him as "a most unfortunate thing that this all-American propaganda should continue," and he believes that "Literature must be judged by language, not by place. . . . . Provinciality of material may be a virtue . . . .; provinciality of point of view is a vice."

Having done what she deemed her duty by the principal American poets of the time, Miss Lowell lost not a moment in pursuing her own creative career. *Can Grande's Castle*[10] revealed her at the height of her enthusiasm for polyphonic prose. Four long poems made up the book—poems which gave the author full scope for her ambitions as a narrator and as a technical experimentalist. "Sea-Blue and Blood-Red" retells, with the dexterous speed of a motion picture, the story of Lady Hamilton and Lord Nelson. "Guns as Keys: and the Great Gate Swings" gives a kaleidoscopic picture of the emergence of Japan from her state of isolation, and indicates by cleverly arranged incidents and symbols, the spiritual conflicts and tragedies resulting from the commercial invasion of the Orient by the nations of the West. "Hedge

[10] New York: Macmillan. 1918. Oxford: Blackwell. 1920.

Island" attempts to portray the passing of Old England, and to bring into the net of rhapsody all the bits of landscape, the snatches of song, the city scenes and sounds, which can serve to awaken memories of an England that is now little more than a dream, and which can form a poetic contrast with the modern order. "The Bronze Horses" is the most ambitious of the four narratives, and occupies nearly half the book. Its conception is unusually good, I believe, and its execution, though uneven, is at times brilliant. Miss Lowell takes as her theme the four horses of Saint Mark's Church, Venice, and from their history weaves a rich tapestry of color and movement. From the days of ancient Rome and Constantinople, we follow the destiny of these horses, finding in them the never-changing symbol of glory and victory, watching with them the rise and fall of empires. We leave them in 1915, when Venice is endangered by German bombs and it is decreed that the beautiful bronze horses must be sent to Rome for safety:

> The boat draws away from the Riva. The great bronze horses mingle their outlines with the distant mountains. Dim gold, subdued green-gold, flashing faintly to the faint, bright peaks above them. Granite and metal, earth over water. Down the canal, old, beautiful horses, pride of Venice, of Constantinople, of Rome. Wars bite you with their little flames and pass away, but roses and oleanders strew their petals before your going, and you move like a constellation in a space of crimson stars.
> So the horses float along the canal, between barred and shuttered palaces, splendid against marble walls in the fire of the sun.

It was a good choice of theme for a pretentious piece of polyphonic writing. It lent itself perfectly to the orchestral effects which Miss Lowell set out to achieve, and it brought into happy union her technical virtuosity and her considerable knowledge of the European scene.[11]

Inasmuch as both *Men, Women, and Ghosts* and *Can Grande's Castle* were limited almost entirely to narrative poems, Miss Lowell now found herself burdened with a tremendous accumulation of lyrics. For at no time had she ceased writing in lyric vein. In the spring of 1919, therefore, she issued as *Pictures of the Floating World*,[12] a collection of short poems written during the preceding five years. As the title indicates (it is a rendering of the Japanese *Ukiyo-e*, a name commonly applied to the realistic color-prints of which Miss Lowell was so fond), many of the poems in this book are on Oriental themes, and some of them are written in imitation of Oriental style. Since the beginning of her career as a poet, Miss Lowell had manifested an unusual interest in the poetry and painting of China and Japan, but not until the publication of *Pictures of the Floating World* did she reveal the full extent of that interest. The short poems which begin the volume are called "Lacquer Prints," and are

[11] It is interesting to find a distinguished post-imagist poet, Archibald MacLeish, bestowing lavish praise on Miss Lowell's polyphonic prose narratives in general and on "The Bronze Horses" in particular. In an essay entitled "Amy Lowell and the Art of Poetry," published in the *North American Review* for March 1925, he says, regarding "The Bronze Horses": "What you have here is not a drama, nor a story, but a ballet in words, a ballet of the Fokine period, a ballet of armies and empires in which the décor is not only written in but becomes part of the action. Phrases of color, of line, repeat and develop themselves as they would be repeated and developed by a great chorographer."

And his general estimate of Miss Lowell's work in these long pieces of polyphonic prose is: "It is her great achievement. And if it is not the greatest invention of an American, American art has pinnacles we have not suspected."

[12] New York: Macmillan; Oxford: Blackwell.

in the spirit of Japanese *hokku* and *tanka*, though no effort
is made to reproduce the actual syllabic pattern of these exotic
forms.   In most instances Miss Lowell succeeds admirably
in attaining the compression as well as the psychological values of her models, and although experts have detected non-
Japanese characteristics in some of them, they agree that on
the whole the poems are valuable examples of the influence
of Japanese art on a Western mind.   In such fancies as the
following we have the authentic spirit of the *hokku:*

TO A HUSBAND:

Brighter than fireflies upon the Uji River
Are your words in the dark, Beloved.

EPHEMERA

Silver-green lanterns tossing among windy branches:
So an old man thinks
Of the loves of his youth.

The pieces written under Chinese influence—"Chinoi-
series"—are fewer in number, and perhaps less convincing
in effect.   Still, they have considerable charm, and their
composition was useful to Miss Lowell as a preparation for
her more extended effort in the same field which resulted in
Fir-Flower Tablets,[13] a collection of translations from the
Chinese, made in collaboration with Mrs. Florence Ayscough.

Whatever else may be said of Amy Lowell as a poetic
interpreter of the Orient, it is undeniable that she went to
great pains to fit herself for such an office.   She steeped herself in the pictorial art of both countries, and read innumerable books relating to their history, life, and culture.
She was in close association with several Orientalists of Bos-

[13] Boston: Houghton Mifflin; London: Constable. 1921.

ton (including her brother Percival, who had lived for several years in Korea and Japan and was the author of four books dealing with the Far East); she learned what she could from Ezra Pound, John Gould Fletcher, and other contemporary poets interested in Oriental poetry; and she derived a considerable amount of help from the French writers of the nineteenth century who had participated in the movement called "Japonisme." This last-named source has been skilfully traced in a recent study by Professor William Leonard Schwartz,[14] and now appears more important than one might have suspected. Professor Schwartz proves, among other things, that in at least three of Miss Lowell's poems she paraphrased prose passages from the work of Edmond de Goncourt, and although she did not attempt to conceal the fact (so literal are the renderings from the French), she made no mention of her indebtedness.

Only a small proportion of *Pictures of the Floating World* is written in actual imitation of foreign models, yet the Oriental influence is dominant throughout the book. Fantastic imagery conveying evanescent moods is the artistic aim involved; an aim which sometimes carried the poet too far, and seduced her into conceits which even to a tolerant reader appear absurd. Such incongruous similes as:

> My thoughts
> Chink against my ribs
> And roll about like silver hailstones.

and

> Little hot apples of fire,
> Burst out of the flaming stem
> Of my heart,

[14] "A Study of Amy Lowell's Far Eastern Verse," *Modern Language Notes* (Baltimore), March 1928.

give no pleasure to the discriminating mind, nor do they plead well the cause of imagism. Fortunately, they are not really typical of the book, though they do illustrate its chief weakness, which is the tendency toward far-fetched and rather puerile imagery.

Miss Lowell's next venture was a return to narrative. Having treated in *Can Grande's Castle* the historical themes which appealed most to her, she now determined to exploit the field of folklore, and the result was a collection of eleven rather long poems published as *Legends*.[15] Some were based on familiar tales, others were inventions. Their settings include China, Peru, Yucatan, England, New England, and the Indian country of North America. How many and what varied sources contributed to their making is indicated in the author's preface, where she specifies a number of reference books, and emphasizes the fact that those unspecified are much more numerous. In other words we have in *Legends* one more example of Miss Lowell's indefatigable curiosity and energy. She was an inveterate explorer of literature, and a tireless creator, or perhaps we should say, re-creator. So fanatical was she on the subject of writing, so ardent in her search for material, that she could not bear to let even the slightest fluttering idea escape her net. The poems in *Legends* are not by any means her worst work, nor are they her best. They stand upon a level of mediocre competency. They represent maturity of technique (in all Miss Lowell's favorite modes), and their subject-matter is legitimate. Yet somehow, it seems to me, they do not get beyond the category of tours de force. Artful but uninspiring, they neither add to nor detract from her reputation as a poet.

[15] Boston: Houghton Mifflin; Oxford: Blackwell. 1921.

Her next appearance before the public was in a mask, and Harlequin as Critic was her rôle. Taking her cue from her illustrious relative, James Russell Lowell, whose *Fable for Critics* had appeared more than sixty years before, she composed *A Critical Fable*,[16] in which she exhibited twenty-one modern American poets (including herself) impaled on the needles of a flashing wit. The book was published anonymously, and so ingeniously had Miss Lowell concealed her personal characteristics of thought and style that few readers guessed the truth of its authorship. Two years later the truth came from the author herself.

A Critical Fable presents Miss Lowell in her most joyous mood, a mood of utter abandon. Taking the rollicking measure of " 'T was the night before Christmas," and riming in couplets and triplets, with plenty of ear-tickling feminine rimes to break the monotony, she races and cuts capers until one is dizzy with following her. How easily she could do this sort of stunt, and what pleasure it afforded her, can be sensed by any reader. But as an amusing comment on her technical facility, I reproduce here a letter (now published for the first time) which Miss Lowell wrote to John Gould Fletcher from her home at Brookline, Massachusetts, on December 6, 1915:[17]

> DEAR J. G. F.: Tonight you said a thing
> Which left me much upset and wondering.

[16] Boston: Houghton Mifflin. 1922.

[17] Mr. Fletcher very kindly furnishes me with the following statement. The letter, he says, "arose out of an argument in the course of which I happened to defend Conrad Aiken's early poetry—Amy took me to task about this, and asked why I liked rime so much in this case. I pointed out that his rime seemed to flow easily—she thereupon wrote this letter and sent it to me next day."

You seemed to feel that riming was so hard,
To have the knack made any man a bard.

To turn out couplets fast as you could think
Was quite a worthy use of printer's ink.

But pointing to your friend whom I'll not name
I said his verse would put a child to shame.

To reach the end within a given time
And wind up sharply on a tidy rime

Seemed to call forth a terrible commotion
And make his brain whirl like a stormy ocean.

Such tricks he used to cause his words to fall
Each on its accent! And that isn't all.

Some verbs expanded with that fearful "did,"
Others condensed; and nothing neatly hid.

Was that a style of which one could be proud?
I asked you, and my horror cried out loud.

You shook your head. "He rimes so easily,"
You sadly murmured, "it amazes me."

I vowed to you that I could do it too.
"But he does not repeat his rimes," said you.

I told you I could rime for half a day,
You doubted me. And now, behold my way!

Not wishing to admit that I'm defeated
I've done the thing, and not a rime repeated.

I could go on like this till you were dead,
But it is late and I must go to bed.

I've proved my point and if these lines don't go well
They took me just ten minutes.

AMY LOWELL.

P.S.   The postscript holds the letter's kernel,
So tell me, did you take the Poetry Journal?

It must be admitted that in *A Critical Fable* she did not allow her pleasure in riming to run away with her intellect. The fact that the rimes came so easily made it possible for her to concentrate on what she had to say. And she had plenty to say. She packed more solid stuff into this crazy jingle than she ever had into her serious prose works. And she was wittier than she had ever been. The frenzied pace of the poem, together with the wild music of its unrestrained rimes, seems to have intoxicated her mind to a degree of extraordinary brilliance.

Particularly interesting to us at this time, of course, is the passage relating to herself. In order to safeguard her anonymity she had, naturally, to adopt the attitude most likely to throw readers off the track leading to her own door. She therefore composed a spirited eulogy of her work, and pooh-poohed those critics who denied her a place among the immortals. The ruse (not unlike those to be found in detective stories) worked admirably. She describes herself as a powerful, bewildering poet, whom few can appreciate:

Conceive, if you can, an electrical storm
Of a swiftness and fury surpassing the norm;
Conceive that this cyclone has caught up the rainbow

> And dashed dizzily on with it streaming in tow.
> Imagine a sky all split open and scissored
> By lightnings, and then you can picture this blizzard.
> That is, if you'll also imagine the clashes
> Of tropical thunder, the incessant crashes
> Which shiver the hearing and leave it in ashes.
> Remember, meanwhile, that the sky is prismatic
> And outrageous with color. The effect is erratic
> And jarring to some, but to others ecstatic,
> Depending, of course, on the idiosyncratic
> Response of beholders. When you come to think of it,
> A good deal is demanded by those on the brink of it.

Yet she is careful to note that technical brilliance does not substitute for, but merely conceals, emotional integrity.

> Despite her traducers, there's always a heart
> Hid away in her poems for the seeking; impassioned,
> Beneath silver surfaces cunningly fashioned
> To baffle coarse pryings, it waits for the touch
> Of a man who takes surfaces only as such.

She is very insistent on the subtlety of her poetry, and expresses much pity for him who cannot divine it. She also spends some time defending her erudition and bestowing praise on her versatility. As for the final judgment on the value of her contribution to American literature:

> The future's her goose and I dare say she'll wing it.
> Though the triumph will need her own power to sing it.
> Although I'm no prophet, I'll hazard a guess
> She'll be rated by time as more rather than less.

Just how much of this egotism was assumed for the occasion and how much was honestly felt is a question which I cannot answer. It must be admitted, however, that Miss Lowell was never lacking in self-confidence.

A Critical Fable was the last book of verse published by Amy Lowell before her death from a paralytic stroke on May 12, 1925. But the last few years of her life were crowded with work. She completed in time for publication shortly before her death a monumental biography and critical analysis of John Keats, and she composed enough poems to form the three volumes which were published posthumously. One of these, *What's O'Clock?*,[18] she herself prepared for the press; the other two, *East Wind*,[19] and *Ballads for Sale*,[20] were edited by her literary executors. On the whole these later poems are less daring than their predecessors. Their tone is quieter, their moods more tender. They reveal less of the note-taking method of composition, and more meditation. The peace of garden-flowers has closed in on the poet's mind and softened the edges of her fancy. She still turns to the far corners of the earth for symbols of beauty:

> So I start, but never rest
> North or South or East or West.
> Each horizon has its claim
> Solace to a different aim.
> Four-soul'd like the wind am I,
> Voyaging an endless sky,
> Undergoing destiny.

But she brings them all back to the New England garden. She will gather pearls from the Orient, and coral from

[18] Boston: Houghton Mifflin. 1925. London: Cape. 1926.
[19] Boston: Houghton Mifflin. 1926.
[20] Boston: Houghton Mifflin. 1927.

distant seas, but their exotic beauty cannot match the beauty
of lilacs:

> Heart-leaves of lilac all over New England,
> Roots of lilac under all the soil of New England,
> Lilac in me because I am New England,
> Because my roots are in it,
> Because my leaves are of it,
> Because my flowers are for it,
> Because it is my country
> And I speak to it of itself
> And sing of it with my own voice
> Since certainly it is mine.

It *was* her country. And when she sang of it she was at her
best. It was then that she sang most with her own voice. In
the eleven volumes of her poetry there are many voices, and
sometimes hers is not the strongest. It is hard to estimate
even now the value of her contribution, for although the
total of her work is before us, its diversity is baffling, and the
personality behind it is still too strongly felt. So dominant
a woman was she, so persuasive a propagandist, so clever a
poetic craftsman, that one prefers to evade the critical issue,
and leave it all to time. Louis Untermeyer once said, "No
poet living in America has been more fought for, fought
against, and generally fought about than Amy Lowell."[21]
That is true, and we are still somewhat blinded by the smoke
of battle.

To Miss Lowell's strongest admirers she was a great
poet, the greatest woman poet of her time; to her detractors
she was only a side show, a specimen of blatant Americanism
—dynamic, superficial, and, in its worst sense, successful. At

[21] *American Poetry Since 1900*, p. 137.

any rate she was, by popular standards, a success. Everything she touched prospered. She was a born promoter, and she was in the right country for the exercise of her talent. But it is not necessary either to elevate her to the plane of the immortals or to set her down a wearer of false fame. One may take a middle course, and agree with D. H. Lawrence that "In everything she did she was a good amateur." That is the course I am inclined to take.

XI ⋘ EZRA POUND: *Poet, Pedagogue,*
Propagandist, etc.

E ZRA POUND was born at
Hailey, Idaho, in 1885, but left the Wild West at the age of
eighteen months, when his family moved to Pennsylvania.
After the customary preparation he entered the University
of Pennsylvania, where he studied for two years. He then
transferred to Hamilton College, and from that institution
he received the Bachelor of Arts degree in 1905. Specializ-
ing in Romance Languages, he re-entered the University of
Pennsylvania for graduate work, and was granted a Master's
degree in 1906. The same year he won a scholarship which
permitted him to travel in Europe in search of material for
a study of Lope de Vega. On his return to America he accepted a position as instructor in Romance Languages at
Wabash College, Crawfordsville, Indiana, and assumed his
duties in the autumn of 1907. At the end of four months his
resignation was requested—the reason given being that he
was a "Latin Quarter type," and therefore ill-adapted to the
requirements of the situation. Nowadays Pound recalls this
experience with considerable amusement, and insists that he
was absolutely innocent of any misdemeanor.

Pocketing the salary due him, he sailed for Europe, land-

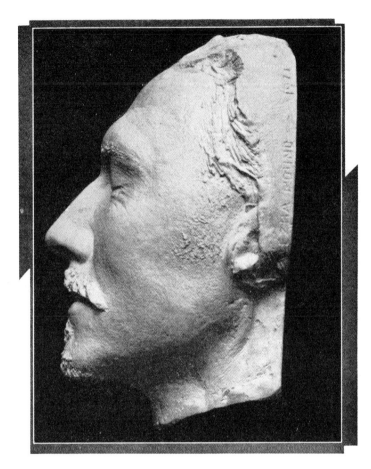

EZRA POUND
FROM A "DEATH-MASK"
BY NANCY COX McCORMACK

ing at Gibraltar with a total capital of approximately eighty dollars. He spent several months in Italy, and at Venice he arranged for the publication of his first collection of poems, *A Lume Spento*,[1] most of which had been written before leaving America. It is typical of Pound that he should have begun his public career as a poet in such a picturesque manner.

In the autumn of 1908 he arrived in London, drawn there largely by his desire to meet and to study with William Butler Yeats, whose poetry he admired more than that of any living writer. He met Yeats, and also other important literary figures in London—among them, Ernest Rhys and Ford Madox Hueffer—who took an interest in his unusual talent. The following spring Pound's early poems (selected chiefly from *A Lume Spento*) were issued in London with the title of *Personae*.[2] They created, within a limited circle, an impression which amounted to a sensation. There were readers who recoiled from the liberties of diction and rhythm which Pound manifested, and one reviewer declared that "At first the whole thing may seem to be mere madness and rhetoric, a vain exhibition of force and passion without beauty," but he adds that "as we read on, these curious meters of his seem to have a law and order of their own; the brute force of Mr. Pound's imagination seems to impart some quality of infectious beauty to his words." And the general verdict among intelligent and liberal critics was that an authentic poet had arisen. This verdict was strengthened by the appearance six months later of *Exultations*,[3] poems written mostly after Pound's arrival in England.

With the publication of these two volumes began, I

[1] Venice: Antonelli. June 1908. (100 copies.)
[2] Elkin Mathews. 1909.
[3] London: Elkin Mathews. 1909.

think we may safely say, the modern vogue of erudite poetry. In the twenty years which have passed, meanwhile, a large amount of writing has been done which requires or at least seems to require of the reader an extensive background of languages, history, and literature, not to mention an agile and tireless imaginative faculty. The bulk of blame (or praise) for this tendency must surely rest on Ezra Pound, though a certain amount may justly be shifted back to Robert Browning, who more than any other one poet gave Pound a method and a poetic psychology. Perhaps, too, we should apportion a share to those pedagogues in Pennsylvania who encouraged a red-headed youth to explore the myriad paths of comparative literature and sent him off in pursuit of the Spirit of Romance.

Having been seduced by Scholarship, and then having yielded to the lure of the Creative Life, Pound has spent his time vacillating between the two. As a consequence there is so much pedantic learning in his poetry that few can follow his references and so much poetic fancy in his critical and expository prose that scholars discredit him. Only a few manage to understand, appreciate, and synthesize the diverse elements of his work. The result of this conflict on Pound himself has been the development of an extraordinarily belligerent attitude, and a combination defensive-offensive technique in controversy which has made him one of the favorite features in the world of literary journalism. Like other thin-skinned egotists he has found invective his natural weapon, and has become a master in its use. He is to the world of aesthetics what Shaw is to the world of politics. Both are militant reformers; both are pedagogues gone wrong (or right). Each has set up a university of his own, and each may boast of a good many alumni.

It is quite possible, I think, to chronicle Pound's life in terms of pedagogy. Having failed to adjust himself to the petty restrictions of a small Middle Western college, he reacted violently against colleges in general. But no sooner had he arrived in London than he began to organize and teach. He gathered about him as many young poets as were susceptible to aesthetic theory, and proceeded to direct their careers. He was even pleased to correct their poems. When they did work that met with his approval, he got it published for them. For all this he took the credit due him, but no one objected to that.

Such teaching earned him nothing but praise and devotion. He was not in the least commercial about it: he did it for love. Which is only another proof that he was at heart a schoolmaster. He lived for years on next to nothing, and did not seem to mind his circumstances. But when funds got so low that something had to be done about it, his first inclination was to teach officially. His father, Homer L. Pound, now assayer at the United States Mint at Philadelphia, recently gave an interview to the Philadelphia *Evening Bulletin*,[4] and took occasion to recount some of the interesting and characteristic episodes in Ezra's life. The following paragraph is particularly pertinent to us at this point:

"He's always had a lot of nerve," said Mr. Pound, the affectionate, reminiscent smile appearing once more, "even the way he met his wife was nervy. He found funds were getting low, as usual, so he went to the Polytechnic Institute in London (he was only about twenty-one years old) and presented his name. 'Do you want to register as a student?' he was asked. 'No,' said Ezra, 'I want to register as a teacher. I want to give a course on the Romance Literature of Southern Europe.' 'But we don't want a course on the

4 Issue of February 20, 1928.

Romance Literature of Southern Europe,' he was told; 'besides, who are you?' 'Let me give the course,' said Ezra, 'and you'll see.' Well, they let him give it, heaven knows why. And among the students who registered for the course was a Miss Dorothy Shakespear and her mother. Ezra promptly fell in love with his pupil, and she with him, and they were married and have lived happily ever after."

Apart from the matter of Ezra's age (understated by several years) the story is probably true. And an even more entertaining document in the chronicle of Pound as professor is hidden away in the files of the *Egoist*, that curious and almost forgotten periodical which served as the English propagandist organ for imagism. In the issue of November 2, 1914, appears an article headed "Preliminary Announcement of the College of Arts," in which it is proposed to establish in London a college offering courses in music, painting, photography, sculpture, crafts, and letters, with a special appeal to American students cut off by the War from intended studies in Continental cities. The wording of the prospectus, the bold and canny nature of the scheme, the personnel of the faculty leave no doubt whatever that its instigator was Ezra Pound.

"We try not to duplicate courses given in formal institutions like the University of London," reads one paragraph, "or purely utilitarian courses like those of Berlitz. London is itself a larger university, and the best specialists are perhaps only approachable in chance conversation. We aim at an intellectual status no lower than that attained by the courts of the Italian Renaissance."

How charming and how Poundesque! And what a pity it never came into being! Gaudier-Brzeska was to have charge of the Atelier of Sculpture; Wyndham Lewis of the Atelier of Painting; Arnold Dolmetsch was to lecture on

Ancient Music; John Cournos on the Russian Novelists. But chief of all (at least claiming most space on the program, and meriting a much fuller biographical note than the others) was the Professor of Comparative Poetry—Ezra Pound, M.A., Sometime Fellow in Romanics of the University of Pennsylvania.

It must have been fun putting this down on paper, and imagining the college in full swing. But of course it was only a dream, born of a full fancy and an empty stomach. It was much more practical that Pound should become his own university, even if the pay was nihil. So for more than fifteen years he has played the part of Master, and at his feet have sat a host of disciples, some of them now enjoying a fame of their own. It is never easy to tell exactly what a writer owes to his instructor, but it is quite certain that many young men are greatly indebted to Pound for technical advice as well as for spiritual encouragement. They have said so publicly. And Pound takes extraordinary pride in his achievements as discoverer and trainer. His eyes are always on the horizon, seeking unknown talent. From a studio in Paris or a roof-top in Rapallo he spies a struggling poet in the wilds of Arkansas and beckons him across the sea. He will not tolerate stupidity; he demands originality—even genius. But if the genius is there, he will do everything he can to nourish and direct it. When asked once if genius was not a rare and seldom-met quality, Pound replied haughtily, and with reproving sincerity, "I have specialized in genius all my life."

In *Personae* and *Exultations* Pound showed that he had learned much from the troubadours, as well as from Browning and Yeats. There were also signs of Latin and Greek study, but none as yet of the modern French poets or the classics of China and Japan. He was fascinated (as he still is) by the possibilities of music in poetry, particularly in its freer, its more variable manifestations; by the revelation of character through speech; and by the richness of archaic diction. He could in those early days compose a whole poem without the use of vernacular, although he did not always do so. His later work is much more strongly marked by the mixture of dignified with colloquial language. But what he did from the very beginning was to vitalize his subjects, whatever their period. To even the tritest theme he brought vigor, and into the dustiest medieval form he breathed tremendous life. In his "Altaforte" he made the sestina ring with lusty music:

> Damn it all! all this our South stinks peace.
> You whoreson dog, Papiols, come! Let's to music!
> I have no life save when the swords clash.
> But ah! when I see the standards gold, vair, purple, opposing
> And the broad fields beneath them turn crimson,
> Then howl I my heart nigh mad with rejoicing.

And so on through the seven stanzas. Never, I should think, did the stately sestina leap to more human rhythm or achieve more boisterous beauty.

Even the familiar ballad form, so often handled weakly by dilettantish modern poets, came to life under Pound's skilful touch. His "Ballad of the Goodly Fere" achieves really dramatic simplicity and a ruggedness which refreshes one of the oldest religious stories:

> A son of God was the Goodly Fere
> That bade us his brothers be.
> I ha' seen him cow a thousand men.
> I have seen him upon the tree.

He cried no cry when they drave the nails
And the blood gushed hot and free,
The hounds of the crimson sky gave tongue
But never a cry cried he.

I ha' seen him cow a thousand men
On the hills o' Galilee,
They whined as he walked out calm between,
Wi' his eyes like the grey o' the sea.

But it must be kept in mind that although Pound, especially in his early work, made use of old patterns, he did so chiefly as a means of developing a personal technique. He did not reproduce mechanically, but creatively. Therefore as soon as he had mastered the technical problems of one model, he moved on to another. Having achieved a felicitous ballad, he quit the ballad form. So with the sestina and many less well-known verse forms. It has been his constant aim to discover the secrets of poetic art and to employ them in an original manner. Most poets, he thinks (all but the most important ones), are victims of arrested development. They score a success with a composition in a certain style, and pleased with the success, they go on repeating this style for the rest of their lives. Hence their work stagnates and their art, though it may continue to be popular, ceases to be significant. Pound firmly believes that he could have stopped at any one of a number of points in his poetic career, and, by repeating himself stylistically, have attained a wide popular following. Instead, he has followed an aesthetic ideal, which has always kept him a good distance ahead of his readers.

Exultations was followed by *Canzoni*,[5] which represents

---

[5] London: Elkin Mathews. 1911.

Pound's most frankly imitative work in the Provençal forms, and which he considers important chiefly as a metrical exercise. And shortly afterward appeared his translations, *The Sonnets and Ballate of Guido Cavalcanti.*[6] In both instances his scholarship was impressively displayed and his technical virtuosity again emphasized. There were critics who objected to this extensive wandering in the paths of the troubadours, and who felt that to do so indicated an unhealthy tendency in a modern poet; but there were others who, unintentionally, replied to this objection by accusing Pound of having brought too much modernity into his translations. To some, in other words, he was too much a scholar, and to others too much a poet. His admirers, of course, insisted he was a happy combination of the two.

But in *Ripostes*[7] there was much more of the author's self—enough to indicate that he had returned to the main line of his development. There are echoes of the past (as there always are in Pound's work) and even some translations, but the personal element is dominant. A clear, lyric note, unaffected and free from erudition or metrical convention, appears in poems like "A Girl":

> The tree has entered my hands,
> The sap has ascended my arms,
> The tree has grown into my breast—
> Downward,
> The branches grow out of me, like arms.
>
> Tree you are,
> Moss you are,

[6] Boston: Small, Maynard. London: Swift. 1912.
[7] London: Swift. 1912. Boston: Small, Maynard. 1913. New edition, London: Elkin Mathews. 1915.

> You are violets with wind above them.
> A child—so high—you are,
> And all this is folly to the world.

And in "The Return" Pound achieved one of his finest effects in beautifully modulated, unmetrical verse. The opening lines will illustrate:

> See, they return; ah, see the tentative
> Movements, and the slow feet,
> The trouble in the pace and the uncertain
> Wavering.
>
> See, they return, one, and by one,
> With fear, as half-awakened;
> As if the snow should hesitate
> And murmur in the wind,
>   and half turn back;
> These were the "Wing'd-with-Awe,"
>   Inviolable.

To those who complained of Pound's devotion to the poets of old Provence he offered in this volume a revivification of an Anglo-Saxon classic, "The Seafarer," and so striking was his version that T. S. Eliot was led to exclaim that "perhaps the 'Seafarer' is the only successful piece of alliterative verse ever written in modern English; alliterative verse which is not merely a clever *tour de force*, but which suggests the possibility of a new development of this form." By other competent critics it was declared to be "unsurpassed and unsurpassable," and "one of the finest literary works of art produced in England during the last ten years." A few lines from the poem will convey an idea of its extraordinary strength:

May I for my own self song's truth reckon,
Journey's jargon, how I in harsh days
Hardship endured oft.
Bitter breast-cares have I abided,
Known on my keel many a care's hold,
And dire sea-surge, and there I oft spent
Narrow nightwatch nigh the ship's head
While she tossed close to cliffs. Coldly afflicted,
My feet were by frost benumbed.

It was in *Ripostes*, also, as readers of previous chapters will recall, that the five poems by T. E. Hulme first appeared, with a prefatory note by Pound containing the earliest mention in print of imagism. The publication of *Ripostes* marks the beginning of Pound's connection with imagism, as promoter, interpreter, and, to a limited extent, practitioner. Two years later he edited *Des Imagistes* and included in it, as one of his own imagistic poems, "The Return." But as has been explained previously, he did not continue to write in the pure imagist vein, nor was he for long the leader of the movement. As usual, he moved on.

His next book of verse was *Cathay*,[8] a series of translations "for the most part from the Chinese of Rihaku, from the notes of the late Ernest Fenollosa, and the decipherings of the Professors Mori and Ariga." Everyone who has read *Cathay* agrees, I think, not only that it is one of Pound's finest accomplishments, but also that it is of major importance as having established the proper manner of rendering Chinese classic poetry into modern English. With subtle discrimination, Pound applied to these poems a technique (a cadence and diction) which no one else had employed and

[8] London: Elkin Mathews. 1915.

which peculiarly suited his material. I quote the opening movement of "The River Song":

> This boat is of shato-wood, and its gunwales
>   are cut magnolia,
> Musicians with jeweled flutes and with pipes
>   of gold
> Fill full the sides in rows, and our wine
> Is rich for a thousand cups.
> We carry singing girls, drift with the drifting
>   water,
> Yet Sennin needs
> A yellow stork for a charger and all our seamen
> Would follow the white gulls or ride them.
> Kutsu's prose song
> Hangs with the sun and moon.

An important point in connection with *Cathay* is that the style employed in it, although derived partly from Pound's study of Chinese poetry, was not invented for the purpose of these translations but was rather a stage in the development of his personal technique. He had used it in original poems (later included in *Lustra*) before the *Cathay* material came into his hands. I quote from an authoritative monograph[9] (published anonymously, but actually written by T. S. Eliot) in which the facts are stated clearly:

The late Ernest Fenollosa left a quantity of manuscripts, including a great number of rough translations (literally exact) from the Chinese. After certain poems subsequently incorporated in *Lustra* had appeared in *Poetry*, Mrs. Fenollosa recognized that in Pound the Chinese manuscripts would find the interpreter whom her husband would have wished; she accordingly forwarded the

[9] *Ezra Pound: His Metric and Poetry.* New York: Knopf. 1917.

papers for him to do as he liked with. It is thus due to Mrs. Fenollosa's acumen that we have *Cathay;* it is not as a consequence of *Cathay* that we have *Lustra.*

And it is quite true that in the poems to which Mr. Eliot refers, "Tenzone," "The Condolence," "The Garret," and "Dance Figure," we find strong evidence of the manner which is often assumed to have been suggested by the *Cathay* material but which should be considered the product of Pound's own experiments in poetic technique, based not upon any one literature, but upon many.

It is interesting to note in this connection that some time after *Cathay,* when Pound reworked the notes and translations of the *Noh* Plays of Japan,[10] also left unfinished by Fenollosa, he felt the necessity of employing an idiom and a cadence already in existence, and, lacking any better, fell back upon the manner of the poetic Irish folk-plays. What he had been able to supply in the case of *Cathay* he borrowed from Yeats and Synge for the *Noh.* And this fact perhaps explains why critics classify the former as original work and the latter as a translation—a judgment, as a matter of fact, with which Pound himself agrees. He "felt" the Chinese poems; he did not "feel" the Japanese plays.

Lustra,[11] as has been indicated, appeared in print later than *Cathay,* but it represents original work done before the translations, as well as work done at approximately the same time. The poems vary greatly in theme and style, but one characteristic stands out prominently, that is, their belligerence. They were written after Pound had tasted acrimonious

[10] *Noh, or Accomplishment.* London: Macmillan. New York: Knopf. 1916.

[11] London: Elkin Mathews. 1916.

criticism, after he had found how thorny is the path of the revolutionary. He had been in London long enough to create a reputation and to acquire as many enemies as friends. No living poet can make enemies as quickly as Pound. It is in his nature to prick with wit or scorn all those who have dealings with him; and his friends he spares least of all. It requires extraordinary patience to put up with his perversities, his poses, his jibes, his silly banterings and nose-tweakings, and to remember him always as an admirable poet and patron of genius. A few possess such patience; the rest strike back in their own way. Yet those who attack a man like Pound are doing him a favor, for he thrives on calumny. Without grievances he would be a sad dog indeed. And so, in spite of the fact that occasionally his temper carries him beyond the limits of art and lands him in senseless vituperation or feeble wit, much of his best work is the direct result of passionate indignation and insulted pride. The first poem in *Lustra*, though a mild phase of Pound's counter-attack on the public consciousness, illustrates the workings of his mind:

TENZONE

Will people accept them?
   (i.e., these songs).
As a timorous wench from a centaur
   (or a centurion),
Already they flee, howling in terror.

Will they be touched with the verisimilitudes?
   Their virgin stupidity is untemptable.
I beg you, my friendly critics,
Do not set about to procure me an audience.
I mate with my free kind upon the crags;
   the hidden recesses

Have heard the echo of my heels,
    in the cool light,
    in the darkness.

This is truly Pound's song. For more than twenty years he has conducted a running fight with the public—a fight in which he, naturally enough, has taken more interest than the public and in which he has done the running. Confident from the first of his ability as a poet and of his importance as an aesthetic philosopher, he has religiously played up to the "Great Man" concept, and has deserted one country after another, carrying Parnassus about with him, and inviting all the worthy to come and climb it, or at least sit about its base. There is nothing incomprehensible in his psychology, and nothing particularly objectionable in his actions, unless one happens to be hit by the rocks which he hurls back from time to time, just to remind the riffraff of his existence.

Lustra is not by any means devoted solely to invective. It contains many of Pound's most charming poems. There are well-turned epigrams:

WOMEN BEFORE A SHOP

The gewgaws of false amber and false turquoise attract them,
"Like to like nature": these agglutinous yellows!

There are images presented in the *hokku* style:

ALBA

As cool as the pale wet leaves
    of lily-of-the-valley
She lay beside me in the dawn.

There are longer poems in which the full-blooded song of the troubadours resounds and in which the modified Browning monologue is developed to a high degree of effectiveness. "Near Perigord" begins thus:

> You'd have men's hearts up from the dust
> And tell their secrets, Messire Cino,
> Right enough? Then read between the lines of Uc St. Circ;
> Solve me the riddle, for you know the tale.

And equally Browningesque is the opening of the second part:

> End fact. Try fiction. Let us say we see
> En Bertrans, a tower-room at Hautefort,
> Sunset, the ribbon-like road lies, in red cross-light,
> Southward toward Montaignac, and he bends at a table
> Scribbling, swearing between his teeth; by his left hand
> Lie little strips of parchment covered over,
> Scratched and erased with *al* and *ochaisos*.
> Testing his list of rimes, a lean man? Bilious?
> With a red straggling beard?
> And the green cat's-eye lifts toward Montaignac.

Lustra is a mixed book. It is filled with echoes from Latin, Provençal, Chinese, and late nineteenth-century English poets. Not mere imitations, but echoes, in which the voice of Pound is blended with older voices.

But in the poems which followed those of *Lustra,* strangely enough, or perhaps naturally enough, Pound discarded his models and burst forth in strictly modern raiment. In a series of sixteen brilliant lyrics grouped under the title of *Hugh Selwyn Mauberley* he revealed a manner so incisive, so finely tempered and glittering, and therefore so admirably adapted to the expression of post-war irony and intellectual sophistication that it was at once adopted by many of the competent younger poets and is still serving to thrill the brighter undergraduates as well as to annoy the lovers of poetic conventionality. The tempo is swift and staccato, the figures are bizarre, the tone is utterly irreverent and mocking. Erudition skips lightly in and out of the dancing verse. A few stanzas chosen from various lyrics will convey an impression of what happened when Pound decided to be modern, the first two acting as prologue and explanation:

> For three years, out of key with his time,
> He strove to resuscitate the dead art
> Of poetry; to maintain "the sublime"
> In the old sense. Wrong from the start—
>
> No, hardly, but seeing he had been born
> In a half-savage country, out of date;
> Bent resolutely on wringing lilies from the acorn;
> Capaneus; trout for factitious bait;
>
> . . . .
>
> The tea-rose tea-gown, etc.
> Supplants the mousseline of Cos,
> The pianola "replaces"
> Sappho's barbitos.
>
> Christ follows Dionysus,
> Phallic and ambrosial
> Made way for macerations;
> Caliban casts out Ariel.
>
> . . . .
>
> Gladstone was still respected,
> When John Ruskin produced
> "King's Treasuries"; Swinburne
> And Rossetti still abused.
>
> . . . .

In the cream gilded cabin of his steam yacht
Mr. Nixon advised me kindly, to advance with fewer
Dangers of delay. "Consider
          "Carefully the reviewer.

"I was as poor as you are;
When I began I got, of course,
Advance on royalties, fifty at first," said Mr. Nixon,
"Follow me, and take a column,
Even if you have to work free."

.   .   .   .

Mildness, amid the neo-Nietzschean clatter,
His sense of graduations,
Quite out of place amid
Resistance to current exacerbations.

Invitation, mere invitation to perceptivity
Gradually led him to the isolation
Which these presents place
Under a more tolerant, perhaps, examination.

It is not at all my wish to do the poems an injustice by reproducing these isolated bits. Mr. Pound will curse me for the mutilation, but, then, he likes to curse. What I wish to do is to furnish the reader with examples of a poetic style which will be recognized at once as the model or at least the inspiration for many modern poets. One can hardly fail to think, in this connection, of T. S. Eliot, Wallace Stevens, E. E. Cummings, William Carlos Williams, Maxwell Bodenheim, and others, many or few, according to the extent of one's acquaintance with post-war poets.

But exciting and satisfying as the composition of these poems must have been to Pound, he dropped their manner and moved on. As usual, he was content to have sown the seeds and to let others reap the harvest.

But what was there for him to move on to? Obviously, to the past, where there is so much to explore, and where he is always at home. A brief sojourn in the modern world seems to have convinced him that it is not worth lingering in. Back, therefore, to ancient and medieval times, with hasty glimpses now and then at the twentieth century, just to get one's bearings and find contrasts and anachronisms. Pound is fonder of anachronisms than Shakespeare ever was. Indeed he holds a theory which justifies them. Of that more later.

Since 1917 his work has been based almost entirely upon the literature and history of past epochs. Its technique is in one sense decidedly modern, for of course it represents the latest development in the work of a master-experimentalist; but in another sense it is traditional, for many of its effects were learned from past masters. To say that it is a difficult technique for most readers is to put the matter mildly. It is so complex that only an adept can appreciate it. By comparison, the darkest Browning poem is crystal clear. For Browning, after all, did stop occasionally to elucidate. Pound scorns doing so.

Homage to Sextus Propertius is a long poem dating from 1917. It represents Pound's attempt to recreate the time and the mind of a classic writer. How successful the attempt is I am not qualified to say. Pound thinks that in most respects it is his best work. John Gould Fletcher, in a recently published critical review,[12] finds fault with it. His argument is as follows:

The difficulty with this poem is that it represents neither Propertius nor Mr. Pound, but only what Mr. Pound might have thought and felt had he *been* Propertius. In the case of the early

[12] See the *Criterion* (London) for April 1929.

translations, he had been content to paraphrase the text. But here he assumes that the text already exists in his own mind and the reader's, and that he is free to comment upon it as if he had written it. The result is an extended criticism of Propertius, written by a modern mind temporarily masquerading as Propertius.

And farther along, the same reviewer objects that: "Mr. Pound's Romans speak as if they had gravitated between modern New York and London."

One of the few men in the world who know Pound's writing intimately and who possess the necessary erudition to understand it is T. S. Eliot, and it is therefore worth noting that in the introduction to the English edition of Pound's *Selected Poems*,[13] Mr. Eliot states that *Homage to Sextus Propertius* has been omitted from the volume because:

If the uninstructed reader is not a classical scholar, he will make nothing of it; if he be a classical scholar, he will wonder why this does not conform to his notions of what translation should be. It is not a translation, it is a paraphrase, or still more truly (for the instructed) a *persona*.

This would seem to limit the audience for Pound's favorite poem to a very small number.

What this strange poet has been working toward since the beginning is a kind of epic, in which "all that matters" can be marshaled in one grand parade. Actual composition of this major work has occupied him intermittently since 1918, and in the eleven intervening years twenty-seven "cantos" have been completed and published in sumptuous

[13] London: Faber & Gwyer. 1928.

limited editions.[14] How many more cantos there will be is a matter for conjecture. Pound himself does not know. He says there may be a hundred. Meanwhile a small circle of "instructed" readers derive considerable pleasure from a study of the "work in progress." It is a poem on a grand scale, and any brief attempt to describe it would be unjust, not to say impossible. It is Pound's Divine Comedy, into which he is pouring the whole of his complex mind and art. But whereas Dante had a neat, compartment-like universe to deal with, the modern poet must write in terms of relativity. Where one conception could be fixed, the other must be fluid. Especially important to an understanding of the *Cantos* is the triple point of view maintained by the poet: (1) the fixed, or eternal; (2) the historical, or accurate; (3) the modern philosophical. These three aspects of life are woven intricately into a pretentious musical pattern resembling a fugue—with themes, counter-themes, and recurrences. Needless to say, therefore, unless one is carefully prepared or "instructed" beforehand, a reading of the *Cantos* will produce little more than bewilderment. Certain lyrical passages may give pleasure, and certain anecdotes may amuse, but the total significance certainly will be missed. And the necessary preparation must include not only a careful reading of all Pound's earlier poems but also his various prose works. It should include, in addition, an intensive study of the Latin poets, several years' research in European (particularly Italian) history, a reasonable knowledge of the Romanic languages, a grounding in the principles of musical

[14] *A Draft of XVI Cantos of Ezra Pound for the Beginning of a Poem of Some Length.* Paris: Three Mountains Press. 1925.

A Draft of the Cantos XVII to XXVII of Ezra Pound. London: John Rodker. 1928.

composition, and an expert understanding of the laws of prosody. Finally, it should include a personal acquaintance with Pound himself, at least by correspondence.

It is possible that some day the *Cantos* will take their place beside the long poems of Virgil, Dante, Goethe, Milton, and Browning. It is possible, I say. Who dares prophesy definitely in such matters? If the *Cantos* end in limbo, then Pound will have failed colossally.

Everything that Pound has written is inseparable from the rest of his writing. For that reason his prose work must be mentioned here, if only briefly. First, there is *The Spirit of Romance*,[15] in which he made his début as critic and scholar. It is the result of his early studies (beginning at college) in the literature of the Romance poets, and contains essays on the troubadours, and on their great inheritors. Dante, Villon, and Lope de Vega are three major figures to whom chapters are devoted. In the preface Pound states with characteristic bluntness and clarity his views toward poetry and scholarship, and also enunciates his theory of time in relation to art: that is, his belief in the "continuous present." He attacks the musty archaeology of the academic scholar, and presents an urgent plea for a more vital approach to the classics. The following paragraphs will convey his ideas:

It is dawn at Jerusalem while midnight hovers above the Pillars of Hercules. All ages are contemporaneous. It is B.C., let us say, in Morocco. The Middle Ages are in Russia. The future stirs already in the minds of the few. This is especially true of literature, where the real time is independent of the apparent, and where many dead men are our grandchildren's contemporaries, while many of

[15] London: Dent; New York: Dutton. 1910.

our contemporaries have been already gathered into Abraham's bosom, or some more fitting receptacle.

What we need is a literary scholarship, which will weigh Theocritus and Mr. Yeats with one balance, and which will judge dead men as inexorably as dull writers of today, and will, with equity, give praise to beauty before referring to an almanack.

Art is a joyous thing. Its happiness antedates even Whistler; apropos of which I would in all seriousness plead for a greater levity, a more befitting levity, in our study of the arts.

In this connection one should read Pound's most recently published essay, *How to Read, or Why*,[16] which he says is the result of twenty-seven years of thinking, and in which he again makes his plea for an intelligent study of comparative literature, going to the trouble of indicating the authors and works which he considers it necessary for a student to read. He is still the professor trying to reform American universities. In the same essay he declares that what is needed for proper study is a twelve-volume anthology of poetry of intrinsic merit, wherein each poem would contain an "invention," that is, "a definite contribution to the art of verbal expression." And he tells how, a number of years ago, he suggested editing such an anthology for an English publisher, and how shocked the publisher was when Pound said, "It is time we had something to replace that doddard Palgrave." The matter was dropped. It has been reopened once or twice since by other publishers, but I think it is doubtful that Pound will ever do the work of preparing the "twelve volumes." He will let one of his disciples do it.

In 1916 appeared *Gaudier-Brzeska: A Memoir by Ezra*

[16] New York, *Herald-Tribune Books,* issues for January 13, 20, and 27, 1929.

Pound.[17] It is a charmingly written account of the life and art of the young French sculptor whom Pound knew in London just before the War, and who died in battle before his genius had been discovered by more than a few. It was Brzeska who, with Pound and Wyndham Lewis, created the movement called vorticism. This memoir contains much that is valuable to one who wishes an introduction to modern sculpture, and it also contains much of value for one who desires a thorough knowledge of Pound. Historically considered, it is an important document in the field of twentieth-century aesthetics.

Pavannes and Divisions[18] is a book of collected essays on various subjects, most of them being reprints from contributions to periodicals: *Poetry, Egoist, Little Review,* etc. There are studies of French and English classics; there are appreciations of outstanding contemporaries; there are re-hashings of the imagist and other Pound-begotten credos; there are some clever translations; there are bits of literary bickering and personal asperity. Altogether there is a good deal of essential Pound scattered over many pages of journalistic writing.

Instigations,[19] published two years afterward, is much the same kind of book, though in it fewer subjects are treated. The first section is a kind of pocket anthology of modern French poetry, prepared for a special number of the *Little Review* in the hope of educating the American public. This is followed by a study of Henry James and shorter comments on the work of Pound's favorite contemporaries: Eliot,

[17] London and New York: John Lane.
[18] New York: Knopf. 1918.
[19] New York: Boni & Liveright. 1920.

Joyce, and Lewis. One study, with translations, of a troubadour distinguishes the latter part of the book, and is followed
by an historical critique of translators from the Greek. The
book closes with an essay by Ernest Fenollosa on the
"Chinese Written Character," an essay which Pound edited
from manuscript, and which he still insists is of fundamental
importance to students of aesthetics.

It was inevitable, of course, that at some time or other
Pound would gather into a volume his opinions on music and
its relation to poetry. He did so in 1924. *Antheil and the
Treatise on Harmony*[20] is a reprint of essays and notes contributed at various times to the *Transatlantic Review*, the
Criterion, and the *New Age*. It does for George Antheil,
the young American-born Polish composer, and for modern
music, what the *Memoir* did for Gaudier-Brzeska and modern sculpture. Besides that, it provides the reader with a
number of epigrams and technical memoranda which are
extremely stimulating to anyone with the faintest interest in
music or in poetry. It is written in the quaintly laconic style
which Pound employs in his happiest moods, and is filled
with his characteristically precise, pricking insults. It comes
nearer than any other of his publications to duplicating his
inimitable epistolary style.

Which leads me to express the opinion (even the hope)
that Pound's letters will be cherished by posterity. They
reveal better than either his poetry or his prose essays what
manner of man he is, and wherein his power as an artist lies.
But of course if a collection of them is ever published, the
age will have to be censorless.

We have spoken of Pound as poet, as critic, and as

[20] Paris: Three Mountains Press. 1924. Chicago: Covici. 1927.

teacher. We have also, in previous chapters, considered him as propagandist. We might go on and write of him as an exile (The Exile), as an editor, as a musical performer, as heaven knows what. I dare say that some day he will be the subject of a very large and immensely entertaining book. He has already been written about in hundreds of articles: he is already a legend. After years in London, and years in Paris, he now lives at Rapallo. He has paid America only one visit during more than twenty years, yet in many respects he is intensely American. In spite of the fact that he is the pioneer exile of this generation, he has never, it seems to me, succeeded in sloughing off his interest in the land of his birth. He has never achieved the cool detachment of T. S. Eliot, whose eyebrows scarcely lift at even the most moving mention of the United States. Pound is always writing home, telling the old folks what is the matter with them. He is still the bad boy who ran away so he could do as he pleased. His hatred of Americanism is honest, but it is interwoven with affection. Either this is true or Pound is an incorrigible pedagogue and reformer who cannot leave anyone, even those he despises, to welter in their own stupidity.

Were I to list here the names that have been hurled at Ezra Pound, I should require many pages more, and the ink would sizzle. And were I to add the eulogies, I should never make an end. That is the point. Pound is a creative force, and has been at the vortex of modern art for a long time. It may be that his chief work is over. No one knows for sure. There are still many "cantos" to be written; there are still young poets waiting to be discovered; there are still the windmills of ignorance beckoning with long arms to the Don Quixote of modern literature.

BIBLIOGRAPHY

BIBLIOGRAPHY

(Titles are arranged chronologically, according to dates of publication. Dates are of first editions unless otherwise noted.)

I. Books of Poetry by the Imagists

RICHARD ALDINGTON

Images. London: Poetry Bookshop. 1915. Boston: Four Seas. 1916. New, enlarged edition, London: Egoist Press. 1919. Reissued, London: Allen & Unwin. 1922.

Images of War. Limited edition, with decorations by Paul Nash, London: Beaumont Press. 1919. New, enlarged edition, London: Allen & Unwin. 1919. Boston: Four Seas. 1921.

Images of Desire. London: Elkin Mathews. 1919. Reissued, London: Allen & Unwin. 1922.

War and Love. (A selection from *Images of War* and *Images of Desire*.) Boston: Four Seas. 1919.

Exile and Other Poems. London: Allen & Unwin; New York: Dial Press. 1923.

A Fool i' the Forest. London: Allen & Unwin; New York: Dial Press. 1925.

The Love of Myrrhine and Konallis, followed by Nineteen Prose Poems. Chicago: Covici. 1926. (Limited edition.)

Collected Poems. New York: Covici, Friede. 1928. London: Allen & Unwin. 1929.

The Eaten Heart. Chapelle-Reánville, Eure, France: Hours Press. 1929. (Limited edition.)

A Dream in the Luxembourg. London: Chatto & Windus. 1930. (Limited and popular editions.)

[253]

Love and the Luxembourg. (Same as *A Dream in the Luxembourg.*) New York: Covici, Friede. 1930. (Limited edition.)

The Poems of Anyte of Tegea. London: Egoist Press. 1919.
Greek Songs in the Manner of Anacreon. London: Egoist Press. 1919.
Latin Poems of the Renaissance. London: Egoist Press. 1919.
The Poems of Meleager of Gadara. London: Egoist Press. 1920.
Medallions in Clay. (A combined edition of the four preceding titles.) New York: Knopf. 1921. (Limited edition.)
Fifty Romance Lyric Poems. New York: Crosby Gaige; London: Faber & Gwyer. 1928. (Limited edition.)

H. D.

Sea Garden. London: Constable; Boston: Houghton Mifflin. 1916.
Hymen. London: Egoist Press; New York: Holt. 1921.
Heliodora and Other Poems. London: Cape; Boston: Houghton Mifflin. 1924.
Collected Poems. New York: Boni & Liveright. 1925.
H. D. (In "The Pamphlet Poets.") New York: Simon & Schuster. 1926. (A selection from her poems.)
Hippolytus Temporizes. A Play in Three Acts. Boston: Houghton Mifflin. 1927.

Choruses from the Iphigeneia in Aulis and the Hippolytus of Euripides. London: Egoist Press. 1919.

JOHN GOULD FLETCHER

Fire and Wine. London: Grant Richards. 1913.
Fool's Gold. London: Max Goschen. 1913.
The Dominant City. London: Max Goschen. 1913.
The Book of Nature. London: Constable. 1913.

Visions of the Evening. London: Erskine McDonald. 1913.

Irradiations—Sand and Spray. Boston: Houghton Mifflin; London: Constable. 1915.

Goblins and Pagodas. Boston: Houghton Mifflin. 1916. London: Constable. 1918.

The Tree of Life. London: Chatto & Windus; New York: Macmillan. 1918.

Japanese Prints. Boston: Four Seas. 1918.

Breakers and Granite. New York: Macmillan. 1921.

Preludes and Symphonies. (A combined edition of *Irradiations—Sand and Spray* and *Goblins and Pagodas.*) Boston: Houghton Mifflin. 1922. New edition, New York: Macmillan. 1930.

Parables. London: Kegan Paul. 1925.

Branches of Adam. London: Faber & Gwyer. 1926.

The Black Rock. London: Faber & Gwyer; New York: Macmillan. 1928.

F. S. FLINT

In the Net of the Stars. London: Elkin Mathews. 1909.

Cadences. London: Poetry Bookshop. 1915.

Otherworld: Cadences. London: Poetry Bookshop. 1920.

TRANSLATIONS

The Love Poems of Émile Verhaeren. Boston: Houghton Mifflin. 1916.

The Closed Door. By Jean de Bosschère. London and New York: John Lane. 1917.

D. H. LAWRENCE

Love Poems and Others. London: Duckworth; New York: Mitchell Kennerley. 1913.

Amores. London: Duckworth; New York: Huebsch. 1916.

Look! We Have Come Through! London: Chatto & Windus. 1917. New York: Huebsch. 1918.

New Poems. London: Secker. 1918. New York: Huebsch. 1920.

Bay: A Book of Poems. London: Beaumont Press. 1919. (Limited edition.)

Tortoises. New York: Seltzer. 1921.

Birds, Beasts, and Flowers. New York: Seltzer; London: Secker. 1923.

Collected Poems. 2 vols. London: Secker. 1928. New York: Cape & Smith. 1929.

Pansies. London: Secker; New York: Knopf. 1929.

Nettles. London: Faber & Faber. 1930.

AMY LOWELL

A Dome of Many-Coloured Glass. Boston: Houghton Mifflin. 1912. Oxford: Blackwell. 1913.

Sword Blades and Poppy Seed. New York: Macmillan; Oxford: Blackwell. 1914.

Men, Women, and Ghosts. New York: Macmillan; Oxford: Blackwell. 1916.

Can Grande's Castle. New York: Macmillan. 1918. Oxford: Blackwell. 1920.

Pictures of the Floating World. New York: Macmillan; Oxford: Blackwell. 1919.

Legends. Boston: Houghton Mifflin; Oxford: Blackwell. 1921.

A Critical Fable. (Published anonymously.) Boston: Houghton Mifflin. 1922.

What's O'Clock? Boston: Houghton Mifflin. 1925. London: Cape. 1926.

East Wind. Boston: Houghton Mifflin. 1926.

Ballads for Sale. Boston: Houghton Mifflin. 1927.

Selected Poems. Edited by John Livingston Lowes. Boston: Houghton Mifflin. 1928.

Poetical Works. 6 vols. Oxford: Blackwell.

TRANSLATIONS

Fir-Flower Tablets. (In collaboration with Florence Ayscough.) Boston: Houghton Mifflin; London: Constable. 1921.

EZRA POUND

A Lume Spento. Venice: Antonelli. 1908. (100 copies.)

A Quinzaine for This Yule. London: Pollock (100 copies); Elkin Mathews (100 copies). 1908.

Personæ. London: Elkin Mathews. 1909. (Includes most of *A Lume Spento.*)

Exultations. London: Elkin Mathews. 1909.

Provença. Boston: Small, Maynard. 1910. (Largely a reprint of poems from *Personæ* and *Exultations.*)

Canzoni. London: Elkin Mathews. 1911.

Ripostes. London: Swift. 1912. Boston: Small, Maynard. 1913. New edition, London: Elkin Mathews. 1915.

Lustra. London: Elkin Mathews. 1916.

Lustra, with Earlier Poems. New York: Knopf. 1917.

Quia Pauper Amavi. London: Egoist Press. 1919.

Umbra: The Early Poems of Ezra Pound. (All that he now wishes to keep in circulation from *Personæ*, *Exultations*, *Ripostes*, etc., with translations from Guido Cavalcanti and Arnaut Daniel and poems by the late T. E. Hulme.) London: Elkin Mathews. 1920.

Poems 1918–21. (Including three portraits and four Cantos.) New York: Boni & Liveright. 1921.

A Draft of XVI Cantos of Ezra Pound for the Beginning of a Poem of Some Length. Paris: Three Mountains Press. 1925. (90 copies.)

Personæ: The Collected Poems of Ezra Pound. (Edition to date of all Ezra Pound's poems except the unfinished Cantos.) New York: Boni & Liveright. 1926.

A Draft of the Cantos XVII to XXVII of Ezra Pound. London: John Rodker. 1928. (101 copies.)

Selected Poems of Ezra Pound. With an introduction and notes by T. S. Eliot. London: Faber & Gwyer. 1928.

TRANSLATIONS

The Sonnets and Ballate of Guido Cavalcanti. Boston: Small, Maynard; London: Swift. 1912.

Cathay. (Translations by Ezra Pound, for the most part from the
Chinese of Rihaku, from the notes of the late Ernest Fenollosa,
and the decipherings of the Professors Mori and Ariga.) London: Elkin Mathews. 1915.

Certain Noble Plays of Japan. (From the manuscripts of Ernest
Fenollosa. Chosen and finished by Ezra Pound, with an intro-
duction by William Butler Yeats.) Churchtown, Dundrum:
Cuala Press. 1916.

Noh, or Accomplishment. (A study of the classical stage of Japan,
including translations of fifteen plays, by Ernest Fenollosa and
Ezra Pound.) London: Macmillan; New York: Knopf. 1916.

II. *Principal Anthologies Containing Imagist Poems*

Des Imagistes. London: Poetry Bookshop; New York: Albert and
Charles Boni. 1914.

Some Imagist Poets. Boston: Houghton Mifflin; London: Constable. 1915.

Some Imagist Poets, 1916. Boston: Houghton Mifflin; London:
Constable. 1916.

Some Imagist Poets, 1917. Boston: Houghton Mifflin; London:
Constable. 1917.

The New Poetry. Edited by Harriet Monroe and Alice Corbin
Henderson. New York: Macmillan. 1917.

New Voices. By Marguerite Wilkinson. New York: Macmillan.
1919.

Modern American Poetry. By Louis Untermeyer. New York:
Harcourt, Brace & Howe. 1919. London: Cape. 1921.

Modern British Poetry. By Louis Untermeyer. New York: Harcourt, Brace & Howe. 1920.

Chief Modern Poets of England and America. Edited by Gerald DeWitt Sanders and John Herbert Nelson. New York: Macmillan. 1929.

Imagist Anthology, 1930. New York: Covici, Friede; London: Chatto & Windus. 1930.

III. Selected References for a Study of Imagism and the Imagists

(a) Books

Poètes d'Aujourd'hui: Morceaux Choisis. By Ad. Van Bever and Paul Léautaud. 2 vols. Paris: Mercure de France. 1900.

The Spirit of Romance. By Ezra Pound. London: Dent; New York: Dutton. 1910.

Six French Poets: Studies in Contemporary Literature. By Amy Lowell. New York: Macmillan. 1915.

Gaudier-Brzeska: A Memoir. By Ezra Pound. London and New York: John Lane. 1916.

Collected Poems. By Ford Madox Hueffer. London: Secker. 1916.

Tendencies in Modern American Poetry. By Amy Lowell. New York: Macmillan. 1917.

Ezra Pound: His Metric and Poetry. (Published anonymously, but written by T. S. Eliot.) New York: Knopf. 1917.

Amy Lowell: A Sketch of Her Life and Her Place in Contemporary American Literature. (Pamphlet.) By Richard Hunt. New York: Macmillan. No date.

Pavannes and Divisions. By Ezra Pound. New York: Knopf. 1918.

Scepticisms: Notes on Contemporary Poetry. By Conrad Aiken. New York: Knopf. 1919.

The New Era in American Poetry. By Louis Untermeyer. New York: Holt. 1919.

New Voices: An Introduction to Contemporary Poetry. By Marguerite Wilkinson. New York: Macmillan. 1919.

Convention and Revolt in Poetry. By John Livingston Lowes. Boston: Houghton Mifflin. 1919.

Some Contemporary Poets. By Harold Monro. London: Leonard Parsons. 1920.

Instigations. By Ezra Pound. (With an essay on the Chinese Written Character by Ernest Fenollosa.) New York: Boni & Liveright. 1920.

American Poetry Since 1900. By Louis Untermeyer. New York: Holt. 1923.

The Doctor Looks at Literature. By Joseph Collins. New York: Doran. 1923.

Fantasia of the Unconscious. By D. H. Lawrence. New York: Seltzer. 1922. London: Secker. 1923.

Psychoanalysis and the Unconscious. By D. H. Lawrence. New York: Seltzer. 1921. London: Secker. 1923.

Speculations. By T. E. Hulme. Edited by Herbert Read. London: Kegan Paul; New York: Harcourt, Brace. 1924.

Antheil and the Treatise on Harmony. By Ezra Pound. Paris: Three Mountains Press. 1924. Chicago: Covici. 1927.

D. H. Lawrence: An American Interpretation. By Herbert J. Seligmann. New York: Seltzer. 1924.

Literary Studies and Reviews. By Richard Aldington. London: Allen & Unwin; New York: Dial Press. 1924.

Contemporary French Literature. By René Lalou. (Translated by William Aspenwall Bradley.) London: Cape; New York: Knopf. 1925.

Littérature française. By Bernard Faÿ. ("Panoramas des littératures contemporaines.") Paris: Kra. 1925.

Men Seen: Twenty-four Modern Authors. By Paul Rosenfeld. New York: Dial Press. 1925.

The Writings of D. H. Lawrence: A Bibliography. By Edward D. McDonald. Philadelphia: Centaur Book Shop. 1925.

Poets of America. By Clement Wood. New York: Dutton. 1925.

Panorama de la littérature americaine contemporaine. By Régis Michaud. Paris: Kra. 1926.

Amy Lowell. By Clement Wood. New York: Harold Vinal. 1926.

Poets and Their Art. By Harriet Monroe. New York: Macmillan. 1926.

French Studies and Reviews. By Richard Aldington. London: Allen & Unwin; New York: Dial Press. 1926.

La Littérature française contemporaine: 1850 à nos jours. By Marcel Braunschvig. Paris: Armand Colin. 1926.

The Imaginative Interpretation of the Far East in Modern French Literature (1800–1925). By William Leonard Schwartz. Paris: Champion. 1927.

The French Poets of the Twentieth Century: An Anthology, with Introduction and Literary Appreciations. By L. E. Kastner. London and Toronto: Dent. 1927.

D. H. Lawrence: An Indiscretion. (Pamphlet.) By Richard Aldington. Seattle: University of Washington Bookstore. 1927. London: Chatto & Windus. 1930.

Time and Western Man. By Wyndham Lewis. London: Chatto & Windus. 1927.

Anthologie de la nouvelle poésie française. Paris: Kra. 1927.

A Survey of Modernist Poetry. By Laura Riding and Robert Graves. London: Heinemann. 1927. New York: Dutton. 1928.

Remy de Gourmont: Selections from All His Works. Chosen and translated by Richard Aldington. 2 vols. Chicago: Covici. 1928.

The Poetry of Amy Lowell. (Pamphlet.) By Charles Cestre. Translated by Dana Hill. Issued by, but without imprint of Houghton Mifflin Co., Boston. 1928.

Bohemian and Social Life in Paris. By Sisley Huddleston. London: Harrap. 1928.

Dialogues and Monologues. By Humbert Wolfe. London: Gollancz; New York: Knopf. 1928.

The Classics and Our Twentieth-Century Poets. By Henry Rushton Fairclough. Stanford University Press. 1928.

Ta Hio: The Great Learning. Newly rendered into the American language by Ezra Pound. (Pamphlet.) Seattle: University of Washington Bookstore. 1928.

English Prose Style. By Herbert Read. London: G. Bell & Sons. 1928. New York: Holt. 1929.

Notes on Language and Style. (Pamphlet.) By T. E. Hulme. Edited by Herbert Read. Seattle: University of Washington Bookstore. 1929.

The Lamp and the Lute: Studies in Six Modern Authors. By Bonamy Dobrée. London and New York: Oxford University Press. 1929.

Our Singing Strength: An Outline of American Poetry, 1620– 1930. By Alfred Kreymborg. New York: Coward-McCann. 1929.

L'Influence du symbolisme français sur la poésie américaine (de 1910 à 1920). By René Taupin. Paris: Champion. 1929.

Pornography and Obscenity. By D. H. Lawrence. London: Faber & Faber. 1929. New York: Knopf. 1930.

Poetry and Poets. By Amy Lowell. Boston: Houghton Mifflin. 1930.

Assorted Articles. By D. H. Lawrence. London: Secker; New York: Knopf. 1930.

D. H. Lawrence. A First Study. By Stephen Potter. London: Cape; New York: Cape & Smith. 1930.

My Thirty Years' War. By Margaret Anderson. New York: Covici, Friede. 1930.

(b) Articles

Contemporary French Poetry. By F. S. Flint. *Poetry Review* (London), August 1912.

Status Rerum. By Ezra Pound. *Poetry* (Chicago), January 1913.

Imagisme. By F. S. Flint. *Poetry* (Chicago), March 1913.

A Few Don'ts by an Imagiste. By Ezra Pound. *Poetry* (Chicago), March 1913.

Impressionism: Some Speculations. (In two parts.) By Ford Madox Hueffer. *Poetry* (Chicago), August and September 1913.

The Approach to Paris. By Ezra Pound. (A series of weekly articles.) *New Age* (London), September 4 to October 16, 1913.

In Metre. By Ezra Pound. *New Freewoman* (London), September 15, 1913.

Modern Poetry and the Imagists. By Richard Aldington. *Egoist* (London), June 1, 1914.

Vorticism. (Manifestoes and articles by Ezra Pound, H. Gaudier-Brzeska, Wyndham Lewis, and others.) *Blast* (London), June 20, 1914.

Blast. A review by Richard Aldington. *Egoist* (London), July 15, 1914.

The New Poetry of France. By Nicholas Beauduin. Translated by Richard Aldington. *Egoist* (London), August 15, 1914.

Free Verse in England. By Richard Aldington. *Egoist* (London), September 15, 1914.

Two Poets. By Richard Aldington. *Egoist* (London), November 16, 1914.

Miss Lowell's Discovery: Polyphonic Prose. By John Gould Fletcher. *Poetry* (Chicago), April 1915.

Imagists and Their Poetry. By William Stanley Braithwaite. *Boston Transcript,* April 21, 1915.

Special Imagist Number of the Egoist (London), May 1, 1915. Contains the following articles:
> *The History of Imagism.* By F. S. Flint.
> *The Poetry of Ezra Pound.* By Richard Aldington.
> *The Poetry of H. D.* By F. S. Flint.
> *The Poetry of John Gould Fletcher.* By Ferris Greenslet.
> *The Imagists Discussed.* By Harold Monro.
> *The Poetry of F. S. Flint.* By Richard Aldington.

The Poetry of D. H. Lawrence. By O. Shakespear.

The Poetry of Amy Lowell. By John Gould Fletcher.

Mr. Fletcher's Verse. By Amy Lowell. *New Republic* (New York), May 15, 1915.

The Place of Imagism. By Conrad Aiken. *New Republic* (New York), May 22, 1915.

Two Notes. By May Sinclair. *Egoist* (London), June 1, 1915.

Imagism: Another View. By William Stanley Braithwaite. *New Republic* (New York), June 12, 1915.

The Poetry of Amy Lowell. By Richard Aldington. *Egoist* (London), July 1, 1915.

A Jubilee. By Ford Madox Hueffer. *Outlook* (London), July 10, 1915.

Vers Libre and Vers Librists. By Alfred Kreymborg. New York *Morning Telegraph,* August 8, 1915.

The New Poetry—A Critique. By William Ellery Leonard. Chicago *Evening Post,* September 18 and 25, October 2 and 9, 1915.

The New Movement in Poetry. By O. W. Firkins. *Nation* (New York), October 14, 1915.

England's Nest of Singing Birds. By Margaret Storm Jameson. *Egoist* (London), November 1, 1915.

Egoism in Poetry. By Padraic Colum. *New Republic* (New York), November 20, 1915.

Six French Poets. A review by F. S. Flint. *Egoist* (London), January 1, 1916.

The Work of Ezra Pound. By Carl Sandburg. *Poetry* (Chicago), February 1916.

An Unacknowledged Imagist. By John Livingston Lowes. *Nation* (New York), February 24, 1916.

The New Manner in Modern Poetry. By Amy Lowell. *New Republic* (New York), March 4, 1916.

How Does the New Poetry Differ from the Old? By Joyce Kilmer. (An interview with Amy Lowell.) New York *Times,* March 16, 1916.

Poetry Today. By Cornelia A. P. Comer. *Atlantic Monthly* (Boston), April 1916.

The New Naïveté. By Lewis Worthington Smith. *Atlantic Monthly* (Boston), April 1916.

Three Imagist Poets. By John Gould Fletcher. *Little Review* (New York), May 1916.

The Latest Quintessence of Imagism. By William Stanley Braithwaite. *Boston Transcript,* May 6, 1916.

John Gould Fletcher. By R. Herdman Pender. *Egoist* (London), November 1916.

A Consideration of the New Poetry. By Amy Lowell. *North American Review* (New York), January 1917.

Ezra Pound. Translated from the French of Jean de Bosschère. (In three parts.) *Egoist* (London), January, February, and April 1917.

Reflections on Vers Libre. By T. S. Eliot. *New Statesman* (London), March 3, 1917.

Vers Libre. (A communication to the Editor.) By John Gould Fletcher. *New Statesman* (London), March 24, 1917.

The Borderline of Prose. By T. S. Eliot. *New Statesman* (London), May 19, 1917.

Drunken Helots and Mr. Eliot. By Ezra Pound. *Egoist* (London), June 1917.

Vers Libre and Arnold Dolmetsch. By Ezra Pound. *Egoist* (London), July 1917.

Reflections on Contemporary Poetry. (In two parts.) By T. S. Eliot. *Egoist* (London), September and November, 1917.

The Rhythms of Free Verse. By Amy Lowell. *Dial* (Chicago), January 17, 1918.

Disjecta Membra. By T. S. Eliot. *Egoist* (London), April 1918.

Some French Poets of Today: A Commentary with Specimens. By F. S. Flint. *Monthly Chapbook* (London), October 1919.

Three Critical Essays on Modern English Poetry. By T. S. Eliot, Aldous Huxley, and F. S. Flint. *The Chapbook: A Monthly Miscellany* (London), March 1920.

Some Contemporary American Poets. By John Gould Fletcher. *The Chapbook: A Monthly Miscellany* (London), May 1920.

Thus to Revisit . . . . By Ford Madox Hueffer. (Published in three installments.) *Dial* (New York), July, August, and September, 1920.

The Art of Poetry. By Richard Aldington. *Dial* (New York), August 1920.

The Younger French Poets. By F. S. Flint. *The Chapbook: A Monthly Miscellany* (London), November 1920.

Poetry in Prose: Three Essays. By T. S. Eliot, Frederick Manning, and Richard Aldington. *The Chapbook: A Monthly Miscellany* (London), April 1921.

The Poems of Richard Aldington. By May Sinclair. *English Review* (London), May 1921.

The Poems of H. D. By May Sinclair. *Dial* (New York), February 1922.

Three Questions and About Twenty-seven Answers. (Regarding the Necessity, the Function, and the Form of Poetry.) By Various Authors. *The Chapbook: A Monthly Miscellany* (London), July 1922.

The Poet and His Age. By Richard Aldington. *The Chapbook: A Monthly Miscellany* (London), September 1922.

On Criticism in General. By Ezra Pound. *Criterion* (London), January 1923.

Amy Lowell and the Art of Poetry. By Archibald MacLeish. *North American Review* (New York), March 1925.

Ezra Pound. Dedicatory tributes by James Joyce, Ernest Hemingway, and Ernest Walsh. *This Quarter* (Paris), Spring, 1925. (See also issue for Spring, 1927, for retraction of dedication by the Editor.)

A Note on Free Verse. By Richard Aldington. *The Chapbook: A Miscellany* (London), 1925. (Annual issue.)

Obscurity. By Leonard Woolf. *The Chapbook: A Miscellany* (London), 1925. (Annual issue.)

Notes on Language and Style. By T. E. Hulme. (Edited by Herbert Read.) *Criterion* (London), July 1925. Seattle: University of Washington Bookstore. 1929. (Pamphlet.)

A Background for Contemporary Poetry. By I. A. Richards. *Criterion* (London), July 1925.

D. H. Lawrence Number of the Laughing Horse. (Santa Fe, New Mexico), April 1926. (Contains a number of contributions by Mr. Lawrence, and articles on his work by various others.)

Amy Lowell as a Poet. By Hervey Allen. *Saturday Review of Literature* (New York), February 5, 1927.

A Study of Amy Lowell's Far Eastern Verse. By William Leonard Schwartz. *Modern Language Notes* (Baltimore), March 1928.

L'Appel de l'extrême-orient dans la poésie des États-Unis. By William Leonard Schwartz. *Revue de littérature comparée* (Paris), January 1928, pp. 113–126.

How to Read, or Why. By Ezra Pound. (In three parts.) *Herald-Tribune Books* (New York), January 13, 20, 27, 1929.

Ezra Pound. A review by John Gould Fletcher. *Criterion* (London), April 1929.

Collected Poems of Richard Aldington. A review by Harriet Monroe. *Poetry* (Chicago), April 1929.

L'Originalité d'Amy Lowell. By Pierre Isoré. *Revue anglo-américaine* (Paris), April 1929.

D. H. Lawrence. By J. C. Squire. *Observer* (London), March 9, 1930.

D. H. Lawrence. By Joseph Wood Krutch. *Nation* (New York), March 19, 1930.

D. H. Lawrence. By Paul Rosenfeld. *New Republic* (New York), March 26, 1930.

The Death of D. H. Lawrence. By Rebecca West. *Bookman* (New York), April–May, 1930.

INDEX

INDEX

Academy (London), 128
"Acon," 111
Adam, Paul, 5
Adam, Villiers de l'Isle, 4
Aiken, Conrad, 49–53, 210, 211, 217 footnote
"Alba," 238
Aldington, Richard: relation to French poetry, 8, 9; first imagist poems published, 12; meets H. D., 25; on *Egoist* staff, 31; contributes to first imagist anthology, 33; writes preface to 1915 anthology, 39; instigates *Imagist Anthology, 1930,* 42; theories of the prose-poem, 75; early life and education, 85; association with H. D., 86; contributions to periodicals, 87, 88; first book of poems published, 88; experience in the War, 93, 94; *Images of Desire,* 95, 96; *Myrrhine and Konallis,* 96, 97; *Exile and Other Poems,* 97–99; settles in Berkshire, 99; *A Fool i' the Forest,* 100–106; *The Eaten Heart,* 106, 107; forsakes England for the Continent, 106, 107; *A Dream in the Luxembourg,* 108; summary of his character, 108; mentioned, ix, 29, 32, 37, 38, 48, 60, 62, 63, 74, 77, 78, 109, 160, 165, 189, 190
A Lume Spento, 225
American Poetry Since 1900, 198
Amores, 171
"Amygism," 38
Anacreon, 96
"An Old Song," 95, 96
Antheil and the Treatise on Harmony, 248
Antheil, George, 248
Anyte of Tegea, 96
Apollinaire, Guillaume, 7
Aragon, Louis, 7
Aristotle, 81
Arnold, Matthew, 74, 81
"At Ithaca," 116
Athenaeum (London), 128
Atlantic Monthly, 67

Whistler, J. M., 246
"White and Green," 201
White Peacock, The, 168
Whitman, Walt, 43, 74, 126, 147, 170, 173, 174, 184
Wilde, Oscar, 18
Wilkinson, Marguerite, 69
Williams, William Carlos, ix, 32, 33, 42, 241

"Winter Night, A," 99
Winters, Yvor, ix
Wolfe, Humbert, 100
"Women before a Shop," 238
Wordsworth, 28, 76

Yeats, W. B., vii, 188, 189, 225, 229, 236, 246
"Young America," 87 footnote